ROMA AND GYPSY-TRAVELLERS IN EUROPE

Research in Migration and Ethnic Relations Series

Series Editor:
Maykel Verkuyten, ERCOMER
Utrecht University

The Research in Migration and Ethnic Relations Series is a joint series of the Danish Centre for Migration and Ethnic Studies, University of Southern Denmark; the Centre for Research in Ethnic Relations, University of Warwick; and the European Research Centre on Migration and Ethnic Relations, Utrecht University. Books in the series are intended to be of interest to students and scholars of migration, nationalism, racism and ethnic relations. The series aims in particular to publish volumes with a comparative European focus, or those nationally-based studies which have a broader relevance to international issues of migration and ethnic relations.

Other titles in the series

Migration Between States and Markets
Edited by Han Entzinger, Marco Martiniello and Catherine Wihtol de Wenden
ISBN 0 7546 4231 3

Nationalism and Exclusion of Migrants: Cross-National Comparisons
Edited by Mérove Gijsberts, Louk Hagendoorn and Peer Scheepers
ISBN 0 7546 3993 2

Transnational Social Spaces: Agents, Networks and Institutions
Edited by Thomas Faist and Eyüp Özveren
ISBN 0 7546 3291 1

International Migration Research: Constructions, Omissions and the Promises of Interdisciplinarity
Edited by Michael Bommes and Ewa Morawska
ISBN 0 7546 4219 4

Roma and Gypsy-Travellers in Europe

Modernity, Race, Space and Exclusion

ANGUS BANCROFT
University of Edinburgh, UK

ASHGATE

Published by
Ashgate Publishing Limited
Gower House
Croft Road
Aldershot
Hants GU11 3HR
England

Ashgate Publishing Company
Suite 420
101 Cherry Street
Burlington, VT 05401-4405
USA

Ashgate website: http://www.ashgate.com

British Library Cataloguing in Publication Data
Bancroft, Angus
Roma and gypsy-travellers in Europe : modernity, race, space and exclusion. - (Research in migration and ethnic relations series)
1.Romanies - Europe - Social conditions 2.Marginality, Social - Europe 3.Racism - Europe 4.Europe - Ethnic relations
I.Title
305.8'91497

Library of Congress Cataloging-in-Publication Data
Bancroft, Angus.
Roma and Gypsy-Travellers in Europe : modernity, race, space and exclusion / by Angus Bancroft.-- 1st ed.
p. cm. -- (Research in migration and ethnic relations series)
Includes bibliographical references and index.
ISBN 0-7546-3921-5
1. Romanies--Europe. I. Title. II. Series.

DX145.B36 2004
305.891'49704--dc22

2004025166

ISBN 0 7546 3921 5

Printed and bound by Athenaeum Press Ltd.,
Gateshead, Tyne & Wear.

Contents

Chapter 1

Europe and its Internal Outsiders

Introduction

From the 'forgotten Holocaust' in the concentration camps of Nazi controlled Europe to the upsurge of racist violence that followed the fall of Communism and the naked hostility displayed towards them across the continent in the 21st Century, Europe has been a dangerous place for Roma and Gypsy-Travellers ('Gypsies'). There are Roma and Gypsy-Travellers living in every country of Europe. They have been the object of persecution, and the subject of misrepresentation, for most of their history. They are amongst the most marginalized groups in European society, historically being on the receiving end of severe racism, social and economic disadvantage, and forced population displacement. Anti-Gypsy sentiment is present throughout Europe, in post-Communist countries such as Romania, in social democracies like Finland, in Britain, in France and so on. Opinion polls consistently show that they are held in lower esteem than other ethnic groups. Examples of these sentiments in action range from mob violence in Croatia to 'no Travellers' signs in pubs in Scotland.

This book will examine the exclusion of Roma and Gypsy-Travellers in Europe. The rationale behind it is that there is a set of processes that connect these phenomena together beyond the fact that they involve groups of people who are called, or call themselves, 'Gypsies' in different parts of Europe.

Historically, there have been times when they have been more explicitly targeted as outsiders, by states and settled populations. These periods seem to be associated with major developments in the emergence and consolidation of the modern, centralized bureaucratic nation-state in Europe – for instance, in the period following the First World War. Europe is currently going through one of those periods in which there is a reordering of nations and states, this time in the context of a supranational body, the European Union, which is developing its own state structures and symbols, along with the globalization of flows of information and capital that revalues space and place. Outsider groups that appear to devalue space and transgress or disturb the meaning of place are reviled and rejected.

In this case there is a particular uncertainty and ambivalence. Outright expressions of racism are considered inappropriate, but hostility is present and unashamedly expressed towards these internal groups that are placed on the moral and political margins. It is vital to develop a sociological perspective on this form of exclusion, what might be called '21st Century racism'. More so, this has to be done in a European context, because many of the developments that affect Roma and Gypsy-Travellers and other outsider groups take place at this level. It is becoming more and more important to adopt a perspective that can link pan-European developments in exclusion and racism to global and local changes.

There are many groups of people living in the European continent who are excluded from the ideological and geographical 'place' of Europe. I will examine the exclusion of one such outsider minority in Europe, Roma and Gypsy-Travellers. Roma and Gypsy-Travellers in Europe have been, and continue to be, the object of assimilation, state coercion, discrimination and racial violence. They have been subject to a variety of regulatory surveillance techniques and structures produced by various institutions of modernity. This book uses their experience to illustrate how certain outsider groups are constituted and excluded within Europe. Its central argument is that the construction of space and identity within Europe as it is constituted excludes outsider groups from a stake in the 'place' of Europe, and this emerging form of exclusion differs in some ways from the racial and social exclusions that have characterized Europe in past decades and centuries. This calls into question the inclusive nature of a common- or pan-European identity, citizenship and rights, by which progressive thought has set much score. The key themes of the book are: narratives of race and ethnicity and nation; legal sedentarization and criminalization; socio-spatial segregation at a local level; the policy of 'fortress Europe' at a national and supra-national level; and the interaction between constructs of globalization and locality.

I place the experiences of Roma and Gypsy-Travellers within the context of recent developments in European societies, institutions and politics that contribute towards new and 'new-old' forms of exclusion, new-old forms of exclusion being those that combine old methods in new forms. The book employs the concept of modernity, understood as a set of systems and sub-systems such as the nation-state based on specific forms of time-spatial order and control, as a theoretical framework with which to investigate their position within European society and to understand recent social changes. Using fieldwork conducted in Britain and the Czech Republic and documentary research, it describes some of the regulatory discourses and exclusions to which Roma and Gypsy-Travellers are subject. It places their experience within the wider contexts of race and ethnicity, changing institutional structures and developing globalization-localization processes.

The book is written from the point of view that it is essential to develop a theoretical perspective that extends past the – important – specific concerns of racial violence, discrimination and so on, expounding on what the most important questions facing Roma and Gypsy-Travellers in Europe are. In spite of the varied nature of the groups discussed in the book, their experiences are connected in important dimensions, both historically and in the present. My premise is that the problems and challenges they faced are different expressions of a common problem or set of problems.

The book takes the perspective that regulatory functions and narratives make and remake Europe as a restricted ideological space and geographic entity. It is a space from which 'outsider' minorities like Roma and Gypsy-Travellers are excluded. This involves processes of race and racialization occurring across the continent; the development of socio-spatial segregation; legal exclusions; the division between mobile objects and restricted subjects; the relationship between globalized space and localized place; and the construction of networks of dark and light zones by socio-economic forces and state practices. Specific issues considered include: the resurgence of anti-Roma violence, mainly in Central and Eastern Europe; the impact of the Criminal Justice Act 1994 on Gypsy-Travellers in the UK; the treatment of Roma asylum seekers in Britain; and the historical criminalization of activities associated with Gypsy-Traveller life.

Race, Space, Modernity and Backwardness: Key Themes

Outsider populations in Europe have been and are racialized, but in different forms at different times and places. Anti-Gypsy action in the Czech Republic has implications for sociological understandings of racism, as well as the concept of backwardness and white identity. An examination of the function of racism in Western and Eastern Europe leads me to suggest that racism in the countries of Central and Eastern Europe is understood in Western Europe as an example of the backwardness of those states, whereas it is in fact intimately associated with their modernization. Western European nations use evidence of racism in Central and Eastern Europe to 'orientalize' racism, in an analogous manner to the way Roma and Gypsy-Travellers are orientialized.

Space is an important factor in the interaction between outsider groups and the institutions and practices of modernity, nation and state. The experiences of Roma and Gypsy-Travellers are examples of struggles over the control and management of space in modernity. In the book I consider processes of spatial management and ghettoization in the Britain and the Czech Republic. In the Czech Republic ghettoization is a factor in the racialization of the Roma. It is a legacy of the Communist era and is fuelled by the ambitions of local politicians in the post-Communist period. In Britain, local politics is also an important factor in the creation and locating of caravan sites for Gypsy-Travellers. The system of local authority sites for Gypsy-Travellers itself has an important role in the sedentarization of nomadic Gypsy-Travellers.

Some of the struggles over control and management of space are played out in the arena of law. Here the focus is on Britain, where a series of legal statutes have been enacted over the course of the 20th Century which have had a severe impact on the lives of Gypsy-Travellers. The law functions to establish moral and social norms and pathologize aspects of Gypsy-Traveller life. Legal principles, sedentarist discourses and bureaucratic agencies combine to construct Gypsy-Travellers as deviant with regard to the moral and social order. Ingrained assumptions about what constitutes a normal way of life leave them out in the cold and often 'on the verge'.

In addition to struggles over local space, there are struggles – even more one-sided – over national and continental space. This can be seen in the experience of and reaction to Czech, Slovak, Hungarian and other Roma who seek asylum in Britain. Amidst the arrival of Roma in the UK and Canada seeking asylum during 1997 the media, public and politicians rushed to label the Roma as 'economic migrants' as opposed to 'genuine refugees'. The British government's reaction is set in the context of a European Union wide attempt to control regional migration. It adheres to the broad EU policy of regional containment of both economic and non-economic migration for the purposes of resource protection and labour market management. Originally the EU created a *cordon sanitaire* of Central European states like the Czech Republic who guaranteed to control immigration on their Eastern borders. With the accession of many of the former Communist states of Central and Eastern Europe to the EU in 2004, the control of population movements from these countries becomes more glaring – but also problematic within the body which theoretically allows for free movement of individuals within it. It was partly concern about Roma migration westwards following accession that put the condition of the Roma minorities in the new member states on the agenda during accession negotiations.

Finally, space and identity are modified by processes of globalization and the changing meanings given to nation and locality. Various developments in the society and the economy are creating and institutionalizing a separation between a network of globalized metropolitan centres, and non-metropolitan localities and peripheries which are unable to participate as global actors. New forms of regionalism and spatial zoning are affecting Roma and Gypsy-Travellers. Examples of this include the spatial cleansing demanded by conservative-national politicians. The emerging globalized European order creates a series of tensions between localities and nation-states, such that we can speak of the emergence of 'post-national states', which are concerned with controlling the mobility of individuals in the interests of maintaining their place in the global economy.

The 1990s and 21st Century have seen increasing encroachment on the lives of Roma, Gypsy-Travellers and other outsider groups within Europe. The exclusion of Roma and Gypsy-Travellers, particularly at a local level, draws on some long-standing prejudices against 'Gypsies'. However, the fact that there is such a long history of anti-Gypsy feeling in Europe should not distract us from the new forms of exclusion that have emerged. There is the establishment of spatial segregation and control of movement on a Continental level, the process of spatial cleansing and ghettoization on a local level, and the formation of a European identity and a European model of citizenship with which Roma and Gypsy-Travellers find themselves in an ambivalent relationship. I use the experience of Roma and Gypsy-Travellers to criticize current sociological conceptualizations. I argue that the problems European modernity creates for Roma and Travellers demands the remaking of a self-critical, open and reflexive modernity which will avoid both the ethnic fundamentalism and cultural essentialism of post-modern neo-tribalism, as well as the bureaucratic and universalist exclusions of classical modernity.

A Note on Terminology

The label 'Gypsy' is problematic. It is sometimes considered to be a pejorative exonym, and its use here has been avoided as far as possible. I include under the term 'Gypsy-Traveller' English Romanichels, Welsh Kale, Scottish Travellers (Nawken) and Irish Travellers (Minceir). I have used 'Roma' to refer to the Gypsies of Continental Europe, including Roma, Sinti, and so on. This division is a rather artificial one, and it subsumes differences between the many groups that I have included under these two headings, but I have used it because there are important historical, cultural, and socio-economic differences which are relevant to their experiences. Although I seek to take a 'European' perspective in terms of theory, the different identities, experiences and circumstances of Roma and Gypsy-Travellers, and the groups which are counted as belonging to those populations, should not be blurred. Linguistic inheritance differs. In addition to the language of their home country many speak a version of Romani.

The term 'gorgio' or 'gauje' is a Romani term referring to outsiders, settled folk, and has something like the force variously of the Mexican 'gringo' or the Jewish 'gentile'. I often use the term 'settled' interchangeably with gorgio or gauje, but again, as many Roma are not nomadic this division has to be drawn with care. It can easily lead to the conclusion that the problems identified stem solely from the existence of a nomadic group living in a settled society, and this is not the case.

Coarse Freedom: The Roma and Gypsy-Travellers of Europe

> He must therefore be popular with his subjects, and he binds them to himself by the charms of the gipsy life under his direction. Coarse freedom, a noisy jollity, and obscenest impudence give attractions to the gang (Marx, 1990: 852).

This section and the next put forward some theoretical and historical perspectives with which to contextualize and examine the experience of Roma and Gypsy-Travellers in Europe. This section describes how the constitution of modernity produces regulatory discourses that create and exclude outsider groups within Europe. These regulatory functions and narratives make and remake Europe as a restricted ideological space and geographic entity, from which Roma and Gypsy-Travellers are excluded. The historical rejection of Roma and Gypsy-Travellers by European society has taken an extreme form in that repeated attempts have been made to either excise them from society altogether, or forcibly incorporate them in a variety of ways, often with damaging outcomes for their culture, not to mention their wellbeing as individuals.

At each stage however they have been able to resist the complete eradication of their cultural and social identity. Partly, the internal social structure of Roma and Gypsy-Traveller groups has ensured their survival, by emphasizing the benefits of the 'Gypsy life' as opposed to a gauje or settled existence. Partly also their structural position, existing in the interstitial spaces of European modernity, has ensured their economic survival within even totalitarian states (Barany, 2002). However, new developments in globalization, the collapse of state Communism in Europe and the emergence of new forms and expressions of racism and social exclusion, present new challenges to Roma and Gypsy-Traveller communities throughout Europe.

I argue that the concepts of place and space are crucial to unravelling the workings of European modernity and its exclusion of outsider groups. 'Space' is usually taken to include place, but this chapter will attempt to disaggregate the two, identifying the association of place with identity, and space with institutional forms, such as the nation state and the bureaucratic institutions of modernity. Subsequent chapters will investigate in more detail some of the forms of exclusion based on these two concepts, the ways in which they intertwine and how they have affected Roma and Gypsy-Travellers in Europe of the 1990s.

For the purposes of this book I divide the population of European commonly referred to as 'Gypsy' into two broad groups. The Roma are peoples who speak various dialects of the Romani language and are part of a recognisable culture, distinct from that of the societies in which they live. Linguistic (Hancock, 1997b), anthropological (Ronald Lee, 1997) and some genetic (Bernasovsky, Jurickova, and Ferak, 1994) evidence indicates they are descended from nomadic groups who were displaced from India beginning in the 10th Century. At that time, they began a great migration north and west, eventually entering Europe through the Balkans and also possibly crossing the Straits of Gibraltar from North Africa. Reflecting their origins, the Romani language still contains elements of Hindi and Sanskrit. However, much of the discussion of their historical origins is, by necessity, speculative; and recent work has revised the assumption that linguistic descent equates with lineal purity (see the discussion in Mayall, 2004).

The majority of Roma are based in Continental Europe, especially Central and Eastern Europe, but various groups of Roma have at different times settled in North and South America, the UK and Australia, among other places. Many of those in Continental Europe have largely ceased to be nomadic in their lifestyle. In some cases this is because of government policies of forced settlement introduced this century, such as those which affected most of the Bulgarian, Czechoslovakian, Romanian and Polish Roma under Communism (McCagg, 1991; Jurova, 1993). In others they had lost their nomadic way of life centuries ago, two examples being the Roma of the Carpathian mountains in Poland (Nowicka, 1997) and the *Gitanos* of

Spain (Quintana and Floyd, 1986). Roma retain a strong cultural identity and intra-group identification. Their sense of separateness is maintained in part by internal processes and in part through the attitudes and practices of the settled, gauje population they live amongst.

Gypsy-Travellers share many cultural characteristics and history with Roma. However, they are a mixture of groups, some Roma in origin, others autochthonous. There are many autochthonous groups of traditional Travellers who are not of Romani origin, mainly originating in Western Europe. These are Travelling people who emerged at some point in the past from sedentary European society. They may have originated as travelling traders and craftspeople, such as metal workers (Gentleman, forthcoming). Over time they gradually developed the internal group complexity that came to differentiate them from the surrounding non-Travelling people as more than an occupational-positional grouping (ni Shuinear, 1994). It is likely that the labelling by the rest of the population of certain occupations carried out by these groups as low status and outcaste encouraged and even necessitated the construction of a strong intra-group identity. This group of Travellers includes the *Jenische* of Switzerland, Dutch *Woonwagenbewoner*, the Scottish and Irish Travellers of Britain and Ireland and the *Quinqui* of Spain.

It is likely that the Travellers' numbers were swelled by the various upheavals that have uprooted large numbers of people in Europe over the centuries, in particular the assorted enclosures of land and clearances of people from it in the name of agricultural improvement. The possibility of their origins in pre-modern times tends to be denied. It is assumed by many that they are socially deprived or delinquent groups resulting from such convulsions as the Highland Clearances in the case of Scottish Travellers, and the Great Famine in the case of Irish Travellers, an assumption reinforced by 'Gypsylorists' (Ronald Lee, 2000). Gypsy-Travellers in Britain have generally been able to maintain their nomadic life with greater success than the Roma of Central and Eastern Europe. They are mainly to be found in Western Europe, but like the Roma many have emigrated to other parts of the world, the USA being an especially popular destination with Irish Travellers who have founded several communities there (McDonagh and McVeigh, 1996).

Non-Romani Travellers even more than Romani Gypsies tend to be viewed as a nuisance to the order of settled society (MacAlister, 1937), and have been subject to similar attempts at settlement as affected the Roma of Central and Eastern Europe (Helleiner, 1998). In the UK at least some leeway is given in popular and elite discourse to 'genuine' Romani Gypsies as true nomads, in contrast to New Travellers and non-

Romani 'tinkers' who are reviled as the dropouts of settled society (Clark, 1997).

The distinction between Gypsy-Traveller and Roma groups is partly an artificial one, although it is one I use to some extent here as it is necessary for my analysis of their situation in Europe. It is probable that there was a large degree of cultural and linguistic interchange between the two after the arrival of the Roma in Europe, and perhaps the example of the Roma was an encouragement for various travelling groups to form a stronger internal group identity. In the light of this, some scholars have questioned the terms in which various of the two groups are identified (Acton, 1994), the imputed Indian origins of Gypsies themselves (Willems, 1998), and the relevance of those origins to Gypsy identity and group boundary maintenance (Okely, 1983). The distinction between Gypsy and gauje is also not as impermeable as is often claimed on both sides. There was and continues to be intermarriage between the settled and Roma/Gypsy-Traveller communities, as well as historical evidence of 'group association'.

Historically, both Roma and Gypsy-Travellers have had an impact on the history of the societies they encountered that often goes unacknowledged, except when they are considered as a social problem. They are seen as a people without history (Trumpener, 1992). Yet national folk cultures were influenced enormously by Roma and Gypsy-Travellers. In some countries, such as Russia (Lemon, 1991), Scotland (Braid, 1997) and Spain (Soravia, 1984), they became indispensable to the survival and revival of the national culture of folk music, storytelling and dance. They have carried out significant economic functions, some groups being nomadic craftspeople whose services were especially important to feudal and early-modern societies. Although traditional trades have declined in utility they have been quick to adapt to changing economic circumstances where possible (Sway, 1984).

Despite the contribution Roma and Gypsy-Travellers have made to European life, across the continent they are reviled as scroungers and parasites, as incorrigibles and, in the words of the former Slovakian Premier Vladimir Meciar, 'social unadaptables' (*Radio Free Europe/Radio Liberty*, 31 June 1998). In Britain, Gypsy-Travellers are increasingly restricted from pursuing a nomadic way of life. In the former Communist countries of Europe, Roma are excluded from the labour market, and are frequently the object of populist violence supported by police indifference (Bancroft, 1999). The arrival of Czech, Slovak and other Roma asylum seekers in Britain during 1997 and 1998 brought their suffering into British news headlines and the considerations of policymakers for a short time (Clark and Campbell, 2000).

Although both groups are called 'Gypsy' by others, at no point was any association made in mainstream political and press commentary between the situation of Roma in Central and Eastern Europe and that of Gypsy-Travellers in Britain. As was intimated earlier, a question which could be asked of the subject matter tackled here is 'What connects these things – racial violence, discrimination, spatial segregation, and so on – apart from the fact that they happen to people called "Gypsies" in different areas of Europe?'. A partial answer is that it is precisely the fact that these developments are happening in different areas of Europe to peoples who are labelled and represented in startlingly similar terms in their home countries that interests me and seems to be worthy of investigation.

The following brief outline of the two areas of from which the book draws most of its examples, which will illustrate in more detail some of the theoretical connections which can be made between the experience of Roma in the Czech Republic and Slovakia and Gypsy-Travellers in Britain.

Roma in the Czech Republic and Slovakia

Roma were well established in Bohemia by the 14th Century (Fraser, 1992). They carried out many functions valuable to the feudal lords of the Czech Lands, serving as blacksmiths, soldiers and so on. However, records indicate an increasing level of hostility towards them from the time when the first anti-Gypsy legislation was passed in Moravia in 1538 (Crowe, 1995). In the upheaval following the Turkish conquest of central Hungary, Roma were targeted as Turkish spies and murdered by local mobs. The situation calmed down somewhat following Maria-Theresa's accession to the Austro-Hungarian throne in the 18th Century. The Roma then became the objects of a reformatory policy instituted by her government, a policy which was designed to sedentarize nomadic Roma and assimilate them into the settled population and which became the model for state sedentarization practices.

The relatively enlightened policies of the Habsburgs were abandoned in the 19th Century. Reactionary absolutism was re-established after the end of the French Revolutionary wars in 1815. The Magyarization of Hungary after 1867 also affected Slovakia and Slovakian Roma badly, though the abolition of serfdom benefited both Roma and the Czechoslovak peasantry. After the establishment of Czechoslovakia in 1918 the Roma made some headway, the new Constitution giving them citizenship and recognition as a national minority. However, dark clouds began to gather with the revival of anti-nomadism ordinances in 1927. In 1928 an anti-Roma pogrom in Pobedim in Slovakia highlighted the worsening of relations between Roma and their neighbours (Crowe, 1995: 45-8). In response to the pogrom the newspaper *Slovak* commented 'the Pobedim case can be characterized as a citizens' revolt against Gypsy life. In this there are the roots of democracy' (Guy, 1998).

With the Nazi annexation of Czechoslovakia in 1939 and the establishment of a pro-Nazi government in Slovakia the net began to close around the Roma. Beginning in 1940, Czech Roma were rounded up and forced into 'labour' camps along with Jews. Some were shipped to concentration camps in other countries, such as Auschwitz, others to the Czech concentration camps at Lety and Hodonin, where they were massacred. Few Czech Roma survived the war. Most were murdered in the *porajmos*, or 'devouring' (Novitch, 1984). Slovakian Roma escaped extermination, the puppet state which the Nazis had established subjecting them to harassment and exclusion but not, for the most part, actively participating in their destruction as a people (Nir, 1993).

After the Second World War the Roma became the objects of an increasingly persecutory state policy under the Communist government. Nomadic Roma were forced to settle, and then pushed into low wage jobs to replace the Sudeten Germans who had been expelled from the country (Kostelancik, 1989). With the exception of a few years following the 1968 Prague Spring they were denied official recognition as a minority. A campaign of forced sterilization of Roma women was put in place in the 1950s. It continued into the 1980s, and some evidence suggests that it continues to the present, though without official sanction (Center for Reproductive Rights and Center for Human and Civil Rights, 2003). There was a deliberate attempt to destroy them culturally through forced assimilation, as much as the Nazis had attempted to eliminate them physically through extermination (Ulc, 1991). After Communism was overthrown in 1989 there was some optimism that the Roma would be able to take an accepted place in national life, with the formation of the Roma Civic Initiative. Although Roma now have many independent political voices, they have paid a heavy price for democracy, in the form of unemployment, discrimination and racial violence. Notoriously, many of them were denied citizenship of the newly formed Czech Republic under the Citizenship Law of 1993. After protests, the law was reformed in 1999, although problems remain. Currently, there are some 250-300,000 Roma in the Czech Republic (Liégeois and Gheorghe, 1995).

The work for this part of the book consisted of a number of interviews with key informants in the Czech Republic, in addition to a period of fieldwork there during 1998. This was supported by an investigation of contemporary newspaper and wire service reports on the situation there, and discussions with contacts via e-mail and newsgroups. It was considered important to investigate the situation of Roma in the Czech Republic specifically for a number of reasons, principally ease of access, but also the nature of the country itself. It occupies a significant position in the mental geography of Europe, having been a part of Communist Eastern Europe, but also considered to be the most Western of the former Communist states.

The Czech Republic's position on the border (Mendras, 1994) – or buffer zone (Wallace, Chmouliar, and Sidorenko, 1996) – between the two symbolic halves of Europe makes it an especially illuminating area to examine. The historical experience of Czech Roma and the history of the Czech Republic itself are both central to establishing it as an important area to work in. At times of rapid state directed modernization, under the Austro-Hungarian Empire and under Communism, Roma were made the object of systematic assimilation. Will Guy (1998) takes state attempts to sedentarize nomadic Roma and make them a part of the settled labour force as characteristic of what he calls the 'Eastern' approach to Roma. Czechoslovakian Roma have also been subject to what Guy calls the 'Western' model, similar to that in Britain, in which they are viewed as social outcasts, at best ignored but more often the object of legislation and state or populist action which is exclusionary rather than assimilative in purpose. He relates the two approaches to the differing histories of state and socio-economic development in Western and Eastern Europe. In terms of the treatment of Roma and wider issues of national and state formation, the Czech Republic can be placed as a part of both Western and Eastern Europe.

Gypsy-Travellers in Britain

> Queen Cleopatra,
> The gypsies' grand matra (Ben Jonson, *The Gypsies Metamorphosed*, 1621).

First recorded in Scotland in 1505, and in England in 1514, were a category of people who were referred to as 'Egyptians' by state authorities. As far as can be ascertained they used the label themselves in dealings with various European powers and with settled folk (Fraser, 1992). It is not clear from the historical record whether these people were Roma who had emigrated from the continent, or indigenous travelling people who had adopted a label useful in terms of seeking legitimacy within the established feudal order. Over the next four hundred years, 'Egyptians' – later to be called 'Gypsies' and 'Tinkers' – became a part of British life.

English and Welsh Gypsy-Travellers are usually considered to be one of the Roma peoples, though their position with regard to Continental Roma is ambivalent and the historical implications of this designation have been questioned. Scottish Travellers and Irish Travellers are autochthonous groups of Travellers. Gypsies and Travellers throughout Britain live in a variety of situations, some on council owned campsites, some on their own or privately owned campsites, some on marginal or disused land, and some in housing. Patterns of residence and travelling are complex, but not aimless. Movements can be voluntary, depending on occupations undertaken, economic opportunities, membership of a specific group, and of a family within that group, or they can be forced, caused by local hostility, police action and evictions or the threat of eviction. These factors constrain patterns of movement, but can also cause severe stress and disruption to individuals and families.

The Gypsy-Traveller population of the UK now includes several distinct groups: Scottish Travellers; Irish Travellers; English Gypsies and Welsh Gypsies. More recently, and seemingly unique to the UK, there has emerged a non-traditional travelling group, New Age Travellers (Lowe and Shaw, 1993). The total population of traditional Gypsy-Travellers is between 90,000 and 120,000 (Liégeois and Gheorghe, 1995). The numbers of New Travellers on the road appear to have declined significantly since 1994.

The fieldwork for this part of the book consisted of interviews with key informants, informal interviews and ethnographic observation on Traveller sites in Scotland and Wales. It was conducted intermittently over a period of three years. In addition, newspaper articles, government documents and historical records were drawn on. It was felt that a variety of methods served the aims of the book best, allowing local experiences to be connected with more wide-ranging themes and concerns.

Disputed Origins and Definitions

Judith Okely (1994) hypothesizes that the foreign origin ascribed to Gypsy-Travellers in the historical record is of doubtful veracity. She states as likely an indigenous, domestic origin for the English Gypsy-

Travellers that she worked with, rather than an exotic, Indian origin. She intends to establish the dynamic, evolving nature of Gypsy-Traveller culture, and rejects the picture of stasis and/or decline painted by 19th Century Gypsylorists among others. During the transition from feudalism to capitalism huge numbers of people were uprooted, creating many wandering bands of former peasants and feudal retainers. They eventually formed the nascent working class. Okely hypothesizes that there were groups of uprooted peasants who refused wage labour, rejected proletarianization, and chose instead to live on the road. Her theory presumes that it is not a coincidence that the presence of Gypsy-Travellers in the UK was first recorded at the time of the collapse of feudalism and the emergence of an absolutist monarchy, precursor to the modern nation state. Certainly, British society appears to periodically throw out groups of people who take to a nomadic life, if only temporarily. It is quite possible that some of these people are reabsorbed into settled society, while others become a part of Gypsy-Traveller society. Hence, the population displacements in the transition from feudalism to capitalism, after the Napoleonic Wars, and the Highland Clearances, could have created and then periodically replenished the Travelling population. People adopting a nomadic life may have found it useful to take on the image of 'the Gypsy' as allowing more freedom and economic opportunities.

Okely suggests that a process of cultural diffusion was at work, with local indigenous nomadic groups at various times adopting symbolic/linguistic practices borne by the 'Egyptian' incomers. Partly this adoption of language and symbol would have had the straightforward advantage of allowing for the ability to control information flow within the group. Word about prices, opportunities and so on would flow along the network lines of trade routes, fairs and stopping places. They would participate in a subsistence information economy. It is probable that this was a factor in the adoption and preservation by Irish Travellers of the ancient Celtic languages of Ireland. Their language could have developed as a subaltern dialect, out of the need to recognise fellow nomads and maintain some distance from the dominant society they lived cheek by jowl with.

Following on from Okely, Wim Willems (1997), associates the emergence of 'the true Gypsy' directly with the Enlightenment. He states that the Gypsies – in the sense of one people with a distinct culture and identity who are related to other groups across nations and continents – are as much a creation of government officials, social scientists and ethnographers as anything else. Groups of people across Europe have historically been labelled 'Gypsy' by authorities and the populace, normally as a precursor to their exclusion, assimilation or persecution (Mayall, 1992; Lucassen, 1999). This does not mean that they were 'real Gypsies', a term which really has no historical meaning. Recently, Roma and Gypsy-Traveller groups have begun to organize internationally and have attempted to present a common ethnic identity as one people. According to Willems they have done so in response to persecution and the real need to articulate some sort of common response to it, rather than from the recognition of a common identity (Willems, 1997). Along with some anthropologists he argues that there is no foundational connection between various 'Gypsy' groups, except insofar as Romani intellectuals seek to create one (Meester, 1992).

These theories are controversial for a variety of reasons, to be examined more closely in Chapter 3. They may be quite neat as far as indigenous Travellers are concerned, but they probably do not account fully for the ancient linguistic survivals in the Romani language among English Gypsies, for example. These survivals may be accounted for by a thesis of combined migration and cultural diffusion. Certainly there has long been an interchange of travelling people between Britain and the Continent and between Ireland and Britain. There is strong evidence that something links the various Roma and Gypsy-Traveller peoples other than a common experience of being the objects of state sponsored social science. Some of the evidence Okely presents to support her thesis, such as that based on court transcripts of the time, may reflect more on the keenness of the authorities to suggest that the 'Egyptians' were vagabonds faking their exotic nature to milk the credulous peasantry rather the actual nature of their origins.

There is a stronger objection to the theory of cultural diffusion made by many Roma and Gypsy-Travellers themselves. Arguments from the above perspective tend to be taken to imply that the 'constructed' ethnic group of the Gypsies can be compared to 'real' ethnic groups, and can be used in a hostile way, to 'de-ethnicize' specific groups of Gypsies. Indeed, Judith Okely has complained of her work being misused in this way. However, Okely's experience underscores the reason why this is such a strong concern. Simply put, the consequences of such interpretations can be harmful for specific groups of Gypsies, who mostly lack the power to seriously challenge them. This can be illustrated with a counter-example. The retrospective construction of the Celts as a unified people has been challenged by recent scholarship, which has suggested that, like so many things we take for granted, Celtic identity is a construction of 19th Century intellectuals and politicians (Dietler, 1994). This has been much to the irritation of Scottish Nationalist Party politicians, who are powerful enough to be able to insist on the 'emotional truths' that Scotland is a Celtic nation and that the Celts are one distinct people united across history and geography (*The Guardian*, 13 March 1998).

Roma and Gypsy-Travellers, however, have mostly been powerless to challenge such scholarly deconstructions of their origins. The 'nationality' of Scots is not in doubt; but the struggle to establish the 'ethnicity' of Gypsies has been a long one, and its objectives have been only partially achieved. Deconstructing 'ethnicity' can be politically damaging to the ethnic group on the receiving end, especially when their deconstruction is followed by a reconstruction as a socially delinquent subculture. This is not to denigrate the important perspectives brought to the debate here, but to acknowledge the possibility of a negative impact on Roma and Gypsy-Travellers. This is particularly relevant if seen in the perspective of the historical construction and criminalization of Gypsies as 'vagrants' in feudal and early modern Europe.

The Historical Context: Vagrancy, Nomadism and the Social Order

Contemporary records of trials, convictions and punishments for vagrancy – the socio-legal discourse which constructed vagrancy as violating the social order – increased enormously in number from 1550 (Beier, 1974). It would be an overgeneralization to say that this was a Europe wide phenomenon. It appears to have been a feature of the countries of North-Western Europe, in particular those that entered earliest into the period of mercantile capitalism, such as Holland and England. They were also the countries that participated in the Protestant revolution, and laid the framework for the early modern state. The construction of and response to vagrancy illustrated two developments which combined to produce a modern idea of spatial control and order. One was the establishment of the unified nation state guaranteeing property rights. The other was the emergence of the work ethic and the reviling of those nomadic individuals who appeared to reject it, and so were a threat to its legitimacy. Commentaries from the time began to subsume Gypsies within a general category of vagrants, and attacked the notion that they were a separate people rather than a rag-bag of delinquents who hung together for self-interest (Fraser, 2000).

Many vagrants were individualist in movement and behaviour. Some were organized into travelling groups, and some of these were identified as Gypsy in the historical record (Pound, 1971), though their actual identity is ambiguous, as was often acknowledged at the time. Though thought by the states to be an especially dangerous criminal element amongst the landless, there were few Gypsies among those arrested under the vagrancy statutes, and none in large gangs. Indeed, most vagrants of any sort still held to a trade, and were not idle wanderers. Despite that, the myth of wandering gangs of Gypsy criminals was current in the Netherlands of the 18th Century (Egmond, 1993), in 19th Century England (Mayall, 1988), and it was revived in the late 20th Century USA (see Chapter 5).

In early modern Britain and Ireland, vagrants were subject to severe repression. The Tudor state, like the Stuart state later on, saw them as a threat to its integrity, and to the moral coherence of English, and later British, identity. They were suspected of plots against the Queen and harbouring Spanish spies in their midst. The Scottish 'Egyptians' in the 17th Century were also accused of harbouring Catholics and plotting against the Protestant state. However, the fear of the vagrant was concerned with the more general threat to the social order which they represented (Beier, 1985). The punishments meted out to 'vagrants and vagabonds' included whippings, public humiliations in the stocks, transportation and so on. There was an essentially moral-symbolic motive behind the punishment of vagabonds, since if they had been seriously suspected of being spies or plotters they would in all likelihood have been executed. Their punishment and segregation authenticated the social order and helped to establish the work ethic (Powell, 1989).

The motivating force for the repression of vagrants at this time was the re-establishment of the social-moral fabric of state and society, which had started to come apart in the reign of the previous monarchs, Edward and Mary. State power was widened in response to bewildering social change. The vagrant transgresses the social order of settled society and symbolizes the weakness of that order. They are removed from any place in the old, paternalistic social hierarchy, but also violate the emerging social order. Nomadic Gypsies were no longer able to pass themselves off as pilgrims partly because the new society had no place for pilgrims, or the 'noble poor'. Instead the poor or the wanderer, the 'sturdy beggars' were a threat.

The treatment of vagrancy and of Gypsy-Travellers in times of state re-entrenchment in Scotland, England and other parts of Europe which were undergoing the transition from feudalism to capitalist modernity suggests that the development of the internal outsider was an important part of the construction of a settled European identity. The work ethic, the morality of property, and civility, were set off against the vagrant, the vagabond and the wandering Gypsy. However, with the development of state authority from the early modern era the governmental response to Gypsies changed from a policy of rejection and punishment to one of forcible incorporation. The differing treatment of vagrants, Gypsies and Travellers in early-modern Europe and in the 18th Century illustrates the development and institutionalization of prevailing modes of social order and social control within European modernity.

Beginning in the 18th Century Roma and Gypsy-Travellers became the objects of corrective, as opposed to punitive, regulation in those parts of Europe undergoing the most rapid and state-directed modernization, such as Austro-Hungary. The changing regulatory discourses to which they were subject coincide with the emergence of the modern, bureaucratic, nation-state in Europe. These novel forms of regulation found in the relationship between the dominant societies in Europe and their 'host aliens' is the key to understanding the relationship Roma and Gypsy-Traveller communities have with European modernity. Modernity is understood in this book as a set of organizing principles which revolutionized the relationship between individuals and society, and especially between internal outsiders and nationalized-states.

Themes and Issues to be Considered

A brief outline follows of the themes that will be pursued in succeeding chapters. Chapter 2 explores the relationship between modernity and its outsiders. Chapter 3 examines the production of race, the workings of racialization and the effects of racial action in relation to Roma and Travellers in Europe. It explores the association between modernity and the racialization of European thought, and inserts the experience of Gypsies into the history of racialized identity formations in Europe. Chapter 4 investigates more closely the creation of spatial structures in which power relations are implicated. The construction of space within European modernity affects the exclusion and marginalization of outsider groups. Chapter 5 places the forms of exclusion discussed in the previous chapters in the context of recent legislation in the UK. Chapter 6 attempts to bring the work of the previous three chapters together by examining the reaction to the Roma from Central and Eastern Europe who attempted to claim asylum in Western Europe and Canada from the 1990s onwards, and response of government and media to them. Chapter 7 seeks to provide a broad theoretical context for some of the forms of exclusion examined in the previous chapters by examining the forces of regionalization, globalization and localization as they affect Roma and Travellers. Chapter 8 concludes by summarizing the main findings of the research and drawing out the wider significance of some of the findings. It argues that from the 1990s there was a retrenchment of regulative discourses affecting Roma, Gypsy-Travellers and other outsider groups within Europe.

Chapter 2

Modernity, Space and the Outsider

Introduction

> Modernity is the belief in linear progress, absolute truths and rational planning of an ideal social order (Harvey 1989: 35).

It is important to distinguish the modern from the project of modernity. The idea of 'the modern' is older than the project of modernity. In the sense of a period in history distinguishable from the Middle Ages it dates from the 16th Century. The project of modernity came into being in 18th Century Europe. I am using the term to mean both an epistemic and an ontological standpoint with regard to humanity. It is the assumption that empirical, scientific truths about nature and humanity can and should be gathered, and in the light of these truths people can and should be moulded to fit in with an overall vision of society. However, modernity differs again from the project of modernity in that it describes a set of social changes, in Nico Mouzelis' (1999) terms the combination of mobilization and incorporation into universal systems such as the free market with a high degree of structural-functional differentiation. These are processes over which humanity seems to have decreasing control over or conscious understanding of.

Anthony Woodiwiss (1997) makes some criticisms of the modish use of modernity within sociology. He argues that sociology has progressively wiped Marxism, class and capitalism from its conceptual chalkboard as these terms have been made problematic by rapid social change. In casting around for a replacement, modernity has been seductive, providing both a large canvas against which to 'do theory', and also a convenient way of describing certain societies and contrasting them with both pre-modern and post-modern formations. He states that the use contemporary theorists such as Stuart Hall (1992), Anthony Giddens (1990), Zygmunt Bauman (1992) and others make of modernity is as flawed as the concept itself. To him it is ill-defined, nebulous and generally unhelpful to effective sociological analysis, and he proposes a return to 'capitalism' as a core concern and tool. He makes some relevant points, but the term will be retained in this work as encapsulating some historically specific formations which the term 'capitalism' does not. In my opinion it provides a far better basis to explain the experiences of Roma and Gypsy-Travellers in Europe, who have found themselves on the sharp end of socialist and capitalist systems. The following discussion of modernity and its application as a theoretical concept will try to avoid the traps identified by Woodiwiss.

Jurgen Habermas (1987) describes and criticizes the project of modernity as privileging damaging forms of reason and rationality which objectify and reify humanity and nature (Guzzoni, 1997). The project of modernity is usually associated with the Enlightenment, although it goes beyond the thinkers associated with the Enlightenment to include the cumulative effect of bureaucracies, planners, and nation-states, from everyday decisions at the local level to strategic plans at the national level. It is a project of institutionalized regulation, and of the internalization of self-regulation (Elias, 1995). The unique feature of modernity is that it creates a body of rules and regulations which most of the time do not have to be enforced by the unprecedented regulative apparatus the state builds up. Individuals themselves adhere to them and regulate themselves. The modern social actor is concerned to avoid the loss of self-control and the resulting shame and embarrassment (Kumics, 1991), and this concern governs everyday life much more than does power, whether naked or disguised.

The combination of the increasing self-regulation of individuals and the investing of regulatory power in institutions was identified by Norbert Elias as the 'civilizing process'. The idea of the civilizing process is often criticized as a naively teleological one, describing progress from an unruly and barbarous pre-modern state, to a neat and orderly civilized society (Engler, 1997), and failing to take into account the role of capitalist development (Robinson, 1987). To understand the civilizing process in this way misconstrues it (Dunning and Mennell, 1998), misunderstanding the ambivalent nature of the process (Burkitt, 1996). As Elias has described it, the civilizing process removes the unseemly – the chaotic – from day to day life while at the same time building up a reserve of power in the nation-state that is unprecedented in history (Elias, 1978). Those that do not fit with the project become the objects of this power, whilst strategies of resistance which were previously effective become obsolete or more difficult to employ. So it should not surprise us, though it does, that the Holocaust took place in what was at the time the culturally and economically most advanced country in Europe (Agassi, 1996).

The project of modernity originated in Europe, and it is in Europe where, in the past two or three decades, it has been radically questioned (Bauman, 1997). In contrast, in parts of the developing world such as South-East Asia and China, a modernization process that is very similar to the classical project of modernity is pursued with a vigour and lack of concern for individuals that would make most post-modernists despair (Tiryakian, 1984; Raymond Lee, 1994). Perhaps it says something about its nature that the project of modernity has often functioned better – as in corresponding closest to its ideal-type – when it has been an export. That is, it has been most successful as both an internal and external export. It has been practiced on outsider and other powerless groups within Europe, and on the presumed *tabula rasa* of colonized and post-colonial states outside it. It is the least powerful who have been most subject to the modernist project of recreating society and humanity from the ground up. Within Europe itself, marginalized populations have been made into that very blank sheet.

Philosophical critiques of modernity have their origins in the work of Nietzsche (1969) and Heidegger (1962). Sociological criticism of the project of modernity can be traced from the work of Weber (1927), though his pessimism is often overstated (Seidman 1985). Horkheimer and Adorno (1973) argued that within the bounds of Enlightenment reason the project of domination of nature is transformed into the domination of humanity. The logic of Enlightenment rationality leads to control and repression of humanity by the forces of instrumental reason, the Nazi terror being merely the culmination of this logic of domination. Without the experience of the Holocaust to learn from, Weber arrived at similarly pessimistic conclusions much earlier in the 20th Century. He saw humanity seeking to emancipate itself through the Enlightenment project by applying universal principles of rationality to nature and to social organization. However the internal logic of modernity means that formal-instrumental rationality wins out over other forms of rationality. Formal rationality and instrumental reason feed off each other until they have created an iron cage of regulation and control (Habermas, 1987b). The Mephistophelian promise turns out to have a limited shelf life, and the creators are devoured by their creation. Much like the Golem of Jewish legend humanity creates a force to serve it, which ends up dominating it (Hill and Pinch, 1993).

The exclusion and ordering of marginal populations within modernity are understood here as intimately spatial forms of regulation. Luce Irigaray (1985a; b) has said that modernity is concerned only with creating and maintaining borders and is not concerned with the spaces within them. This is not entirely accurate.

The project of modernity does seek the ordering of space, and the way in which space is ordered is changing as modernity evolves. In its classical form it was concerned with making spaces under its gaze ordered as well as bordered. Increasingly however, the institutional processes which govern contemporary societies make some places into ordered zones and leaves others to their own devices, as dark zones. This development is a move away from the Foucauldian concept of the Panopticon. Rather than all individuals being monitored, or behaving as if they were being monitored, the landscape of modern society is transformed into dark and light zones, the latter protected against undesirable individuals in a variety of ways (McKinlay and Taylor, 1998).

Much – indeed most – work about the transformation of the landscape within modernity concerns the urban landscape (Gottdiener, 1991). There are quite good reasons for examining the city as the prime location of the institutions of modernity. The city is both the ultimate achievement of modernity, its supreme statement in its constant chaos and remoulding of itself, and the biggest problem for the modern project for precisely these reasons. For example, urban renewal projects are targeted at the re-creation of city space as governable space (Sorkin, 1992). The re-construction of Paris by Baron Haussmann had the specific aim of editing out the mob and the de-stabilizing crowd (Fabijancic, 1995), and the creation of greenfield capital cities (like Abuja and Brasilia) are in part attempts to overcome the disorder and chaos of the city space. Less often examined, but equally relevant to the way space is actively formed and regulated, are the constructions of the countryside that are produced within European modernity.

The rural countryside within modernity has been subject to similar forms of constrictive control to the city (Bantjes, 1997). It could be argued that in Britain at least institutional modernity has been more effective in regulating, zoning and ordering the countryside than the city. Certainly since the end of the Second World War and the rapid transformation of the countryside into a factory floor for the agricultural-industrial complex the extent and complexity of regulations affecting the countryside has increased exponentially. The British countryside is now strongly zoned and policed. Rural areas are designated for either residential or agricultural/industrial use. The home is separated from the workplace. Gypsy-Travellers in the countryside have faced increasing pressures because of this, since they fall between the two zoning principles. Gypsy-Traveller society does not traditionally employ the level of mental and spatial division between work and home that characterizes settled society. Some of the competing and conflicting constructions of the rural locale will be considered in following chapters, with regard to the imputing of the rural locality with competing narratives of meaning and to the geographical, physical and social isolation of Gypsy-Travellers.

To the extent that Gypsy-Travellers have managed to maintain an arm's length relationship with the project of modernity they have been able to maintain a distinct socio-cultural space, a space for cultural survival. To the extent that they have been enclosed by it, they have found their culture under threat. Sometimes the threat has been deadly, as in the Nazi Holocaust (Eiber, 1998). To focus solely on the Holocaust is somewhat misleading, as there have been many less dramatic attempts to systematically wipe out their way of life under otherwise democratic regimes (Milton, 1998). Throughout the post-war period certain European countries, such as Switzerland and Ireland, had state-sanctioned programmes whereby Traveller children were removed from their families and placed in foster care, for the sole reason that they were Travellers (Helleiner, 1998). One of the reasons they have been subject to so much state action, particularly during the 20th Century, is that they have been construed by politicians, professionals and the public as a 'backward' section of the population. For the nation-state to have an internal population which rejects some of the key principles of modernity shows up the mismatch between the universalizing principles of modernity and the inequalities which it creates and sustains. Modernity includes an idea of backwardness as a counterpart to the idea of the modern.

Modernity and Backwardness

It is in its continuous revolutionizing of human society and its relationship to the natural world that the period of modernity stands apart from other periods in history. Modernity revolutionizes much more than society's productive capabilities, recreating the uses humans make of time and space. The ways in which modernity organizes society and individuals according to time is important for the view taken of outsider populations, especially in the way they are constructed as backward peoples who are threatening to the moral order, and how it establishes Western Europe as civilized by comparison (Agnew, 1996; Wolff, 1994).

Modernity has been notable for the way it imposed a unity of backwardness on the recent past and on non-modern societies contemporaneous with European modernity (Gellner, 1987). Nothing was quite so modern as European modernity, and nothing quite so backward as the non-European societies that were encountered in the evangelical expansionist stage of European history, which involved the conversion of non-European societies to this idea of progress. 'Backwardness' became a moral category, and the moral imperative – the new white man's burden – was to rid the world of backwardness. A moral imperative to intervene against backwardness was created. Certain social groups were branded as backward and proceed to be subjected to a process of forced modernization.

Some of the greatest human disasters of the 20th Century have come in the name of progress, and of excising obstacles to that progress. In this way, backwardness is the original sin of modernity. It should come as no surprise that the European nations most keen to modernize, most acutely aware of the catching up they have to do, are those quickest to stereotype Roma in particular as backward, 'socially unadaptable' and so on. In the service of this idea, social science is in constant danger of becoming the science of backwardness, through its continual concern with the marginal and the deviant, which can be at its most intrusive when taking the form of a concern for their wellbeing.

Roma and Gypsy-Travellers especially are seen as out of time in this way. It is in these terms that they have been the object of assimilation programmes under both absolutist, Communist and democratic states in Europe. In the first two, they were an embarrassing reminder of backwardness in a rapidly modernizing society. In the last they were the objects of the welfare capitalist state. Since the revolutions of 1989, the former Communist states have undergone a rapid transition, producing a politics of memory which has scapegoated ethnic outsider groups in these countries and sought to (re)establish the ethnic homogeneity of the nation (Wydra, 1998). The tools developed by Communist social sciences for the assimilation of Roma were equally useful for establishing their exclusion under post-Communism (Kohn, 1995). The apparent discontinuity between the treatment of Roma under Communism and the post-Communist era may hide a deeper continuity, explicable in terms of the way in which the modern nation state functions as a social-engineering state, focusing its energies on 'out of place' peoples.

Necessary Cruelty and the Gardening State

Zygmunt Bauman (1989; 1991a) uses the metaphor of the gardening state to illustrate the social-engineering ambitions of Enlightenment philosophers and statesmen. The conflict between order and ambivalence is fundamental to modernity. The garden is quite an apt metaphor for the treatment of individuals defined as non-functional. Like weeds, they inhibit the growth of the finer specimens. They must be removed not because they are inferior *per se* but because they inhibit the development of the superior individuals, and so society's progress. In this vision of society there is no scope for co-existence, and everything which is dysfunctional or non-functional must be removed from the garden one way or another. Progress requires the removal of what holds society back from attaining its fullest development. The ambition of creating a 'universal man' through the establishment of order and the permanent removal of ambivalence came to be realised in the totalitarian visions of the Soviet Union and Nazi Germany.

The time-space distanciation characteristic of modernity allows for strong action at a distance (Giddens, 1985). According to Bauman it removes the individual both from having to make a moral choice and having to face the consequences of his or her actions. It allows for the application of necessary cruelty by bureaucrats without them having to face or feel the consequences of their actions. Milgram's voltage experiment illustrated how individuals will with few qualms inflict an immense amount of suffering on another individual when it is sanctioned by an expert system (Milgram, 1974; Lutsky, 1995; Miller, Collins, and Brief, 1995). Necessary cruelty – cruelty limited only by necessity – is an instrument of the gardening state. This necessary cruelty is one way of describing the relationship the state has to outsider groups. It applies various forms of coercive assimilation, interfering in their lives with little restraint, when it is felt necessary to do so (for criticisms of Bauman's position see O'Kane, 1997; Freeman, 1995).

Marx wrote in the Economic and Philosophical Manuscripts (Marx 1964) that the uniqueness of the human condition lay in humanity's ability to act upon the external world, to create plans in the mind which would be recreated in nature. For him, progress in human affairs rested on increasing this architectronic facility. For Marx and many other thinkers adhering to the Enlightenment project the extent to which humanity's existence is defined by natural forces outwith its control equates to the degree to which it is still fettered to the past. The extent to which social-technological forces are able to dominate nature and society is equated with progress. The Promethean standpoint exemplified by Marx has been much criticized for the way in which it creates an intellectual separation between humanity and the environment, and removes any limitations on the impact of human society on the ecosystem (Gorz, 1993.) In doing so it opens up enormous risks and dangers for human survival (Beck, 1987).

Humanity's pursuit of modernization with little regard for the rest of nature is not necessarily entirely negative. It is likely that even hardened postmodernists would, if pressed, admit to preferring to live in a world with electric light and Internet access. The negative aspect of the promethean vision outlined above which is important here is the way it leads to an unlimited domination of humanity by social and institutional forces. What escapes social control becomes defined as a problem for order, and groups such as Roma and Gypsy-Travellers who appear to stand in the way of modernization are transformed into a social problem. The policies created and applied by European nation states to 'solve the Gypsy problem' are intertwined with the character of European modernity.

State Policy Towards Travellers: From Elimination to Assimilation

> Policies [towards Roma/Gypsies] can be broadly grouped into three categories: exclusion, containment and assimilation ... these categories are not mutually exclusive: they can operate side by side during the same period in different states, or even simultaneously, seemingly in mutual contradiction, within a given state (Liégeois and Gheorghe, 1995: 8).

Strategies directed towards coercively re-making the Roma and Gypsy-Traveller populations started to be put in place during the 18th Century, after long centuries of Europe-wide persecution of Roma (Hancock, 1987a). It would seem that the adoption of these various strategies – in particular assimilative strategies – were associated in both time and place with the formation of modernity. On the one hand, established states which were following a path of 'enlightened' modernization, such as Austro-Hungary, adopted policies designed to turn Roma into national citizens. Later on, in the 19th and early 20th Centuries, nation-states which were forming on ethnic lines began to emphasize policies designed to contain or exclude Roma, along with other non-national ethnic groups. This was especially the case with the states of Central and Eastern Europe (Livezeanu, 1995). After 1945, assimilative policies came to the fore again in Europe. What follows is a brief overview of a few of these strategies, which are relevant to following chapters.

The first attempt by a modernizing state to forcibly assimilate Roma was in the Austro-Hungarian Empire. The Habsburg Empress Maria Theresa instituted in 1758 a set of policies intended to sedentarize nomadic Roma and assimilate them into the population as 'new Magyars'. They were barred from wearing their traditional dress, using the Romani tongue, owning horses and wagons and were restricted in their movements and the trades they could follow. Children were forcibly removed from their parents and placed with Hungarian families. They resisted these assimilative polices and in this they were assisted by much of the populace, who did not wish to accept the Roma within their communities. The policy spawned imitations in Prussia and Spain at around the same time.

Assimilative and repressive measures in general seem to have fallen into disuse during the 19th Century. Population upheavals, war and revolution gave the elites of Europe much more to worry about in terms of maintaining the social order. There were some gains for Roma. Romanian Gypsy slaves were freed in 1864. Austro-Hungarian Roma benefited from the general emancipation of the serfs. There were also forebodings of things to come in the 20th Century. During the 19th Century race science was developed by European and North American intellectuals, its appeal spreading rapidly and forming the basis for categorical distinctions between peoples. It was a part of a wider racialization of European thought, the development of a racial science of humanity feeding the populist eugenics movement. The consequences of this were to be felt in the 20th Century, when they became the basis for the thinking behind Nazi racial science (Barondess, 1998).

It was during the first three decades of the 20th Century that two types of state policy on outsider groups began to crystallize. One was to institute regulative and assimilative policies based on their conception of Roma and Gypsy-Travellers as a social problem. The other sought the removal or destruction of them as a racial other. In practice, both often made use of similar instruments, the Nazi state being able to rely on the anti-Gypsy regulative apparatus built up under the Weimar Republic and preceding regimes. It was the Nazi government which brought the project of modernity to its zenith and nadir. The German bureaucracy, its scientists – both social and natural – its police, its civil service, were all mobilized towards the complete destruction of two ethnic groups, Jews and Gypsies (Hancock, 1987b; Hancock, 1988; Lutz, 1995). They were identified, enumerated, segregated and finally annihilated (Huttenbach, 1991). The destruction of the Gypsies is the forgotten Holocaust, and it is seldom remembered or commemorated (Bauer, 1994). Survivors have had great trouble getting compensation from either the German government or the Swiss banks which appropriated their savings (Kenrick, 1998).

Most of the Communist states of post-war Central and Eastern Europe have pursued policies of coercive assimilation that have had a lasting and deleterious effect on their Roma populations. One example is Poland, which began its programme of forced settlement in the 1950s (Mirga, 1993). Poland contained some groups of Roma who had been long settled. However it still had at the time a large number of Roma who lived in trailers and were nomadic or semi-nomadic, and who were the target of the Communist government's assimilation policy. The assimilative measures carried out included the removal of wheels from trailers and shooting of horses. In this it was typical of the assimilative measures aimed at Roma and Gypsy-Travellers which attack nomadism. The Roma of Poland refer to this time as 'the Great Halt'. The programme of the Polish state was typical of some other Communist countries, such as Czechoslovakia.

Zoltan Barany (2002) highlights the variety of policies pursued by Communist governments. He identifies four approaches, the first, consistent coercion, was adhered to by Czechoslovakia and Bulgaria. Laws directed against them were promulgated at a national level and enforced across the board. The second was erratic intrusion, common to Poland and Romania. There were similar policies as in the first two, but their implementation depended on local authorities. Romania practiced forced proletarianization, confiscating gold coins that were the main form of wealth that Roma possessed. The third was decreasing pressures, exemplified by Hungary. Initial assimilation was modified by the increasing account taken of the Roma identity and recognition of autonomy. The assimilation policy was official ended in 1984. Finally, constructive interference was the lot of Yugoslavian Roma.

Yugoslavia was an exception to the assimilative orientation of most European Communist states. The policy was integrative. Roma had many organizations that were autonomous from the state. They were a visible, recognized ethnic minority. By the 1970s the federal government had given them recognition as a national minority, and the state funded various programmes to promote Roma culture. In 1981 the government granted them national status. The individual republics pursued their own policies, with Slovenia practising segregation in contrast to the relaxed policy of Serbia and Macedonia. Several factors combined to allow Yugoslavia to be among the most progressive of European states with regard to Roma. There was the fact that it was a completely new state. Unlike Romania, for instance, its cultural politics were not defined as the expression of ethno-national supremacy (Roth, 1995; Gallagher, 1992). Perhaps because of its multi-national makeup it needed to emphasize accommodation of minorities, including the Roma. The federal system was sufficiently pluralist to allow for a political culture accommodating to ethnic-minorities. Its relative independence from the Soviet Union seems to be relevant here, in light of the 1956 Soviet government decree that nomadic groups should be settled.

Yugoslavia has now fragmented, and the *de facto* principle whereby rights inhere in ethnically homogenous territorial units has been established to succeed it (Rabrenovic, 1997). This development was not the inevitable result of long buried tribal hatreds, as Western European opinion has often represented it. Rather, it was in part the outcome of actions and decisions made by politicians such as Slobodan Milosivec and Franjo Tudjman (Denich, 1994), as well as Western European governments and international bodies who largely accepted the new ethnic order (Kumar, 1997; Hudis, 1996), and the longer term process of economic development (Calhoun and Pfaff, 1998). The fragmentation of the country has destroyed the rights of those who did not belong to any of the territorially based ethnic groups, or who belong to one of them but are in the wrong place (Hayden, 1996). Many Bosnian Roma became refugees in Western countries. They were made to return to Bosnia on the grounds that peace has been established. However, the Dayton peace agreement accepts the parcelling out of the country on ethnic lines (Bass, 1998), and the Roma have found that they have no place in the ethnic structure (European Roma Rights Center, 2004b).

Croatia is not an easy place for Roma either. The creation of a homogenous ethno-national state by Tudjman deliberately excluded Serbs, Roma and other minorities from the vision of the nation, drawing on the imagery and rhetoric of the short-lived wartime Nazi puppet state which was enthusiastic in its cleansing of Jews, Serbs and Roma (Mirkovic 1996). Roma in Kosovo are in an ambivalent situation regarding the conflict between Serbs and Albanians. Many were victimized when Albanians were dominant, and some Roma organizations identify primarily with the Serb minority there, although others support the Albanian autonomy movement. Continued problems exist in Kosovo following the 1999 war, with Roma being targeted along with Serbs (European Roma Rights Center, 2004a). In general, being a Rom seems to mean being at the bottom the status ladder of all ethnic groups, and being discriminated against by whatever group is in power.

Yugoslavia's legacy, however, is not solely one of ethnic cleansing and warlord banditry. One of its successor states, Macedonia, appears to have reached a broad accommodation between all ethnic groups, including the large number of Roma in the country. According to Zoltan Barany (1995), the Roma there have managed far better than in other post-communist states. They have not had to endure the level of discrimination or the violence that Roma in the rest of Central and Eastern Europe have faced. The government of Macedonia has implemented effective measures to support the Roma, and the Macedonian majority group does not see them as threatening. In part, this is due to the existence of well-organized and vocal Roma political parties, but also to the makeup of Macedonian society and the actions of political leaders (Marks and Fraenkel, 1997). The largest ethnic groups are the Macedonians and Albanians, followed by the Roma. Neither one is capable of achieving dominance of the other two, so an accommodation between the different ethnic groups is not only desirable but necessary.

However, findings of the European Roma Rights Center (1998a) suggest that there is pattern of exclusion of Macedonian Roma which is similar to that which Roma face in other parts of the region. There have been instances of police violence reported recently (2002). Roma are held in low esteem by both ethnic Albanians and Macedonians (Kanev, 1996). Many were rendered stateless by the 1992 Act on Citizenship. As in other parts of Central and Eastern Europe, Roma have been deprived of basic rights and marginalized by the law. Unemployment is also rife, the Roma having borne the brunt of the economic problems which followed the break up of Yugoslavia.

There has been an equally long record of assimilative legal and bureaucratic measures in post-war Western Europe, though their magnitude is far less than that in Communist Europe. Totalitarian Communism allowed for no restraint on the part of the state. The weakness of civil society under Communism meant that few limiting factors on the power of the state were present. Liberal democracy has allowed Roma and Gypsy-Travellers a little more breathing space, even if more by default than intention. Assimilation in Western Europe has taken different forms. Networks of official sites were set up in Britain and the Netherlands, partly with the intention of brining nomadism to and end. Since these state owned sites were set up, nomadism fell and dependence on the welfare state increased (Sandford, 1973; Cottaar, 1998). In other cases much more coercive and regulatory methods were applied, such as the forced sterilization of Roma and other social outcasts in Sweden.

It is impossible to put one broad categorization on state treatment of Roma and Gypsy-Travellers in 21st Century Europe, but there are some trends emerging. In former Communist Europe, policy at a local level seems to have turned back towards exclusion on ethnic lines, while national governments make policies aimed at increasing integration of Roma (Government of the Republic of Hungary, 1997; Government of the Slovak Republic, 1997; Government of the Czech Republic, 1997). Most sources for this book were cynical about the effectiveness of these policies in counteracting the resurgence of anti-Roma violence and discrimination. There seems to be an emerging divergence between the policies of the national state towards Roma, and the actions of the local state and populace. However, these developments do suggest hope for constructive, local, national and international dialogues in which Roma have a recognized voice.

Michael Meyer (1969) describes the clash between the creation of universal human rights in the Enlightenment and the actual implementation of them with regard to Jews. Gentiles were abstractly in favour of granting Jews full citizenship, but when faced with the actually existing Jew, 'the flesh-and-blood Jew with his beard, strange garments and wholly irrational ceremonial law', many balked at the implications of recognizing them as full human beings. His description is analogous to the situation of Roma today, especially in Central and Eastern Europe. The nation-state is capable of granting them full citizenship and human rights, including ethnic minority rights, in the abstract. Yet when it comes to granting them full humanity in the concrete, at the level of the local state where the actual enactment of such rights is carried out, conflict remains.

Yet the conflict between 'abstract universal ideals' and local particularisms also ran in the other direction. Bauman (1989) describes the way that, under the Nazi regime, Germans were often quite capable of expressing generalized anti-Semitic sentiment whilst defending or being unwilling to attack Jewish neighbours and colleagues, 'our Jews'. The Nazi government found this a great source of irritation, complaining that non-Jewish Germans showed insufficient enthusiasm for instances of organized anti-Jewish hysteria like the *Kristallnacht*, even defending Jewish neighbours from attacks. In this instance racism was the 'abstract universal' which came up against the obstacle of localism. The Nazis had to actively had to construct an 'abstract Jew' to make their destruction possible.

In the case of the Roma of Eastern Europe the opposite is the case. They are granted abstract rights within the nation-state yet the police, local councillors and so on balk when confronted with having to apply them to 'their Gypsies'. Opinion surveys in the post-Communist states indicate that the imputed negative characteristics of Roma are uppermost in the minds of the populace (Tomova, 1995). Public opinion of Gypsy-Travellers there is little different from the rest of Europe. In many of the former Communist countries there is a prevailing tendency to think the national government is 'a bit soft', divorced from the reality of the situation in its effort to pay lip service to the equally unrealistic ideals of the international community.

In Western Europe a concern at government level with the situation of Roma in Central and Eastern Europe seems to disguise a lack of action concerning Gypsies in their own countries. In Britain, the planning system is stacked against Gypsy-Travellers being granted the right to live on their own land. The legal system pushes them off the verges of the road and out of longstanding traditional – but unauthorized – encampments on unused land. Their spatial movement is restricted by the institutional structure of British society, as well as by local hostility from settled folk.

Constructions of Space and Identity: Geographies of Exclusion and the 'Place' of Europe

> If Irish Travellers want their ethnicity, they should go and do it somewhere else. Irish local councillor (MacLaughlin, 1999b).

Roma and Gypsy-Travellers are recurrent objects of institutional regulation. They have historically been at the sharp end of processes and structures of legal control, bureaucratic surveillance, racialization and nation state building. They can be seen as a paradigmatic outsider group. There are many different groups of Roma and Gypsy-Travellers in Europe and the rest of the world, many of whom do not recognize any commonality between each other. Yet their experience, of being accorded the lowest social status, of enduring persecution and exclusion, spans the differences between the separate groups and the countries they live in.

This book is seeking to interpret how the matrix of surveillance and symbolic mobilization impacts on marginalized populations in Europe. It now develops in two broad areas: governance, regulation and the monitoring and control of space in European modernity; and the development of status, ethnic and national identities and hierarchies. It finds that the exclusion of Roma and Gypsy-Travellers from European society can best be described and explained by examining the constructions of space and place within Europe. It can be seen that the social order is a spatial order, and that the ordering of place at a European, national and local level functions to exclude outsider groups like Roma and Gypsy-Travellers. It argues that these processes underpin social integration and exclusion within Europe in the 21st Century, relating not only to Roma and Gypsy-Travellers but affecting the wider structures of modern society. Although primarily concentrating on Britain and the Czech Republic, since these are the two main fieldwork areas, the focus moves from the local level to the European, seeking to explain the complex associations of inclusion and exclusion.

Chapter 3

The Gypsies Metamorphosed: Race, Racialization and Racial Action in Europe

Introduction

This chapter examines the narratives of race and racialization in European modernity. It considers whether and to what extent Roma and Gypsy-Travellers have been subjects of racism, and uses their experience to problematize common sociological understanding of the origins, meanings and functions of 'race' and 'racism'. It begins with a discussion of the concepts of whiteness and blackness, and finds that Gypsies were associated with the latter in early modern English literature. It comments on the usefulness of the term 'ethnic group', and suggests that the concept of 'status' better explains some aspects of internal group maintenance. It relates anti-Gypsy-Traveller and anti-Roma sentiment to Simmel's concept of 'the Stranger'.

The focus of this chapter is the formation of ethnic and racial identity and the process of racialization in European life, considered from the perspective of Roma and Gypsy-Travellers. The extent of anti-Roma violence in Europe will be described, and related to particular processes of state and nation formation, as well as practices which constitute 'white' and 'settled' identities. These practices will be traced through this chapter. It will use them to challenge the way racial violence and ethnic cleansing is associated in West European political discourse with the 'barbarous East'. In contrast, the particularly modern and European nature of anti-Roma and anti-Gypsy-Traveller sentiment and action will be established. To provide some historical context the chapter begins by examining the construction of racial archetypes in the history of Europe, making specific reference to the creation of a racialized 'Gypsy' identity in relation to intellectual discourse and state and social conventions within European modernity.

'Gypsies' and the Idea of Race in European Thought

The meaning of race and the significance of phenotypical differences has varied enormously throughout modern European history (Solomos and Back, 1996; Banton, 1980). Categories of whiteness and blackness are not fixed but are formed and deployed as practical strategies of boundary maintenance. Racial categories, like any other social categorization, are constituted in terms of state structures, intellectual and everyday discourses and balances of social power. They are a part of social life within European modernity because they have the particular utility of providing an ideological and practical way of dealing with the tensions between universality and specificity which characterize modernity. The development of European modernity and of the concept of race are intertwined, the project of modernity including race as a core innovation in its conceptual framework (Goldberg, 1993; but see also Malik 1996).

Roma and Gypsy-Travellers in Europe have been the object of racial practices and racialized conceptual structures. However, they have existed at a curious juncture between racial categories, sometimes held up as romantic bohemian outsiders, at other times subject to rapid processes of racialization and destruction. Nazi ideology combined both perspectives, romanticizing 'true Aryan Gypsies' at the same time as Roma and Sinti were herded into the concentration camps (Willems 1997). The historical construction of 'Gypsy' as a meaning laden term in Europe has occurred within the context of the prevailing social-intellectual structure of different periods and places. The changing categorical significance and social meaning of the term 'Gypsy' illustrates how identity and difference have to be repeatedly reconstructed, and the ways in which the continual recreation of Roma and Gypsy-Travellers as an outcast group is affected by social and political pressures and conflicts within European societies. The following example of one historical meaning constructed around Gypsies is used to illustrate the reification of a racial category within European thought:

> CORVINO Has he children?
> MOSCA Bastards,
> Some dozen, or more, that he begot on beggars,
> Gipsies, and Jews, and black-moors, when he was drunk.
> Knew you not that, sir? 'Tis the common fable,
> The Dwarf, the Fool, the Eunuch are all his.
> (Ben Jonson, *Volpone*, 1605: Act 1, Scene 5, Lines 40-45).

Ben Jonson's *Volpone* or *The Fox*, is set in Venice. The theme of the play is justice. Mosca is a parasite (a self-ascribed status) and is called a devil by Volpone. Corvino (the Crow) is a merchant. Both are seeking to benefit from the estate of Volpone, who in the above scene is close to expiring. Comparisons with Shakespeare's *Merchant of Venice* spring to mind, especially similarities and differences between the representation of Jews in the latter and Gypsies in the former. Both plays contain what appear to be particularly pre-modern representations of the two, having them as both outsiders in European society and at the same time acknowledged playing a necessary part within it. To modern eyes the plays seem paradoxical, their representation of the racial outsider being very different from the discourse of racism that prevails in modernity. The point can be made clearer by examining Jonson's masque *The Gypsies Metamorphosed* of 1621, in which Gypsies turn up again.

> CHORUS: To see a gypsy, as an Ethiop, white.
> (Ben Jonson, *The Gypsies Metamorphosed*, 1621: Epilogue, Line 1386).

The masque was presented to King James the Sixth on three occasions. Gypsies play an important part in the masque, and there is one specific aspect of it that is relevant to this chapter. At the start of the play they have black faces. At the end they are redeemed by Royal intervention and their faces turn white. They are metamorphosed, transformed into membership of another social category. Their treatment in the masque illustrates both how race, conceived of as skin colour, had some significance in pre-modern and early-modern societies and how its significance was qualitatively different from that prevailing within modernity.

It is the case that a fair amount of the critique of 'race' in the sociology of racism has involved arguing that race is not only a social construct, but a thoroughly modern one as well. It is argued that societies in Antiquity, and those of medieval Europe, did not think in terms of 'race' (Weinerman, 1994; Scammell, 1991). Yet here we have two clear references to colour, 'blackamoors' and black Gypsies. At first sight this seems to falsify the assumption that race, understood as moral and/or social differences imputed to phenotypical characteristics, is purely a feature of European modernity alone. However that may be a mistaken conclusion. To give the reading that references to skin colour in the two texts suggest the existence of a modern racial taxonomy is to look at Jonson's works – and similar evidence (Dikotter, 1990; 1994) – through modern eyes. Rather, they demonstrate some of the pre-modern formations which fed into the production of modern racial consciousness (Orkin, 1987) and illustrate some differences between pre-modern and modern social configurations.

Colour, along with other aspects of physical appearance, certainly had some sort of social evaluation in many pre-modern civilizations, and conversely social evaluations were coloured (Bonnett, 1998). However the fact that coloured judgements existed in pre-modern times doesn't necessarily mean that the idea of race, as it is conceived of in modernity, also did. In the play, the outsiders' otherness is not eliminated by them being expelled, or destroyed. Although these measures were employed against Jews and Gypsies in pre-modern England and throughout Europe, they were not deployed as part of strategy of racial cleansing, there being no idea of race as we understand it on which to base such a strategy. In the play the outsiders are transformed, pre-modern social formations having a transformative potential. By considering works such as *Volpone* and *The Gypsies Metamorphosed* we can see the process by which imputed physical differences stopped being merely one characteristic to differentiate between people and eventually became the major characteristic by which they were divided (Lorimer, 1988; Banton, 1988). The unevenness of this development is central to understanding how Roma and Gypsy-Travellers are the objects of differing racial and social representations and exclusion in different parts of Europe.

In different circumstances, imputed physical differences and assumed social characteristics are given different weight in the racial and social representations of outsider grounds. Both elite and popular discourses around these two forms of representation actively construct the position that Gypsy-Travellers, along with other power minorities, have within and in relation to European societies. The position these groups have within each society is the concrete accretion of these historical discourses, and varies accordingly. It is the contention of this chapter that in Central and Eastern Europe the Gypsies have been broadly represented as a racialized outsider group. In contrast, in the UK and some, maybe most, countries of Western Europe they have been represented as a social problem group. The difference between countries and regions within Europe is partly the result of the de-racialization of elite language in Western Europe since 1945, but it is also due to the contrasting histories of state formation, civil society and developing national identity between the countries.

Whiteness as a Contingent Construct

It is argued that Europe was the place in which racial identity was formed (Hannaford, 1996), and modernity was the time in which it was formed. The reified racial identities produced in modern Europe were novel, replacing previous social-cultural constructions of group identity, and eventually influencing the way non-European societies thought of themselves on a deep level (Anthias, 1995). A seldom examined question is why it was that racial labels came to correspond to skin colour, rather than to other physical characteristics. It might seem counterintuitive to imagine that physical appearance has or could have no impact on the judgements people make, especially given the amount of time people put into managing it (van den Berghe, 1997). That does not explain why it was that colour become the marker of racialized group differences, even if it is a symbolic marker more than anything else.

One answer is that other physical characteristics do play a part, but skin colour became the central marker of racial different because of a number of associations it has had. For example, there are clear associations between class and skin colour. Photos of European peasants from the turn of the century show them to be dark and swarthy. The urban middle class in Victorian literature was often characterized – unflatteringly – by the figure of the pale and gangly clerk, in contrast to the rural middle class who were sunburnt and earthy. It has been suggested by literary critics that the character of Heathcliff in *Wuthering Heights* was variously black, Irish and a Gypsy (Michie, 1992; Eagleton, 1995). Through the book he gets paler as he becomes more civilized. These examples show how judgements of what black and white means remain contingent and relative. They are often wholly unrelated to 'actual' skin colour: Roma and Southern Italians in Northern Italy are called by a term meaning 'black', and there are plenty of other examples of 'racism without colour' (Gupta, 1983). Such a cursory examination should alert us to the unsettled and contingent nature of white identity.

And yet, as Alistair Bonnett (1996) points out, 'whiteness' is seldom regarded even by anti-racists as a contingent and fluid identity in this way. It is more often taken as read, assumed to be unquestionable and given. Even anti-racist criticisms of whiteness have tended to take it as something of a monolith, a universal standard. It is assumed that everywhere the white mind is intent on imposing the same colonial order, imperialist mindset or racial hierarchy. Indeed, left wing anti-racist thought has often actively constructed whiteness in this way. In Britain the left has been particularly attached to the idea that whiteness is inherently racist, that racism is built into Britishness, and Britishness is built on racism (Shukra, 1998). Whiteness is a historically, societally specific category however, as an examination of the racialization and rehabilitation of the Irish shows (Curtis, 1997).

Taking an approach to the question of whiteness and European ethnicity which assumes that it has such a monolithic character limits the scope of research on ethnic and racial issues. For example it closes off considerations of the interactionist construction of identity, and the many forms racism takes in specific circumstances depending on social and economic forces, discursive constructions and individual interactions (Banton, 1988). It takes the concept of 'whiteness' as being without history, and ever-present. By way of contrast there is widespread acknowledgement of the development of non-white consciousnesses, though there is also a tendency to frame them in primordial terms at the same time as the attempt is made to instil consciousness of race. There was the attempt by the anti-racist left in Britain during the 1980s to redefine black Britons as 'African'. This was unsuccessful partly because it did not allow for felt differences within black communities. Black Afro-Caribbeans in particular felt left out of this attempt at re-definition. It exemplified the way in which anti-racist discourse employs, perhaps out of necessity, a primordialist paradigm.

It can be seen then that as well as minority or outsider identities being historically specific and socially constructed, so are powerful and insider identities. The practices and discourses which constitute both powerful and powerless races or ethnic groups are intimately intertwined. Though not exactly two sides of the same coin, they interact with the same flows of power and social change, and often reflect similar concerns and needs on the part of individuals to explain their social situation, to provide a strong group identity and individual narratives, and to cope with rapid and bewildering social change. The most striking difference lies in the way that the more powerful identity is generally taken as given, the less powerful contested, challenged and struggled over. Possibly one aim of anti-racist practice should be to make whiteness a site of struggle and contest. The changing constitution of European racial whiteness will be returned to later on in the chapter, which will now examine some struggles over Roma and Traveller ethnicity.

Contesting and Constructing Ethnicity

Like the variable nature of whiteness, the definition of Gypsy or Roma is contingent and reflects changing social pressures on the community. Roma activists debate whether those who do not speak Romani, such as Scottish and Irish Travellers or Swiss Jenische, are part of the Romaniya (Hancock, 1997a). For some purists, only a few Romani groups count. There is a common distinction made between those who belong inside the 'Big Tent' and the 'Little Tent', between a core of Romani speaking groups and a wider set of traditional Travelling people, which includes English Romanichels, Scottish Nawkens and Irish Minceir. The Big Tent-Little Tent distinction is not one that informs the research framework of this book. I am also more interested in the way outsiders have been considered to distinguish the 'true Gypsy' from 'Tinkers', a distinction which is still present today, notably in statements of British politicians, press commentary and in popular opinion. This distinction is telling. Romanticization of a group assumed to be following a pre-modern way of life still has some strength in contemporary society. It coexists with the demonizing of a pariah out-group, who are described as having no culture, apart from shared criminal ways, no group cohesion, apart from that required to scam the unwary housedweller, no identity, except that assumed as part of a cunning ploy to claim 'ethnic rights'. In reality, the image of the true Gypsy recedes quickly in the minds of the local gauje population whenever some real life Gypsy-Travellers are present but unwanted.

In addition to the efforts of activists and intellectuals, Gypsy-Travellers in day to day life make distinctions between groups as to whether they are Gypsy or not (Salo, 1979), usually referring to their behaviour to make these distinctions, especially the occupations they engage in and their adherence to the *mochadi* cleanliness-purity regulations.

Such judgements are made all the time, but are also contingent. Some will make the claim to be Gypsy at some times, not at others. The much examined *mochadi* system of cleanliness-purity distinctions likewise changes over time and between groups of Gypsy-Travellers, between families and between individuals, often being applied more strictly when it is felt that their identity or way of life is under threat.

Identities can also be adopted and articulated anew. For example, in Macedonia and Kosovo what appears to be a previously unknown ethnic group has emerged since 1990, the Egyptians (*Roma Rights*, 6 April 2004). They are assumed by observers to be Roma who are adopting a novel ethnic identity for pragmatic purposes, but they categorically deny that they are Gypsy, and claim to be descended from Egyptians who had settled in the Balkans in the 4th Century (Duijzings, 1997). It is possible that either they are high status Roma who are seeking to mobilize around an identity more acceptable to the dominant ethnic groups, or that they have long identified themselves as Egyptian in a local context, but are only now looking to differentiate themselves in national debates from the category of Gypsy on the grounds that it is a low-status classification.

Neither option would be unusual. Roma have often chosen to identify themselves with higher status or more powerful ethnic groups, which tends for them to mean almost any ethnic group. They may do so as a matter of survival (Popov, 1992), or because upward social mobility makes them ambivalent about their 'Gypsy' identity. In a situation such as the one prevailing in Kosovo the importance of ethnic identity is paramount. As the Serbs and Albanians have struggled for hegemony, a powerless minority like the Roma have had to find ways of representing themselves, either camouflaging their background, identifying with a more powerful group, or in this case constituting a novel ethnic identity. One's own sense of ethnic difference may not matter one jot however:

> In Kosovo, the Ashkaelia reject an association with the Roma; but because they are perceived as 'Gypsies' by the nationalizing Albanian majority, they were subjected to the same ethnic cleansing as the Roma in the aftermath of the 1999 NATO war against Yugoslavia and the mass return of the Kosovo Albanian refugees to their homeland (Petrova, 2004).

It is in many parts of the former Communist world a matter of life and death to correctly insert oneself into the symbolic structure (Taras, 1993). Although in the rest of Europe the situation is not as dramatic, identity is also vital, and appears to be increasingly important to individuals with the rise of identity politics and ethnic nationalism (Miles, 1994).

Much of the ethnographic work on Roma and Gypsy-Travellers has spent a lot of time looking at the construction and maintenance of Gypsy-Traveller or 'Gypsy' identity, and not very much on the way settled society has gone about its business of creating and maintaining its identity. Jim MacLaughlin (1996) in his study of the evolution of anti-Traveller racism in Ireland makes a start on examining how European nation-states create national closure in opposition to ethnic, social and status outsiders, of which Roma and Travellers are a prime example (Welsh, 1994). In this case, Irish Travellers share the same language, religion and nationality as the settled majority, yet are subject to severe exclusion (Carlson and Casavant, 1995). MacLaughlin links their exclusion to the creation of a national identity in the years after the Irish civil war. The process of nation formation involved rejecting the radical and non-sectarian nationalism represented by leaders like Michael Collins, in favour of a Catholic-Peasant vision of the nation (Dowling, 1997).

Irish Travellers were not merely excluded from this vision of the nation. The settled-national identity was created in direct opposition to them and their way of life, as nomadic outsiders violating the cleanliness of a settled and closed society (MacLaughlin, 1999b). The recent industrialization and modernization of Ireland has changed this somewhat. Irish Travellers continue to be associated with primitiveness and backwardness (see comments on the Czech Republic below), but are also increasingly likely to be seen by the rest of the Irish public as a separate group, rather than as just cultural or social delinquents (Gmelch, 1986). To complicate the matter a little, these divisions are mixed in with more 'traditional' distinctions between insider and outsider communities, re-forming the connection between blood and soil (MacLaughlin, 1998).

One form anti-Traveller exclusion has taken is to delegitimize Gypsy-Traveller identity, especially in the UK and Ireland (Williams, 1986). For example, the Northern Ireland Government reports on Travellers (Ministry of Home Affairs, 1948; 1955) did not allow them an identity except as a social problem, that of itinerancy. The government of West Germany after the Second World War refused compensation to Roma concentration camp survivors on the grounds that they had been persecuted as a – delinquent – social group, rather than an ethnic group (Margalit, 2002). It was a common tactic among local authorities in Britain who wished to avoid their obligations under the 1968 Act to claim that they had no Gypsy-Travellers in their area, or that those who were there 'weren't proper Gypsies'. The discursive dismissal of Gypsy-Traveller identity is ongoing and further adds to their exclusion. This does not always involve denying that there is some connection between groups of 'Gypsies'. In some sections of the British press, the misdemeanours associated with one encampment are used to discredit all Gypsy site applications. Here, discrimination works by connecting members of this group together, though not to their benefit.

This highlights an ethical and methodological quandary the researcher is placed in. Questioning the assumed primordial origins of Gypsies or Travellers is often taken to be yet another attack on Roma. The motives of the sociologist are to produce original work, and part of this process involves questioning and deconstructing categories they are presented with. Yet work produced by these rules can have the effect of only questioning and deconstructing one half of the relationship, and unconsciously reifying settled identity and delegitimizing that of Roma and Gypsy-Travellers. Valuable scholarship will hold these two in balance, and hopefully the next part of the chapter avoids the trap of endless deconstruction, whilst also challenging some of the terms in which the debate on race and ethnicity has been conducted.

Ethnic Minority or Status Group?

Michael Banton (1983) has many criticisms of the way the term 'race' is applied in a taken for granted manner (see also Rodriguez and Corderoguzman, 1992; Gilroy, 1998). Many academics and policymakers fight shy of the term altogether, preferring the term 'ethnicity', which lacks the unhappy associations of race and is applicable to a far wider set of communities. However there are several criticisms to be levelled at the use made by academics of the term. The use of the term in Europe tends to be one-sided, hiding the 'ethnicity' of the white majority (Ballard, 1997). It begs some questions concerning what makes for an ethnic group, how group closure operates, why ethnicity is maintained even when it would appear advantageous to abandon it, and the ways in which ethnicity relates to other aspects of individual and social identity. These questions are more often than not covered up by the use of the term.

According to Richard Jenkins (1994; 1996), social science and anthropology tends to over-privilege ethnicity. In the last analysis there is not much to separate 'ethnicity' from the Weberian concept of the status group (Weber, 1968b). Status group is a concept which gives the researcher a handle on more aspects of inter- and intra-group behaviour than ethnicity does. If applied with care it can do so without submerging identities into an overarching concept, like class or gender, or over-privileging and ossifying them as the discourse of identity politics tends to do. It may be productive to employ the concept of status group to explain certain aspects of the position of Roma and Gypsy-Travellers in modern society, rather than ascribing all exotic or opaque behaviour to the catch-all of 'ethnicity' and all conflict to 'ethnic conflict'.

The difficulty with the concept of ethnicity is it tends to be used as a black box, hiding some key internal processes which explain group attachments. The concept of status group can have more utility because central to it is the positive social estimation placed on honour (Weber, 1968a). This can allow us to understand much more of individual behaviour, and to draw out the ways in which individual actions are patterned by and reaffirm the values of the status group. What is considered by the group to be honourable and proper is what is valued, striven for and competed for by group members. Individuals who do not accept the values of what are honourable to the group have to take their place outside it or in a subordinate position within it (Kornblum and Lichter, 1972). The concept can encapsulate both the power status values have over group members, and the active role they as individuals have in maintaining those values, policing boundaries, sanctioning negative behaviour and so on. It can also help explain how status groups form around marginal or peripheral positions in society, which appear at first sight to restrict group members' life chances.

The socio-economic niche Gypsy-Travellers in the UK and Ireland occupy is represented as a marginalized position. If sympathetic, non-Travellers say that they are pushed into it by external group closure and forced to maintain a marginalized position with regard to settled society. Unsympathetic accounts say that they are delinquent and suffer from a failure to internalize what are clearly the more valuable values that the larger status group maintains. The latter is the 'culture of poverty' thesis which has often been applied to Irish Travellers (McCarthy, 1994; Collins, 1994). Both these attitudes are part of a status hierarchy which places Gypsy-Travellers at the bottom. Gypsy-Travellers, however, do not see it that way, and do not necessarily share the same status hierarchy that values long formal periods of education and paid work. The Gypsy-Traveller status community emphasizes values such as family, sociability and independence, consciously contrasting these with the practices of the settled community (Okely, 1983).

An examination of the history of Gypsy-Travellers in many societies shows how they have been forced or have chosen to seek out and occupy a position which is marginal or peripheral in the eyes of the settled majority. Partly they are forced to do this because of the social closures operated by the power groups and agencies in settled society upon their arrival, be they the state in capitalist modernity or the guilds in feudal society. Like other outcast minorities, Gypsy-Travellers develop and sustain status options dependant upon occupying this position. It is internally valued among some Gypsy-Traveller groups that individuals do not engage in waged or apprenticed labour, or that children do not attend school beyond a 'decent' age. The values of settled society are seen as the low status ones (Oliner and Hallum, 1978). Analogously the Indian Untouchable castes were marginalized into a low wage, low status occupation. Although they seem relegated to an exploited position, there is some marginal utility in it for them. What is seen by the castes above them as negatively valued allows them to maintain an exclusive access to certain types of work (Weber, 1968a). The positive social estimation placed on that type of work inside the caste has its own internal rationale and limited functionality. The case of Gypsy-Travellers is more complex in that they can often make a good living while remaining outside what are for settled society the higher status occupational categories (Laitin, 1995).

What makes the concept of status group most useful when applied to Roma and Gypsy-Travellers is the part their structural position in society plays in the formation of their ethnic identity, which is not the case with other ethnic minorities. Most ethnic minorities do tend to occupy a specific, identifiable structural position within the larger society of which they are a minority. That is part of what makes them ethnic minorities. However, in most cases the structural position is not a part of the process by which their ethnic identity is reproduced. Indeed, they would mostly view being placed in low-status occupational positions as an offence to their ethnicity, as a mark of being misjudged by a racist society. In the case of Roma and Gypsy-Travellers, their economic role is more important to their identity, which is closely intertwined with status formation and socio-economic position. Many of the names of Roma groups relate to occupation.

The concept of status group is useful because it can account for the two-way process of social exclusion. What is seen by the minority group as good and positively status valued can be alien to the majority and vice versa. It can provide a basis to explain how the divide between two communities is maintained on both sides. The host society finds its sense of 'status community' violated by the presence of threatening Gypsy-Travellers and proceeds to blame all goings on that are negatively valued on them. Hence it is able to minimize its own problems regarding the inability or unwillingness of its own group members to adhere to what the group positively values. The awareness that group adherence to high status behaviour is as a whole bound to be less than perfect can be projected onto the out-status group.

Gypsy-Travellers are a convenient 'other', who can be used to throw the values of the dominant settled community into sharp relief (Okely, 1994b). To Gypsy-Travellers, it is the gauje who is the 'other'. Gypsy-Travellers maintain their group boundaries through the practice of the *mochadi* regulations. It governs many aspects of social behaviour, from washing and cooking, to relationships with gauje. It is necessary because Gypsy-Traveller society cannot merely avoid contact with whoever and whatever is considered to be impure, as closed religious or quasi-religious communities can. Gypsy-Traveller men and women must engage in everyday economic and social intercourse with members of settled society. It is a system which is a practical guide through these contacts with gauje, as well as governing power relations within Gypsy-Traveller communities. It maintains the status hierarchy within the Gypsy-Traveller community, as well as reassuring Gypsy-Travellers of the lower status of the gauje, who unthinkingly violates the *mochadi* boundaries.

Describing Gypsy-Travellers as a status-group rather than an ethnic group is controversial because a lot of the activist work with Gypsy-Travellers concerns their recognition as an ethnic minority as a basis for opposing discrimination and harassment. In most European countries the achievement of ethnic status would allow legal action to be taken in defence of Gypsy-Traveller rights under each country's race discrimination laws. A long campaign persuaded the UK government to include Irish Travellers as an ethnic group for the purposes of the Race Relations (Northern Ireland) Order 1997 (Noonan, 1997). Its initial reluctance to do so was in keeping with that of most European governments.

It is with wariness that social scientists should do anything which appears to question the ethnicity of Travellers, as this can be seriously damaging to their interests. It should be remembered that the assertion of the importance of status relates to sociological, rather than political, practice. Anti-Traveller government officials, commentators and activists do seize on any research which suggests that Travellers are not an ethnic group. The following quote shows how their status as an ethnic minority is actively resisted by some:

> [Italy is full of] Gypsy children who poke you in the ribs with pieces of cardboard so they can ransack your pockets while you are distracted by the mini assault ... Oh, I forgot. I'm not supposed to refer to them as Gypsies because they're now a disadvantaged minority. Nor am I supposed to comment on their extraordinary skills of thievery. How easy for those who have never been set upon by a pack of prepubescent vipers to characterize them as social victims (*The Toronto Star*, 8 March 1999).

Of course, the point being made in this chapter is very different. In the sense in which Gypsies can be said not to be an ethnic group, no community can be said to be an ethnic group, or for that matter a nation. Status-group may be the more useful tool for social theory, whilst it can be acknowledged that Gypsies constitute an ethnic group in the terms framed by law and common understanding. It is illuminating, though, to see that ethnicity is treated as an achieved status, and something which is resisted in anti-Traveller discourse in which it is asserted that they are merely a delinquent sub-group.

Despite the importance given to ethnicity by activists as a basis for political mobilization, there is some reluctance among many Travellers to take on the label of an ethnic group themselves. Scottish Travellers are usually reluctant to engage in ethnic mobilization. This is the case with many Travellers across Europe, such as Norwegian Roma

(Halvorsen, 1997). The end point of any collective ethnic action is likely to be increased visibility, and many Travellers are reluctant to engage in any action which will increase visibility as being likely to invite further persecution. Travellers often feel that their traditional way of life serves them better than gorgio concepts of ethnic and civil rights, which have largely unproven value to them. The work of various voluntary groups in Britain and other countries has over the past two or three decades shown that there are some gains to be made from this form of action, however. Given the extent of anti-Roma and anti-Gypsy-Traveller feeling in European societies, to be examined next, the work of establishing their status as an ethnic minority is more vital than ever.

Anti-Gypsy Sentiment: Origins and Persistence

> Gypsies have moved in next door [to us]. They throw all their rubbish out [into the street]. They all sit out on the road (Resident of Margate, *The Guardian*, 4 October 1998).

> There is no problem of racism in Albania. Roma live in segregated neighbourhoods, which is good for their security. Roma are presently very poor, dirty and noisy, so they have fewer problems if they live separately (Albanian government official, Petrova, 1997).

Despite the heterogeneity of Roma and Gypsy-Traveller populations, there is one constant between almost every group in Europe and America: the low position in which they are held by settled people. It is not an exaggeration to say that anti-Traveller and anti-Roma feeling permeates the consciousness of every European society, as evidenced by the rising wave of racial violence against them that has spread since the revolutions of 1989 and the resurgence of nationalism in Europe.

Several theses have been postulated to account for the origin and constancy over time of anti-Gypsy sentiment. Barth (1969) investigates the formation of ethnic groups and boundaries to describe the production of the pariah in European society. The 'pariah group' is a minority which carries out certain functional tasks within a larger society. It is the object of generalized rejection by the majority but at the same time carries out a necessary economic role which the members of the majority group are unwilling or unable to fulfil. One such group he mentions are dealers in horseflesh in early modern Britain, another Gypsies. According to Barth the symbolic boundaries of most pariah groups are maintained by the host society, with the exception of Gypsies who operate internal border maintenance, and actively differentiate themselves from the gauje.

Another perspective is offered by Marlene Sway (1975) who uses Simmel's concept of 'the Stranger' to explain anti-Gypsy sentiment. The Stranger group embodies certain specific characteristics – not owning land, being a middleman or trader group and so on. It is easily made into a scapegoat for problems of the majority group (Simmel, 1950). One historical characteristic of the Stranger cited by Simmel is that she or he is a member of a group which has been subject to a special tax. Simmel had in mind Jews in medieval Frankfurt who were required to pay a fixed tax, in essence a poll tax on Jewishness, whereas non-Jews paid an income and wealth related charge. The Stranger is regarded as parasitic, taking from the community and not giving to it, and hence can be taxed arbitrarily. Sway finds an analogy in Roma in St. Petersburg in the late 18th Century, who had to pay a special charge to enter the city.

The examples Sway and Simmel quote seem to apply more to pre-modern states and state practices. In modernity Stranger minorities are the subjects of unique regulations – rather than taxes – which encapsulate an abiding suspicion of them. Several examples from legislation in the USA are listed in Hancock (2004). There are numerous examples of special state monitoring of Roma and Gypsy-Travellers in Europe, such as the German police unit which was dedicated to monitoring Gypsies. It was set up in 1899 and remained in place until the 1970s. The key difference between the Stranger in pre-modern and modern Europe relates to the distinction made at the start of this chapter between pre-modern (mutable) and modern (immutable) racial categories. For the pre-modern state the Stranger was quite convenient – a permanent scapegoat and a source of revenue which could not object to being taxed. For the modern nation-state the Stranger is a social problem, to be regulated, assimilated or removed.

> [How about] a demonstration of synchronized scrounging by Czech and Slovakian gipsies dressed in their traditional costume of Adidas shell suits? (*The Daily Mail*, 23 October 1997).

The above quote encapsulates the way in which the Stranger in modernity embodies a terrifying ordinariness – wearing shell suits rather than the exotic traditional Gypsy costume – and a problem for order. The Czech and Slovak Roma asylum seekers in the UK being written about above were resented because they were potential 'scroungers' and because they upset the spatial order of modern Europe. As Strangers, they were permanently out of place.

> Barrons Great Outdoors, Britain's biggest retailer, has banned the term [caravan] in showrooms. It says the word is 'associated with gypsies, traffic jams and greasy spoon cafés' (*The Times*, 12 February 1997).

> Polish gipsies infested with lice slept in a public concourse at Heathrow because immigration chiefs had no room for them (*Mail On Sunday*, 5th January 1997).

Mary Douglas (1966) writes of the terrifying nature of that which is felt to be slimy, the slick spilling over bounded categories. Dirt is matter out of place, and when settled people across Europe characterize Roma and Gypsy-Travellers as 'dirty' it is not with regard to their presumed hygiene habits.

Roma and Gypsy-Travellers may violate gauje boundaries, but of course they see things the same way as well. Ignorant gauje happily transgress some important categorical distinctions of Roma and Gypsy-Traveller society, which is why they have to be guarded against in the mochadi system. Some Roma and Gypsy-Travellers have mentioned that they were afraid to have a gauje in the house in case there was such a violation. However the exclusion of Gypsy-Travellers from European society is not directly mirrored in the practices of Roma and Gypsy-Travellers themselves, whose relationship with settled society is fraught with difficulties and contradictions which have to be resolved on a day to day basis.

Conclusion

Roma and Gypsy-Travellers are frequently represented as being outwith society. It is acceptable to many to suspend prevailing norms of obligation and mutuality with regard to them, including that individuals be judged solely by their own actions. This sometimes extends to claimed sympathizers, producing an odd ambivalence in even 'pro-Gypsy' commentary. This is an excerpt from an article in *The Scotsman* newspaper, which presented a broadly sympathetic account of the situation of Czech Roma:

> Gypsies are not all thieves. But the prejudice is based on fact. Let's not pussyfoot around. No amount of political correctness can obscure the fact that certain Roma clans are very much involved with petty crime (*The Scotsman*, 21 August 1999).

The discourse of racism and anti-racism becomes slippery when applied to Roma and Gypsy-Travellers. It becomes acceptable to lay part of the blame for the out-group's pariah status on them and their behaviour. The principle of 'joint liability' is applied to them, so all have responsibility for the supposed actions of some group members.

Chapter 4

Segregation of Roma and Gypsy-Travellers

Introduction

Modernity creates spatial structures in which power relations are implicated. The construction of space affects excluded and marginalized groups, both fixing their position as modernity's other, and also providing spaces of resistance to marginalization and exclusion, spaces of survival. Here, competing constructions of space in Britain and the Czech Republic are examined in terms of their impact on Gypsy-Traveller and Roma communities. The processes of creating and locating Gypsy-Traveller sites in Britain is examined, as are issue of site design and the ways in which Travellers are compelled to take up settled housing. In conclusion, it is found that in the UK, Gypsy-Travellers have been the object of a number of forces which have restricted their travelling. However they have found a number of ways to resist these forces. Roma in the Czech Republic have found it more difficult to do so, for a number of reasons which include their relative visibility.

Every society creates narratives of space. A unique feature of modernity has been its proselytizing of what happens to be a culturally and historically very specific understanding of space. The history of modernity is the history of the triumph over space (Eagleton, 1997). Within the project of modernity, progress – social, economic and technological – is equated with the control of space: bridging it, shrinking it, binding it. Space was perceived either as a passive and static object to be moulded, or as an obstacle to be overcome. It was not encountered as something rich and textured. Mostly considerations of space were pushed out of the frame. The narrative of time dominated modernist discourse, although there were exceptions. Georg Simmel among others was aware of the effect of different spaces on social relations, and vice versa.

More recently social theory has begun to draw on this subterranean tradition, examining space not as static and empty but as structured and richly textured with meaning, boundaries and so on, the locus of power networks and the focus of discourses of meaning and subjectification, the site of power and the source of resistance to it (Lefebvre, 1991). It is that approach which will inform this chapter. Space is both the object of forces which empty it out of non-hegemonic social structures and the site for the production of counter-hegemonic narratives and practices. This chapter will examine some of these narratives of space as they concern Gypsy-Travellers and Roma in Europe.

> The chronic evil of Scotland, an oppressive multitude of idle, wandering people and beggars (*Domestic Annals of Scotland from the Reformation to the Revolution*, 1665).

Throughout history there have been struggles over space and its meaning. From the expulsion of Jews from England in 1290 to the ethnic cleansing of Bosnia and Croatia, dominant forces have sought to purify it by removing in one way or another those that were disturbing to the social or ethnic order. Roma and Gypsy-Travellers have been subject to forced movement as the result of such forms of social-spatial exclusion. 'Egyptians' were transported from Scotland to the Americas during the second half of the 17th and the early 18th Centuries, as recorded in the *Books of Warding and Liberation* of the Edinburgh Tolbooth Prison. The Edinburgh records mention 'the King's Plantations in the Americas' as their destination, and the records of the Privy Council indicate that this meant 'Gemaica and Barbadoes'. Records of Glasgow city taken from the early 18th Century state that the Court of Justiciary sentenced a number of individuals, including at least one married couple, to transportation to the Caribbean 'for being habite and repute gipsies, sorners &c' (*Minute-books of the Burgh of Glasgow*, 1 January 1715; MacRitchie, 1894).

They were part of a general panic over 'wandering bands of vagabonds', something which has occurred time and time again throughout the history of Europe. Significant numbers of nomadic people are threatening to the social and moral order. They tend to appear, or become more visible, at times of social upheaval, and are easy scapegoats for the widespread uncertainty and insecurity brought on by rapid social change. There are some apparent parallels with the moral panic over New Travellers in Britain during the early 1990s. To understand this we need to consider the use of space, and the place of British Gypsy-Travellers within it.

Space in Late Modernity

Zygmunt Bauman asserts that the final years of the 20th Century saw capital win its longest struggle: the 'war of independence from space' (Bauman, 1998a). The effect of globalization has been to remove capital from the rule of the locality – locality meaning any space of identity below the nation-state. In a world of footloose capital the function of the nation-state is increasingly oriented towards the management of space and the creation of benign zones, quiet spaces for the insertion of international capital. The intensified institutional management of space has opened up a sphere of struggle and contest over the occupation and surveillance of space. When these space wars are fought between the excluded and the institutions of the nation-state or capital they are mostly conducted in a one sided fashion, with the rights of surveillance and spatial management asserted as overriding any notion of civil liberty or democracy, in the name of creating 'safe zones'. The social atomization resulting from state non-intervention in the regulation of capital requires that the state expands its regulative capacity in the social sphere. One aspect of this increased regulative intervention is the extended control of space. The actions of the nation-state in making space safe for capital bring out the ambivalent contest between empowered, or partially empowered, localities and the nation-state of which they are a part regarding the control and management of excluded populations. These issues relate to the operation of socio-spatial segregation of Roma in the Czech Republic and the spatial restrictions placed on Gypsy-Travellers in the UK.

Kevin Hetherington (1996) reflects on the use of space and particularly of sacred sites made by New Travellers. They use sacred sites such as Stonehenge and Glastonbury which have resonance for their group identity and the articulation of their belonging not to one place but to the Mother Earth. They especially gather at those sites which hark back to a pre-modern and pre-Roman Britain. He uses the Foucauldian concept of 'heterotopia' to describe the New Travellers use of space (Hetherington, 1993). Hetertopic practices bring together various mythologic strands in places that have been marginalized within modernity. The practices of heterotopia act to symbolically construct an alternative social order. The sacral-spatial practices of New Travellers contrasts with the uses traditional Travellers make of space.

Gypsy-Travellers tend to look on marginal spaces for their utility, rather than as a vision of an alternative society – a place to stop without harassment, a place with work nearby etc. In the UK, Gypsy-Travellers who have to stop by the roadside prefer relatively private and hidden places (Gmelch and Gmelch, 1988), understandably enough since they are less likely to attract the ire of the local police and populace. However the extent to which they can make use of these places has shrunk enormously. Increasingly, and in particular since the introduction of the Criminal Justice And Public Order Act 1994 (the 1994 Act), they have had to resort to unused public land. Often on public land they are able to gain a month's grace to stay, which they are no longer able to get on private land. However, this grace is entirely at the discretion of the local authority in whose boundaries they happen to stop. Some local authorities have created set procedures for Gypsy-Travellers pulling on to public land, while others deal with it on a purely ad hoc basis. As a result there is a great deal of uncertainty, with Gypsy-Travellers on the verge commonly subject to harassment and forced movement.

One example of the foreclosure of space is the fate of the old Gypsy-Traveller fairs. These are continuations of the ancient fairs of Britain. Gypsy-Travellers are now among the last people to be actively keeping this old tradition alive. The fairs have an important function in binding the Gypsy-Traveller community. Annual fairs – such as the famous one at Appleby – are times for exchanging both goods and information, news, taking part in competition and forming and cementing relationships. They renew and revitalize the complex set of social and economic relationships which underpin Gypsy-Traveller society. However, all the Gypsy-Traveller fairs are coming under increasing pressure, mainly from councils who would generally prefer it if Gypsy-Travellers did not occupy their town centres (*The Times*, 28 March 1995). As a way of accommodating the demands of local authorities, Gypsy-Travellers who regularly attend the Barnet, Appleby and Stow fairs have clubbed together to buy or lease land outside the town centre, but doing this has not meant that they are free to hold the fair.

Stow-on-the-Wold fair was granted a Royal Charter by Edward IV in 1476. It evolved from being a general market fair to become a horse fair attended mainly by Gypsy-Travellers. In recent years local settled people have increasingly objected to the disruption caused by having the fair in the town centre. The council then said that they could no longer park in a field in the town centre. The Gypsy-Travellers then bought a site on the edge of the town so that they could hold the fair without causing disruption to the town centre. In 1991 the council gave the site temporary planning permission to be used by them for the two or three days of the fair. However, objections by some townspeople caused it to reverse its decision. The council took out an injunction banning them from using their field, and since they broke the injunction in 1996 the council obtained a High Court order, meaning that any Gypsy-Traveller pulling on to the site can face prison (*The Times*, 5 May 1998). After the ruling, the only option the Travellers had was to camp on the roadside in the town itself, making them liable to prosecution under the 1994 Act. This is one of many instances of Gypsy-Travellers' practical use of space being curtailed.

Unlike New Traveller gatherings there is little overt symbolism or use of ritual in traditional Gypsy fairs. It is the use of space and time which is central to distinguishing the relations between European modernity and Gypsy-Traveller society. Nomadism demands a high level of endogamous distinction practice. The strongest of the distinctions made, and the most immutable, is that between 'white' Czech and Roma, or Flattie and Nawken – between Gypsy-Traveller and settled person. These distinctions are based on genealogy and an elaborate set of cleanliness/purity regulations. Travellers also have strong group spatial boundaries, and the pure-impure distinction can be taken to apply to space as well as the body. The active maintenance of the spatial boundary between gauje and Gypsy is sustained on the opposite side as well. Settled people set up 'Gypsy Site Action Groups' whenever a proposal for a Gypsy-Traveller site is announced. The appearance of groups of Gypsy-Traveller often becomes the focus for mobilization of the community and closure of the group against them.

A particularly explicit instance of this was the symbolic burning of a 'Gypsy caravan' in the English village of Firle in October 2003, as part of its Bonfire Night celebrations. Every year, the village traditionally burns an effigy, an 'Enemy of the Bonfire', someone who has offended them. In this case, Gypsies were alighted on. A group had stayed near the village previous summer and were blamed for killing local pheasants and causing environmental damage. They were evicted in September. Memories were long enough for them to feature in the following season's bonfire in October. The bonfire organizers created a caravan with the number plate 'P1KEY' ('pikey' is a pejorative term for Gypsy) and a picture of a 'Gypsy family' inside it. Following complaints, the 12 organizers were arrested for incitement to racial hatred. After a nine-month investigation The Crown Prosecution Service announced it had decided not to prosecute them.

A common feature of commentary in the press was a combination of briefly voiced regret over the bonfire along with sympathy for the motives behind it. *The Daily Mail* (15 November 2003) commented irritably on the 'political correctness gone mad' involved in the arrest of the organizers. It also reported negatively on the Gypsy-Travellers, based on some of the villagers' accounts:

> Among the trailers and rubbish was a fleet of new luxury cars, including a Porsche 911 Targa ... How a group of travellers came to acquire such

expensive vehicles is a question that the police, no doubt, might have liked to ask them.

This kind of insinuation is common in reporting on Gypsy-Travellers. The symbols of their affluence can only be a sign of criminality, a suspicion hinted at but never directly stated. When they have expensive cars and trailers this is suspicious. When they do not, it is evidence that they possess a culture without value and symbols without status and, in the words of *The Sun*, 'trundle from place to place in dilapidated caravans with raggedy children and mangy dogs' (24 July 2001).

The authors of these actions and statements are engaging in a collective action to maintain the socio-spatial order, the purity of social space and the identity of the locality. These boundaries are maintained in the absence of the racialized phenotypical differences which exist between Roma and non-Roma in the countries of Central and Eastern Europe.

Space, Deviance and Exclusion

Donald Carter (1994) describes the formation of the Italian state in terms of a process of cartographic control and taxonomic mapping of vagrants, beggars and Gypsies. The modern nation state asserts it existence symbolically in its documentation, bringing into being its power as a nation-state. Laws are the clearest such combinations of statements of being and creation of face, but in addition there is the minutiae of civil life – the drawing of administrative boundaries, map-making, rule making and so on. The Italian state had a problem with banditry from its formation, a direct challenge to state authority. Against this the Caribineri engaged in systematic categorization and classification of social deviance. The establishment of the state's hegemony was not achieve by surveillance and criminalization of the whole subordinate population, as in totalitarianism, but through the identification and elucidation of deviant categories. Modernity imposes conceptual frameworks which map time and space in the interest of the settled majority. There are many more recent examples of state action to affirm the distinction between settled society and the deviant or recalcitrant nomad (Shamir, 1996).

The past marking of space is a powerful myth in modern society. The casual use of the term 'white settler' by some Scottish and Welsh nationalists to describe 'recent' arrivals from England, and the activities of organizations like *Scottish Watch* which advocated the use of violence to drive English migrants out of Scotland, are two instances of the ethnic identification of space (*The Guardian*, 3 November 1992). Political developments such as the passing of the 1994 Act may be taken to embody the drive for the purity of space, re-mythologizing the countryside as a pure rural idyll. As Andrew Gamble (1988) showed in his work on Thatcherism, the ideology of the free economy and the strong state gained political currency as a response to what was seen as excessive permissiveness in the moral sphere and excessive societal control in the economic sphere. To the new right spaces of freedom and choice were to be confined to the marketplace. Politics is to be taken out of the state's remit, its functions being to guarantee a quiescent labour force and to secure the social order.

According to David Sibley (1994), the sections of the 1994 Act concerned with public order are a response to the perceived transgression of boundaries. British society in the 1980s and 1990s had been subject to an increasing number of boundary problems, leading to a boundary crisis (Erikson, 1966). Society attempts to resolve its boundary crisis by staging a confrontation with deviant groups who are seen as transgressing the zoning of space. In this instance the opprobrium was directed against New Travellers and hunt saboteurs. Both groups are seen as composed of those who leave the city and violate the rural idyll. They transgress the boundaries of city and country. The 1994 Act is intended to restrict this movement. Space is purified and rendered homogenous through the establishment and reinforcement of protected boundaries (Sibley, 1988).

The 1994 Act was intended to assert the robust policing of space. It was intended to prevent certain gatherings and movements, such as New Traveller convoys and festivals. The myth of the rural idyll was employed in the Parliamentary debates on the 1994 Act, an idyll shattered by New Travellers and hunt saboteurs (Halfacree, 1996). The place of Gypsy-Travellers in this social representation of rural society was accepted by many of the MPs contributing to the debate, mainly in order to contrast them with New Travellers, city folk who were felt to have no rights of access to the countryside. The countryside in Britain was represented as an idyllic arcadia, a fundamental part of English ethnic identity. That rural arcadia is distant to most members of society, urban and rural, actual life in the countryside bearing little resemblance to it. The representation of the countryside as an idyll contrasts with its operation as a factory floor for the agricultural-industrial complex, a space as almost as zoned, regulated and closed to the public as an urban industrial estate.

The production of socio-spatial segregation within modernity became also recreates a more established form of segregation which in some forms pre-dates modernity, that of the ghetto. Louis Wirth (1966) describes the old European and American ghettos, and the ways in which they offered security and a measure of social solidity to their residents. It was a familiar space, in both senses of the word, containing networks of kin and acquaintances. There would appear to be a problem with this description, because it could be applied to most working class neighbourhoods, and not merely to Black areas of American cities and Jewish areas of European ones. However, the traditional racial ghetto contains the vertical as well as the horizontal layers of a society. It contains a middle class. It is a microcosm with many institutions which parallel those in the rest of society, such as more or less informal welfare systems, social organizations and so on. It is the container of a whole set of social relations which give the ghetto its own life. In contrast the modern ghetto – perhaps 'post-modern ghetto' is a better term – is articulated by the forces of socio-spatial exclusion described above, which empty it out of most of these vertical relationships and produce what is known as the hyper-ghetto (Wacquant, 1991), or impacted ghetto (Hughes, 1990).

Ghettoization was applied by the Nazi government in the period leading up to the Holocaust. The spatial segregation of undesired social groups was the first aim of the bureaucracy, rather than their outright destruction. It appears to have been originally the intention of the Nazi government to physically remove Jews and Roma from the cleansed space of Nazi occupied Europe. Deporting them to Madagascar was one suggestion. Whatever the seriousness of its intentions in this respect it is the case that the physical elimination of the racial and social others was only implemented after their spatial separation from society had been achieved. The ghetto was first emptied out of socio-economic relations and then destroyed. Roma were pushed into the ghettos after they were cleared of Jews, to await deportation to the camps.

Whereas the Holocaust destroyed the Jewish ghettoes of pre-war Europe, de-segregation and wider socio-economic change spelt the end of the Black American ghettoes as they had existed, and the beginning of their transformation into hyperghettos. It started a process whereby the vertical networks and ties which had held together the ghetto as a heterogeneous socio-economic space were fragmented as better off and more motivated individuals departed for the suburbs. The much vaunted 'white flight' from the cities was said to have weakened their social fabric, relegating the cities to the poor relations of white America's polity, and increased the level of racial homogenization in the inner city (Wilson, 1983).

In addition there was the less often noticed phenomenon of black flight, with black middle class families departing the traditionally black areas, creating a spiral in which class segregation and race segregation came increasingly to coincide, bringing with it a wide range of social problems (Liska, Logan, and Bellair, 1998). However, many authors have criticized the assumption that de-segregation led automatically to white flight and the associated problems of the American inner city (Cunningham and Husk, 1980; Frey, 1980; Farley, 1982). They point to a complex of social changes associated with the restructuring of capitalist societies during the 1970s and 1980s which explain many of these phenomena (Wilson, 1987; 1997). Likewise the increased conflict between Roma and Czech society is not directly due to the increased racial sorting of the two groups, but rather that sorting is the function of deeper processes of socio-economic restructuring which have re-constructed social spaces as impacted ghettos.

Ethnicity, Racialization and Ghettoization

Peter Jackson (1998) describes the role of geography and space in constructing and naturalizing whiteness. Processes of boundary construction and the imagination of the locality are combined in the production of white ethnicity. The conception of whiteness as a universal construct has declined however, as has been mentioned earlier in this book. White identities tend to be asserted increasingly as minority ethnicities, and employ some of the same spatial practices of non-white ethnicities.

> With our colouring, you can pass as [white] English, as gauje. But in Czechoslovakia, where the Gypsy stands out, they call you a nigger (English Gypsy-Traveller, *Radio 4,* 8 February 1999).

The racialization of the Czech Roma plays an important part in the process of ghettoization to which they are subject. Many Roma and Gypsy-Travellers find that they have to 'pass' as gauje at some time or other. Because of the hostility and discrimination they encounter, many hide their ethnicity at certain times. Some do so throughout their whole lives, and are warned by their parents never to reveal their true origins to other people. The British Gypsy-Traveller quoted above describes how this is possible and often necessary for day to day survival. He was also aware of the different situation pertaining in other parts of Europe, where tactical invisibility is often not an option. In mainland Europe, and particularly Central and Eastern Europe, many Roma have significantly darker skins. They are labelled 'blacks', especially in these countries, and non-Roma are referred to as 'whites'. Many have quite light colouration and are able to 'pass', but most are not. Accent and dress are also elements that have to be managed, and many Roma in the former Communist states claimed membership of another national minority, such as Turks in Bulgaria.

Under Communism a high degree of spatial segregation between Roma and non-Roma was developed and maintained. There was a two way process behind this. Government housing allocators kept Roma apart from other citizens. They stated that Roma would wreck newer flats and put them into old ones, and were also concerned to keep 'decent' people separate from the Roma. In addition there were the choices made by Roma themselves, who preferred the older type of accommodation, being more suitable for large families. The result is that Roma in may cities of Central and Eastern European countries live with a high level of spatial segregation, which paradoxically appears to have increased as the result of the efforts of Communist governments to change their way of life. In Hungary the numbers of traditional Roma settlements had fallen by a great deal during the 1970s, due to action by the Hungarian authority in clearing them. The extent of Roma segregation in Budapest actually increased as a result of the influx of Roma from the countryside who had been made to leave their traditional settlements (Ladanyi, 1993). They had been forced to abandon their settlements as part of the government's modernization programme.

Communist policy was on the one hand to settle nomadic Roma and on the other to erase the traditional settlements of Roma who had been settled for a significant time (Stewart, 1990). The policy, which was intended to disperse the Roma among the rest of the population, had the unintended effect of reproducing their segregation. There is a comparison to be made with the efforts British local authorities have made to counter the concentration of New Commonwealth migrants in certain areas of their cities from the 1950s onwards. At each stage their attempts at dispersal reproduced the prevailing situation (Rex and Tomlinson, 1979; Rex, 1981; 1988). On the other hand segregation was also frequently reproduced by deliberate discrimination on their part.

Segregation and Isolation

> We simply want to separate the decent people from those who are not (Ladislav Hruska, Mayor of Usti nad Labem, Reuters, 3 June 1998).

Usti lies in a gorge of the Elbe. It is a classically Soviet industrial town. With the exception of a recently repainted Baroque church, it combines run down 19th and early 20th Century buildings such as the train station with Stalinist concrete monstrosities such as the shopping centre. Soviet era apartment blocks are stacked up the sides of the gorge. 30 or 40 Roma families live one of these apartment blocks on Maticni Street. City officials were to spend around £7,000 on erecting a four metre high wall around the apartment block. In addition there were to be 24-hour police patrols (*International Herald Tribune*, 27 May 1998). After 18 months of controversy the wall was finally built in October 1999. It was destroyed soon afterwards on the orders of the Czech government. Further ghettoization is another move in the cycle of repression and exclusion of Roma. Even liberal intellectuals in the Czech Republic demand that the Roma mend their ways, but it is hard to see at what point the cycle could be broken and by whom:

> The fence will separate this problematic community from those people who have private houses on the road [Maticni Street]. The wall will not stop [the Roma] from moving about. It will not be a ghetto enclosed on four sides (Milan Knotek, Usti city council spokesperson (*The Independent*, 27 May 1998).

The council said the wall was part of an urban renewal programme. The wall was more of sight-screen than an enclosure – as one Roma said much later on, 'It was silly, really, as we could get out round the back' (*The Guardian*, 23 February 2004). In appears that the wall was partly intended to severely limit the Roma's movement, and more importantly ensure that the problem is hidden from the neighbours. The non-Roma residents of the street complained of a variety of low-key anti-social behaviour, mainly noise and rubbish being left around the apartment block. The Roma complained that the council did not bother to collect their rubbish, and said the apartment is without hot water, heat, showers or baths. The deputy Mayor of Usti, Jan Kocourek, was asked about possible violations of Roma civil rights if this project went ahead and replied:

> Rights? Are you serious? What civil rights? They can vote, but they don't. They can work, but they don't. They can pay rent, but they don't (*The Independent* 27 May 1998).

In response some Roma representatives pointed out that the city council could provide them with services, but didn't.

In Usti the intention was to confirm what was an already existing ghettoization, concretizing the social divide into a physical one. What was sought was not the reform of the 'recalcitrant community' but only its physical separation from the rest. In Plzen local officials put forward a proposal to create a monitored ghetto. An area on the edge of the city was to be set aside and used by 'low income residents'. This plan was closer to the classic Panoptic concept of having a monitored population held within a sharply defined spatial zone. Under the plan, several hundred people from public housing are to be placed in a series of prefabricated houses akin to portakabins. It would have a single entrance which would be monitored by the on-site police station. A warden will supervise the area and he will:

> Have the right to enter any room [in the compound] whether the resident agrees or not (Petr Cekal, Plzen city council, *Mlada Fronta Dnes*, 24 May 1998).

It was expected that the compound would be largely filled with Roma.

From when it was proposed in 1998 and built in 1999 to when it was knocked down it became a symbol in the British press and in the EU for the relationship between the former Communist countries and Roma populations. It was a powerful symbol, with echoes of the Berlin Wall, concentration camps, wartime Jewish ghettoes, and ethnic cleansing, a frightening term that entered the European vocabulary during the 1990s. It symbolized the 'ethnic tensions' assumed by many in Western Europe to be a fundamental fact of life in Central and Eastern Europe. There was also a certain amount of playing to the gallery by local authorities involved, which could be seen again in 2001 when the mayor of the Romanian town of Piatra Neamt unveiled plans for another attempt at urban renewal. A chicken farm well outside the town would, he said, become home to a barracks-like 'District of Hope' where Roma would be relocated to. Initially bullish about this 'genuine ghetto' for the 'black plague' he changed his spin following national and international condemnation.

If there is such a thing as folk memory then in Europe it is one of atrocities, some hidden, some half remembered. Usti itself – although this was never mentioned in the media coverage – was the site of a massacre of Sudeten Germans during the expulsion. Every historical memory of European atrocity was lit up by this. Mattijs van de Port (1998), writing of the Third Balkan War, notes Western European's fascinated repulsion with the 'bloody dramas' of dark Europe.

Usti had been a symbolic flashpoint earlier in the 1990s. In 1993 the then mayor, Lukas Masin, along with other town mayors in North Bohemia, asked for powers to expel 'unwanted elements' 'back' to Slovakia – powers which would be used almost entirely against Roma. Local officials stated that Slovak Roma had moved into North Bohemia prior to the Velvet Divorce and were responsible for a crime wave. Evidence for this was difficult to come by. In 1993 an entrant to a beauty queen competition coming from the town, when asked about her goals in life, said that she wished to become a public prosecutor in order to 'cleanse' the town of its 'dark skinned' inhabitants. In fact, these sentiments were probably more relevant to the segregation of Roma in Central and Eastern Europe than the examples of enclosure mentioned above. It raises some broader issues about the far more insidious and widespread ghettoization that in fact proceeds more prosaically, and mostly without the need for walls.

Most Czech Roma live in rented apartments. Rents in 90% of apartments are controlled, but are being gradually deregulated, with the result that rents are increasing above inflation. However, both public and private housing is allocated on a de facto racially discriminatory basis, with Roma placed in substandard, segregated accommodation. Roma endure discrimination in housing, both by local authorities and private landlords. Housing segregation was rife under Communism, where Roma were assigned to old, crowded blocks of flats with inadequate services, and this continues. Roma are increasingly ghettoized. The EU Open Society Institute has noted that 'local authorities apply a range of discriminatory practices, ranging from arbitrary tenancy requirements disqualifying Roma applicants to the segregation of many Roma into substandard "social housing"' (Open Society Accession Monitoring Program, 2001). Local authorities allocate Roma to the poorest housing, with no money for repairs or improvements. Housing declared unfit for human habitation is considered adequate for Roma. In general local authorities try and encourage Roma to move out of the area.

Many municipal apartment blocks where Roma are in the majority are overcrowded and lack the most basic facilities, including sewerage. There is the practice of allocating Romani families to 'holobyty' or 'bare apartments', housing for those who are unable to pay their rent but who are eligible for state housing. This housing is severely below standard. Private landlords often try and constructively evict Roma tenants using massive rent increases. The Czech government has not yet introduced anti-discrimination legislation in housing.

Although rules for housing allocation are ethnically neutral, they are applied in a way which discriminates against Roma. For instance, Ondrej Gina, a former member of the housing committee in Rokycany, said that, 'when [the committees] came to a Romani applicant, they would stop and start looking for reasons to deny them the apartment, saying, for example, that the available apartment "is not suitable" or "too small" for a Romani family'. It is also not unusual for neighbours to use accusations of petty crimes to get rid of Roma neighbours, since a conviction will result in their lease not being renewed by the municipality. This kind of low-level discrimination has not been affected by the recently stated intentions of the Czech Government to reduce and eventually end anti-Roma discrimination. The government has not introduced anti-discrimination legislation in housing, nor has it taken steps to tackle the discriminatory attitudes of housing committees and local officials. The failure to tackle housing discrimination represents a violation of the stated government policy on housing. Roma are not made welcome in housing blocks mainly occupied by non-Roma Czechs.

Patterns vary across Europe and within countries. For instance, Roma in Czech and Western Slovak towns commonly live in 'ghetto' areas. In Eastern Slovakia, Romania and Macedonia they are more likely to occupy separate villages, many of which are in a run down state. Several towns in Eastern Slovakia banned Roma from entering them (*Christian Science Monitor*, 3 January 2003). In 1997 the mayor of Kosice in Slovakia, Rudolf Schuster, now president, had Roma removed from their dwellings in the city centre in order to beautify the place. Peter Schultz, described as 'a leading local political analyst', said of this policy:

> I am glad they are gone. You can't have a beautiful city with Roma, because they destroy beauty. They have a different mentality. It is impossible to integrate them into Slovak society ... The only option is to forcibly move them out of town.

Separation is also maintained by racial action on the part of the white citizenry:

> Every Saturday evening there comes a group of 25 skinheads with armbands, torches in their hands and drums. They march through our town and shout 'Send Gypsies to be gassed' (Roma from Most, *The Guardian* 20 August 1998).

Chanov is a suburb of Most, considered by one contact to be in the worst situation regarding relations between Czech and Roma. Few Roma come to the town centre. They prefer to stay in their own area. The town centre is actively policed by the 'skinheads', who voluntarily maintain the ethnic segregation of the town. In many other areas of the Czech Republic skinhead organizations actively contribute to socio-spatial segregation by violence, harassment and the threat of violence (European Centre for Research and Action on Racism and Anti-Semitism, 1994).

Placing Difference in Britain

In Communist Central and Eastern Europe Roma were dealt with by being forced into a settled way of life, one such act being the 'Great Halt' in Poland of the 1950s. However it is a mistake to think that Travelling forms a great part of the identity of most Roma. Some groups have been settled for hundreds of years. In some of the countries of Western Europe where Gypsy-Travellers still travel, the object of governments of all political shades has been to create a network of official sites, which would work to render them sedentary and encourage them to give up the travelling life (Cottar, Lucassen, and Willems, 1992). Although considered an achievement of liberal legislation, many Travellers are severely critical of the British site system, often expressing their misgivings in terms like 'Being here is like living in a house', 'You can't really travel if you're in one of these places'. Some of their criticisms relate to the mismatch between the structures and forms of Gypsy-Traveller society and those of modernity.

It is usual to assume that the makeup of contemporary landscapes is largely determined by the powerful, by flows of capital, constructions of power, ways of seeing and doing. However subtle these arguments, ranging from the straightforwardly materialist to the socio-cultural constructionist, they tend to underestimate the active agency of minority groups in determining their place in the city and the country. Both social scientists and government planners fail to appreciate the role agency plays, even – perhaps especially – amongst the most excluded groups in society. David Sibley (1990) examines the spatial pattern of Gypsy-Traveller residents in London. Gypsy-Travellers face substantial popular hostility as not fitting into the spatial order of modernity.

Increased provision of official sites in London during the 1980s did not have the expected effect of reducing the extent of unauthorized camping in London. Illegal settlement is a historical and persistent feature of the London landscape, and something that the designation of London under the 1968 Caravan Sites Act had done little to change. Designation (giving councils power to evict Gypsy-Travellers from roadside campsites) was effective for a short period in controlling illegal settlements, but their agency soon reasserted itself. There seems to be a cycle in the spatial relationship between the British state and Gypsy-Travellers, with the state asserting methods of spatial control and then Gypsy-Travellers finding ways to subvert it. This may sound a little optimistic in the light of recent developments – most reported that the 1994 Act did real damage to them. On the other hand they seem to have bounced back in a number of ways, such as by relying more on housing to support a travelling life.

The 1994 Act exemplifies the role the British government established for itself during the 1980s as socially authoritarian and economically libertarian. Sibley (1994) argues that it asserts the role of the strong state, which 'subordinates local political interests to the economic and political project of the centre'. The 1994 Act was an attempt to resolve British society's ongoing boundary crisis, creating the spectacle of confrontation with some minority groups. It was aimed in particular at those groups who transgress spatial boundaries, especially that between urban and rural spheres. It concerned movement which is danger of violating the sanctified rural space. It marks one battle in the ongoing war of space, and it has had a detrimental effect on New Travellers, perhaps because they do not have the experience of facing state hostility that Gypsy-Travellers do. Like most hasty legislative responses to moral panics it turned out to be often unworkable in practice, but it is arguable that the 1994 Act wasn't intended to 'work' in legislative terms, rather it was a way of symbolically re-establishing the boundaries of decency.

Unauthorized Sites

Unauthorized sites, roadside sites, traditional stopping places, illegal encampments, depending on who describes them the term is different. Alongside proposals for new official sites, roadside sites (as they will be called here) are the focus of most of the direct conflict between Gypsy-Travellers and settled society. For settled communities and authorities they are the most outrageous imposition of Gypsy-Travellers onto their protected space. Gypsy-Travellers feel much the same about the practices of settled society in blocking off or rendering unusable their traditional roadside stopping places (Brookes, 1995).

One roadside site in South Wales is the focus of extensive and continuous conflict. Police will not allow anyone to pull on to it, and they will only allow trailers to leave. In this instance the site is actively controlled. This is quite an extreme example, and generally there is not this degree of active hostility. However the introduction of the 1994 Act has led to a reduction in the number of people on roadside places. There are a number of reasons why Travellers still wish to maintain their roadside sites, some practical, some preferential, as in the words of a Scottish Traveller in this excerpt from my fieldnotes:

> I have fifty horses. There isn't anywhere to put them on a council site. I have to use the roadside.

Many council and private sites simply do not cater for Gypsy-Travellers' needs. Most council and private sites have a ban on work being conducted on site. Gypsy-Travellers often combine their home and workplace, so scrapbreaking will be done in a yard in which the trailer is parked. Children are involved in work from what is (for settled society) a young age and will often be present while it is being carried out. Settled society creates a strong spatial separation between residential and industrial areas, a separation that is not such an important part of the spatial management structure of Gypsy-Traveller society.

Private Sites and Discrimination

> Some [private caravan sites] you pull onto, they look at you and think 'Gypsy', and that's it, forget it mate. They're terrified of you (Fieldwork Notes, 1998).

In Scotland it is not uncommon to see pubs with signs declaring 'no Travellers'. Likewise in the Czech Republic signs saying 'no Gypsies' are common in restaurants and pubs. There is widespread and largely unchallenged discrimination against Gypsy-Travellers in service provision. It is particularly acute with regard to Scottish Travellers' admission onto private caravan parks (Lloyd and Morran, 1998). Many site owners are quite upfront about this, with signs declaring 'no Travellers' or more euphemistically 'no Traders' (Bancroft et al., 1996). In other instances Travellers are told directly that 'we don't take Gypsies', 'we've had trouble with your sort before', or (a classic) 'we already have our quota of Gypsies'.

Ideally, private sites should provide some slack in the system for Gypsy-Travellers who are not able to use council sites or the roadside. They certainly give Scottish local authorities some slack when providing accommodation for Travellers, as they are included in the assessment of the number of pitches available to Travellers. Under the Scottish system, each local authority was set a 'Pitch Target', a quota. Until it is reached the council had its powers of eviction limited under the Toleration Policy. Grants were provided to assist councils in building sites. Councils are allowed to include some private sites in their Pitch Count. An investigation by Save the Children indicated that they often included sites which were non-existent or which discriminated against

Travellers. This was not just an argument about numbers. If the council was deemed to have reached its target Travellers stopping on the roadside may be prosecuted on the grounds that officially designated pitches are available, when in fact they may not be. This was ended in 2001, and councils are now expected to include Travellers in their Housing Strategy.

Discrimination against Travellers in this instance increases the level of socio-spatial segregation. It closes off an option which is available to settled people travelling with caravans, and leaves Gypsy-Travellers with the choice of either risking a roadside site and conflict with the law, or moving onto a council site, with the associated problems discussed below. The combination of discrimination by members of settled society against Gypsy-Travellers, and the institutional discrimination they face, makes it harder for them to travel by choice (Advisory Committee on the Framework Convention for the Protection of National Minorities, 2002). By way of contrast, settled people are able to travel by choice, able to park overnight on caravan sites and so on. The structure of the British state and society combines to foreclose the degree of choice open to Gypsy-Travellers, often giving them a choice between forced movement or forced settlement. In 2002, the Deputy Prime Minister announced that he intended to give policy stronger powers to clear roadside sites where they judged that there was adequate legal site provision locally. In 2004 the Scottish Executive recognized a general presumption against prosecution for unauthorized camping by Travellers.

Out of the Way and Out of Mind

> How do they decide where to build council sites? On industrial wasteland, next to a railway track, under an electric pylon, above a sewage farm (Scottish voluntary worker, Fieldwork Notes, 1998).

It is normal to find Gypsy-Traveller sites in Scotland and the rest of the UK placed where no settled housing would be built.

> 26 per cent of the [Gypsy-Traveller local authority and private] sites are situated next to motorways, 13 per cent are next to runways, eight per cent are next to commercial and industrial sites, 12 per cent are next to rubbish tips, and four per cent are next to sewage farms (Baroness Sharp of Guildford, *Hansard*, 2003, Vol. 648, Col. 1574).

Councils opt to build Gypsy-Traveller sites on marginal land partly due to cost restrictions, but the main motivation is that it is easier to get a planning application for a Gypsy-Traveller site when it is as far as possible from the settled community. There are simply too many political problems with any other choice. It illustrates the imbalance of power between the two communities, and the almost complete lack of a political voice that Gypsy-Travellers have. The political opposition created by proposals for new sites meant that local authorities preferred to build one very large site:

> The concept of building large sites, simply because it was just as difficult to get it through the planning, if you got one large site through, rather than five public enquiries for five small ones, with all the hassle and opposition, you went for the one big one, and only had one political storm to deal with. We would now go for a large number of family sites, instead of the large sites which have three or four families on, where there's always a difficulty with families, and it reflects the same difficulties that exist in social housing. You start mixing families on housing estates and you get the same problems. But I think small family sites are the way forward and we support them. If we were ever in a situation where funds were made available for the building of them we would go for small family sites ('Matt', Gypsy Liaison Officer, February 1998).

The emergence of a post-fordist labour market, the decline of heavy industry and the globalization of the British economy, has meant large changes in land use over the past two decades. There has been increasing pressure on the zoning system created by the 1947 Town & Country Planning Act. De-industrialization meant that many once vibrant areas fell into disuse; globalization and post-fordism mean that new uses are constantly being sought for them. Council sites have been built on out of the way land, land which in many cases has now been designated as industrial estates or for re-development. In some instances this has been at the root of increasing conflict between Gypsy-Travellers and local authorities.

The planning system works against Gypsy-Travellers, both when they apply for permission to build their own sites, and when councils try to create statutory sites (Hawes, 1987). In part it reflects the power imbalance between Gypsy-Travellers and settled people, but it also signifies something more about the problematic relationship between the two communities. Each time a site is proposed there is a high level of heartfelt and vocal opposition from the local community. A site proposal is usually greeted by the formation of a residents' 'Gypsy Site Action Committee' to oppose it. Wilton (1998) examines similar opposition and anxiety created over the siting of an AIDS hospice. He argues that the internalization of the distinction between normality and difference relies upon the maintenance of protected local space. A threat to the local spatial order is felt as a very real threat to one's sense of identity, but it is also the space which is perceived as having an identity. A particular place is identified as British and hence populated by whites, or as Welsh and populated by Welsh speakers: immigrants or others who are out place threaten the identity of the place.

One case in point is that of June Buckley. Like many British Gypsy-Travellers she had lived illegally on her own land which she had bought in 1988, and had been refused planning permission for (Eli Frankham, *The Daily Mail*, 26 September 1996). The council, South Cambridgeshire, rejected the site application on the grounds that the site was, in its view, an 'eyesore'. A long appeal to the European Commission of Human Rights on the grounds that her right to a home was being violated failed (European Commission of Human Rights, 1995), and in the light of it the council suggested that she move onto and empty pitch on the nearby council site. Ironically the site it requested she move on to is considered a far worse eyesore (*The Times*, 26 September 1996). The cumulative impact of the various planning decisions made over the years has been to underscore the view of Gypsy-Travellers as out of place, as violating the spatial order of city and country.

The Impact of Sites on Gypsy-Travellers

> The council site is almost as bad as being in a house. When they built it they didn't think of young folk. It's boring, ten miles from the city and two miles to a wee village with one shop ('Claire').
>
> It's not really travelling [living on a council site]. There's no community, everyone's out for themselves ('Susan', Scottish Travellers, Fieldwork Notes, 1998).

Council sites are sites owned and managed by local authorities. Most of them were built under the auspices of the 1968 Caravan Sites Act, which obliged local authorities in England and Wales to provide for Gypsy-Travellers 'residing in or resorting to' their area. Despite the legal obligation, various circumstances meant that few sites were built until the introduction of a central government grant for site-building in 1979.

> I've been on this site for twenty years, ever since it was built ('Donna').
>
> It's almost like being settled ('Pat', Fieldwork Notes, 1998).

There was and is an expectation among some government officials that Gypsy-Travellers who have lived on a site for a large part of their lives would move into housing. It was felt that there was no difference between living in a trailer on the same pitch for years and moving into a house. For many Gypsy-Travellers however, there still was a great difference between the two. They feel that moving into housing permanently is dangerous for their identity.

The geometry of modernist planning and its desire for ordered space has a negative effect on the lives of groups not engaged with the project of modernity, of which Gypsy-Travellers are perhaps the most persistent example (Sibley, 1998). Gypsy-Travellers tend to be ambivalent about local authority sites. Some consider it to be like being settled. Most people said they used them because of the convenience, or because there was nowhere else to go. However, others were glad of the stability they offered:

> I like the peace of it. If you've got any problems you can go to the warden ('Tom', Scottish Traveller, Fieldwork Notes, 1996).

There are some very good, well run council sites, and some very bad ones, just as there are better and worse council housing estates. One South Wales site has a very broad social mix, with rich and poor Travellers. It part this is due the operation planning system which makes it very difficult to establish private sites. Prosperous Travellers who would have bought their own sites have to live on council sites instead. Paradoxically this discriminatory outcome has the effect of ensuring a greater social mix. This is an exception to the general effect of council sites, which has been to segregate Gypsy-Travellers from the settled population and from non-Romani Travellers (Acton, 1991).

Ideally there would be a half way house, with sites which give Gypsy-Travellers a stable home, but which are flexible and accommodating. For a number of reasons however this is not very likely. There are too many institutional imperatives which push things in the opposite direction, and for many there is less to be gained from travelling.

Housing Travellers

The thrust of state policy across Europe throughout the 20th Century has been to encourage nomadic Travelling people to settle, with varying degrees of coercion. In the UK the council site building program was introduced with the intention of integrating Gypsy-Travellers into settled life, with the expectation that they would give up travelling and move into housing. However there was and is a high level of resistance to housing on the part of Gypsy-Travellers. Some face psychological difficulties when moving into housing.

> When I'm in the house I just sit by the fire all day. I feel like I'm dying, dying of boredom. There's no-one to speak to, nothing to do. In a trailer, there's less space but then that doesn't bother me. That's where I'm happiest. I was born in a trailer ('Nick', Scottish Traveller, Fieldwork Notes, 1998).

Many previously nomadic Gypsy-Travellers have to cope with some very real problems when moving into housing, some psychological, some sociological. Feelings of depression and isolation are common experiences, and it is not surprising that the move into housing is often merely temporary. Housing has the function for many Gypsy-Travellers of providing a temporary stability and shelter for a time, such as when a child is due, or when a family member is very ill for a long period.

> The Health Visitors get them into the house, but then their brief ends, but that's when they need you the most. They get into the house, feel imprisoned, don't get on with neighbours. It's a very isolating environment for them. The only solution for them is to go back on the road ('Penny', Voluntary Sector worker, interview, 1998).

It is not uncommon for Gypsy-Travellers to face discrimination and harassment from their neighbours, which can make the isolation of living in a house all the worse. However there are signs that Gypsy-Travellers are adapting to use housing without losing their identity and way of life. It is increasingly common to buy or rent a house and live in it for part of the year, while spending the rest of the time travelling. Certainly moving into housing does not mean that they cease to be Gypsy-Travellers, and it gives them some freedoms that are not available to them when living on sites.

Hyperghettos and Impacted Spaces

Many of the processes described above combine to segregate Roma and Gypsy-Travellers and to turn their sites or housing areas into hyperghettos. The hyperghetto is the ghetto emptied out of many of the institutions and quasi-social structures that those living outside it take for granted, such as banks (Pollard, 1996), and the residents of which are viewed with an automatic suspicion by the coercive arm of the state (Kushnick, 1999; Chambliss, 1994). Surveillance of the hyperghetto is one element of state control and monitoring of the recalcitrant subject. CCTV and other surveillance technologies are generally welcomed for their practical effects, reducing crime in public spaces, controlling traffic flow and the like. Yet their apparent neutrality masks a deeper shift in the relationship between state and individual. The state is able to use new technology to penetrate day to day life to a far greater extent than ever before, its totalitarian impact masked by the benefits and benign uses of the technology, its character masked by the objective and neutral form of the technology (Fiske, 1998).

The use of surveillance technology in advanced industrial societies increases the extent of ghettoization, creating 'safe zones' – usually zones occupied by those with most power and wealth – and 'dark zones', which are unsurveilled and with which the police use a policy of containment. This thesis could be pushed a bit further, and could be a basis for explaining how the surveillance superstructure impacts on the relationships of almost all individuals to the state, comfortable and poor, black and white. The term 'impacted spaces' was originally coined to describe spaces emptied out of social structures and its subjection to totalitarian state action (Lash and Urry, 1994). However the ubiquity of surveillance technology suggests that many more spaces are being impacted, being processed through the apparently impartial gaze of the surveillance society. All individuals are paying a price in terms of their personal freedom, though some may be paying a higher price than others.

The extent of surveillance technology and the implementation of hyper-carceral regimes brings to mind an obvious parallel with Foucault's description of the Panopticon. The Panopticon renders its occupants seen but unseeing (Foucault, 1992). The many are watched by the few, and, being unable to perceive when they are being watched or not, must behave all the time as if they are under constant surveillance. Their bodies are rendered docile, and the Panoptic regime of correction renders them as civilized subjects. Looking at the forms of socio-spatial segregation that have emerged recently, one is tempted to talk of the Panopticon.

A closer look reveals that this may be an unreliable assumption. Panopticons are houses of correction (Bauman, 1998a). They were concerned with ordering their inhabitants, ensuring the maintenance of a disciplinary regime. The word 'penitentiary' contains this definition within it: it is concerned with the production of penitents, individuals repenting their former ways and prepared to become self-disciplining subjects. Yet many of the spaces are examined in this chapter are not about order, or correction. They are concerned with confinement, certainly: yet it is not the production of an ordered labour force that is sought. Rather it is the segregation of irreducible subjects, incorrigible others. It matters not what they do, as long as it is done somewhere else. It is a kind of reverse Panopticon, with the safe zones under constant watch, and the unsafe zones walled off and largely ignored, except on the occasions when they erupt into hot zones, as in the Los Angeles riots of 1992.

Restricted Places, Interdictory Spaces

The social problems caused by social divisions have throughout the 1990s and into the 21st Century led increasingly to societies which are segregated and fortified (Garland, 1996). Much of the interaction that takes place in public spaces is characterised by mistrust and defensiveness; or rather, it is predicated on the assumption that there are others to be mistrustful of or to defend oneself against. Mike Davis (1992) describes the spatial sorting and zoning in Los Angeles, a globalized city in which ghettos of the rich are created alongside monitored spaces of the poor. Public spaces are privatized and hygienized. Shopping centres are provided with the level of security that prisons could enjoy, and libraries are built with huge security walls and without windows. The extent to which public and quasi-public space in Britain is subject to surveillance is increasing constantly, with government grants and encouragement to implement CCTV. Newcastle City Council in 1995 introduced the first publicly provided surveillance system of a residential area, in this case a council housing estate (Crang, 1996). Again, the thrust of this chapter is that these developments are not merely about ordering space, but about ordering subjects within it (but see also Parson (1993) for a description of processes running counter to those described by Davis).

Stephen Flusty (1997) defines several types of interdictory spaces. These are spaces and buildings designed with the intention of filtering individuals. The nation-state of the past filled its cities with monumental spaces; libraries, council chambers, concert halls, and so on were designed to impress the individual with the power and wealth of the city and the nation. In contrast, the globalized city is a community to be sold, rather than admired. Hence spaces are built to withstand certain types of individual. He defines five types of interdictory space. They include slippery space, which is designed to be unreachable from certain approaches; prickly space, space that cannot be occupied for any length of time due to features like sprinkler devices installed to soak loiterers; and jittery space, which is continually monitored and observed by surveillance technology. These spatial forms contribute to socio-spatial segregation. They make certain spaces uncomfortable for individuals who are discomforting to the ideal the city or community wishes to project. Social mixing is built out of the architectural script, creating a series of segregated monotopias. The dominant society actively engages in constructing immobilized subjects, and it is against this immobilization that the attrition politics of New Travellers and environmentalist movements is directed.

Left over from the construction of these private and quasi-private spaces are what are termed here residual spaces, unmonitored, uncontrolled, and decreasing rapidly in number. Residual spaces include the verges of highways, wasteground, commons, any land which is unclaimed and little cared for – 'land' which has not been turned into private or public property. The process of enclosure of residual space has been carried out in Britain by local authorities. The closing off of Gypsy-Travellers' traditional stopping places has been one aspect of this. It has meant that throughout the past thirty years there has been a steady decline in the number and variety of spaces open to them. They have often worked around the restrictions imposed by the foreclosure of residual space, but there can be no doubt that it has affected their economic independence to some extent. However, it tends to be the case that as some spaces are closed down others are opened up, so there is an ongoing process in which spaces are recycled by Gypsy-Travellers after they are deemed economically unviable by settled society (Sibley,1981).

Immobilizing Travellers

One of the ways in which Gypsy-Travellers have historically been forced to give up Travelling is through control of their children. Throughout the 20th Century many European states have instituted strategies to control the reproduction of Roma and Gypsy-Travellers. Their children have often been on the sharp end of state action. Sterilization without consent was practised by Sweden from the 1930s until the 1970s and may also have been a part of the social engineering programmes of other European states (*The Times*, 28 August 1997). In their eugenic programmes, Roma and Travellers were lumped in with the mentally subnormal, as unfit to reproduce. Post-war Czechoslovakia also practised sterilization of Roma women without their consent (Brearley, 1996). In a similar fashion to the carceral vision of the mentally ill, being a Roma or a Gypsy-Traveller was to possess a social disease to be excised for the patient's own good. The actions of the state were presented in terms of a benign concern for the well being of its subjects.

Similarly, instances of state sanctioned kidnap of Roma and Gypsy-Traveller children were defended as for the child's own good. The countries which operated these policies ranged from the progressive welfare states of Scandinavia to the eliminationst social engineering state of Nazi Germany.

European states have long operated policies of kidnapping Gypsy children. Hungary in the 18th Century sought to turn Gypsies into 'New Magyars'. Part of the policy involved removing Gypsy children from their parents and putting them in the homes of the settled Hungarian population. The children often tried to escape and return to their parents. During the 20th Century policies of the forced removal of children from their parents came to the fore. The Swiss charity *Pro Juventute* between the 1920s and 1973 removed *Jenische* children from their families. Under the 'Children of the Open Road' project *Jenische* children were put into psychiatric clinics, children's homes and with foster families. The charity officials and psychiatrists who commanded it adhered to the theory that the *Jenische* exhibited criminal and anti-social tendencies to which they were genetically prone. Likewise, the Norwegian state had an effective policy of forced separation of *Tattare* children from parents wherever possible (Barth, 1974). It has been suggested that Norwegian mental hospitals practised the lobotomization of *Tattare* in the 1920s and 30s (Okely, 1997).

In the Republic of Ireland several Christian charities made it their business to do the same with Traveller children. In contrast to the Norwegians and Swiss they tended to justify their policy in terms of a religious, pre-modern ideology. The Traveller children were said to be in a sinful state, in contrast to the modern ideology that they were genetically or socially programmed into socially maladaptive behaviour, propounded in the liberal progressive welfare states of Scandinavia and in Communist Eastern Europe. In Continental Europe and Ireland direct state operated kidnap of Roma and Gypsy-Traveller children seems to have been less common than that carried out by charities sanctioned by the state. In Britain during the 1950s, Gypsy-Traveller children were labelled members of a delinquent subculture by social workers, and many were taken into local authority care (Okely, 1997). The control of children by the state was instituted to deal with what was viewed as the primary delinquency of Gypsies, their nomadic lifestyle.

Conclusion

This chapter has illustrated the forces and practices which spatially order the lives of Roma and Gypsy-Travellers and which reproduce socio-spatial segregation. It was seen that the socio-spatial ordering system implemented by local authorities and the nation-state played a central role in reproducing the problematic relationship between Roma and Gypsy-Traveller and settled communities, as well as constructing and mapping their difference and deviance. The bordering practices of both communities also had an important role, sometimes confirming this mapping, sometimes violating it. However it would be better for both Gypsy and settled society not to be engaged in a continual game of cat and mouse with each other but rather to reach an accommodation which would open up a socio-cultural space for them.

Chapter 5

The Law of the Land

Introduction

This chapter examines the place of British Gypsy-Travellers within the legal system. It considers the function of the law in establishing moral and social norms and pathologizing aspects of Gypsy-Traveller life. It examines how a variety of legal principles, discourses and bureaucratic agencies combine to construct Gypsy-Travellers as deviant with regard to the moral and social order. It considers the attempts in British law to control Gypsy-Travellers' accommodation, and the ambivalent nature of legislation in this area. The origin and impact of the 1994 Criminal Justice and Public Order Act is assessed, as are attempts to establish Travellers as an ethnic minority with associated rights. It is contended that the criminal justice system has its own rationality which may conflict with both that of the formal law and other parts of the state. The development of the category of 'Gypsy Crime' in America is used as a comparison. It is argued that institutional discrimination exists within the legal system, based on ingrained assumptions about what constitutes a normal way of life, but that there is scope for the establishment of a framework of civil rights with which to form the basis for the empowerment of Gypsy-Travellers.

The legal system both reflects and constitutes a specific social order. For the citizens of modern society the law is a powerful arbiter which constructs and delimits large parts of social life, but also a strangely elusive and esoteric narrative, carried out in an arcane and obscure language by a small and relatively closed elite. It has an elusive double nature, at once constructed by social conventions but also rendering them concrete. It appears to us as both active and passive, definite yet malleable. Much sociological writing about law oscillates between the two sides of the equation, unsure of where 'the real power lies' with regard to deviant or outsider groups within society.

When tracing the construction of deviance in law Roma and Gypsy-Travellers recur regularly. The historical record shows them to be one group which have been perceived as violating the social and moral order of feudalism, of early capitalism (Mayall, 1992b), of industrial society (Gronfors, 1979; 1981) and of postmodernity (MacLaughlin, 1999b). Throughout their presence in Europe they have been subject to periodic attempts to legislate their lifestyle out of existence (Puxon, 1977; Hancock, 1987b).

> Since 1948 a series of [UK] Acts of Parliament and other developments have made life progressively more difficult for Gypsies (European Court of Human Rights ruling, 1991).

This chapter concerns the construction of Roma and Gypsy-Travellers within the criminal justice network, and in particular the social forces behind the introduction of the Caravan Sites Act 1968 (henceforth the 1968 Act) and the Criminal Justice and Public Order Act 1994 (henceforth the 1994 Act). A possible basis for civil rights to be developed within a European-wide legal framework will be sketched out. It begins with the examination of some theories of law, deviance and punishment in which to set developments affecting Gypsy-Travellers.

Punishing Society

Durkheim describes the development of modern law as the outcome of the transition from the retributive system existing under mechanical solidarity, to the restitutive one necessary for maintaining the social order of organic solidarity (Durkheim, 1933). At first glance Foucault's distinction between purgative and carceral regimes seems to draw strongly on Durkheim's differentiation of retributive from restitutive juridical practice. However Foucault, in adopting an inverted Whig theory of history, rejects the idea of progress inherent in the distinction Durkheim makes. Instead he sees in modernity the development of an apparatus of power-knowledge, which in the prison system operates to produce 'docile and useful bodies' (Foucault, 1992). Law in modernity establishes carceral reason, forming a punitive rationality through its discourses and practices (Hunt and Wickham, 1994: 40-1). Foucault is probably closer to Marxism than he would have accepted in arguing that law masks domination, but his theory works at a much deeper level. Law is closely involved in the day to day production of domination, and is not merely the mask for, or instrument of, power.

Leon Sheleff (1975) criticizes Durkheim's categorization of pre-modern law, citing historical evidence to highlight the non-punitive and restitutive character of many pre-modern legal systems. The evidence he presents draws into doubt Durkheim's assumptions about progress from repression to restitution as an organizing principle of the organic division of labour. Sheleff argues that the law has in fact moved in the opposite direction, the individual losing power to centralized governments. There is certainly no shortage of evidence concerning the repressive aspects of modern legal systems. In the light of the 1994 Act it does appear that Durkheim was overgenerous about the extent to which society has moved from being a state of punishment to a state of correction, but this criticism applies to Foucault also, as he draws a similar distinction, even if his conclusions are different.

For Marxists the rules of law constitute and formalize the rule of capital (Quinney, 1978). The legal superstructure is constructed by and in the interests of the ruling capitalist class (Collins, 1982), though the legal system in practice has some autonomy from the state and material interests (Cain, 1974). Property rights are secured by law, and the morality of property is secured also. 'Deviance', 'crime' and other apparently neutral or common sense categories are actions or practices which violate that morality (Hay, 1975). Popular sentiment for firm action on law and order issues is so much false consciousness, obscuring the real function of the judicial system, which is to punish violations of the capitalist order (Garland, 1994). At the risk of caricaturing them, Marxist interpretations, and sociological interpretations more generally, take the popularity of such 'tough on crime' measures as extended jail sentences for certain classes of criminal to be in a sense unreal. They are presumed to be a set of impulses displaced from the real source of disorder and crime, the class system.

Such a stance seems to be slightly patronizing and dismissive of very real fears about personal safety. However it does introduce the important understanding that legal categories are constructed terms defined by social processes and balances of power and interest, material and ideological (Sims, 1997). To assume that enthusiasm for harsh judicial sanctions is constructed solely – or even mostly – in the interests of capital mistakes how such sentiments are often held in opposition to actual government and judicial policy, which has often been perceived as being weak, too liberal and too sympathetic to the criminal. Those with relatively little property understandably feel quite strongly about property rights, and those who are most likely to be the victims of violent crime might be more concerned with direct measures to prevent it than middle class liberals. The divergence of elite and popular opinion over the death penalty is just one example of this difference.

From this perspective, what was unusual about John Major's insistence in 1993 that criminal justice policy 'condemn more and understand less' (*The Times*, 22 February 1993) was that it represented a break from a long period of liberal, anti-prison sentencing policy under both Labour and Conservative governments. It eventually led to a 'sentencing auction' being established between the two parties (Ashworth, 1997). It was a populist measure which aroused the ire of the judicial and criminological establishment, although it was instructive how it largely failed in its attempt to play to the gallery and drum up popular support for the Conservative party or unify its members. An important question is whether the punitive turn in judicial policy – the 'decivilizing of punishment' (Pratt, 1998) – was a short term political strategy on the part of the Major government, or part of a long term dynamic in modern society affecting 'out' groups and collapsing together social and penal discourses around these groups (Downes and Morgan, 1997). The thrust of this chapter, and this book, is towards the latter interpretation, although it has to be borne in mind that the character of the 1994 Act was formed by specific elements which were unique to the Major government.

Whatever the limits of Durkheim's teleology, Foucault's anti-progressivism and Marxist class determinism, their conception of law as a social product is a valuable one. Taking his lead from them, David Garland (1994) examines the development of law – and its necessary counterpart, crime – from the social order, and the way in which the application of punishment sustains a particular moral order (Garland, 1985). Pushing this further, he proposes that punishment be considered as a cultural and representational agent, as an active player in the creation of cultural standards and norms (Garland, 1991). It constructs categories which inform social knowledge, and operatives which impinge on social practice (Sandland, 1996).

The legal and the criminal justice systems have many functions, ideological, practical and symbolic. They are both part of the 'core' state (Jessop, 1990), the assertion of its territorial monopoly of violence, and the primary means whereby the exercise of that monopoly is restricted. They assert the primacy of property relations and allow for the redistribution of wealth (Cooper, 1997). In the judicial process the characters of the state and the citizen are measured and asserted, and the boundaries of their relationship defined. The law, in both its criminal justice and planning manifestations, is a paradigmatic zone in which the relationship between Gypsy-Travellers and settled society is mapped out.

British Law and Enclosure

> [Asks] the Home Secretary if his attention has been called to frequent complaints of the delinquencies of gangs of gypsies, especially in the

> south and eastern counties ... seeing that the police are unable to protect the public against the depredations of these people, he will consider the advisability of introducing legislation for the accomplishment of that purpose? (T. Bennet MP, *Hansard*, 1923, Vol. 163, Col. 492).

It has been asserted that possession is nine tenths of the law, to which can be added the statement that most of the other tenth is the construction of deviance as a moral marker. Although this chapter will also examine the construction of deviance and delinquency with regard to Roma and Gypsy-Travellers in the category of 'Gypsy Crime', it is primarily concerned with the relevance the law of enclosure and the legal structure of land use – the 'law of the land' – has to Gypsy-Traveller society in the UK. It will be seen that with Gypsy-Travellers the law of spatial enclosure is still an operative principle. As shall be shown, permanent possession and ownership of land are valued in legal statute whereas rights of intermittent access are not. Almost by definition Gypsy-Traveller society in Britain requires some measure of the latter to thrive, or merely to exist. This has been the source or the focus of much of the conflict between the two communities (Niner, 2004).

Succeeding periods in history have produced different forms of legislation relating to Travellers in the UK (Mayall, 1995). Both official papers and 'rogue' literature in the early modern period constructed Gypsies as a delinquent social group and a separate race (Mayall, 1997). The first Act of Parliament relating to them was the Egyptians Act 1530, which gave notice to all 'Egyptians' to leave England and banned any from entering the country (Mayall, 1988). Similar Acts followed in 1552, 1554 and 1562, suggesting that the original Act did not have a great efficacy in reducing the numbers or visibility of Gypsies in England. However, the Acts were not complete dead letters. In York in 1596, 106 Gypsies were sentenced to death by the 'Quarter Sessions', although most were later reprieved (Ministry of Housing and Local Government, 1967). The next legislative spurt came in the 18th Century with the Justice Commitment Act 1743, which declared that all Gypsies practising palmistry were to be treated as vagabonds. The Rogues and Vagabonds Act 1783 strengthened anti-vagabond measures. Reflecting the function the law had as primarily a defender of liberty and property, up to the end of the 19th Century legal measures were mostly directly punitive of Gypsies.

In Christopher Hill's description of 17th Century struggles, Gypsies were a symbol of common liberty to the poor (Hill, 1996). The traditional liberties of the labouring poor and the peasantry were opposed to that of the encroaching law, which was seen as securing the liberty of property. Gypsies' appearance in the written record occurred in tandem with an upsurge in social disorder. Moral panics about vagabonds and heretical or millennial sects swept the country in the 16th and 17th Centuries. The large itinerant population was a source of fear to the authorities (Gerking, 1973). The lower classes looked to the Gypsies as a symbol of defiance of the wage labour system that the state was seeking to impose, sweeping away feudal rights and *noblesse oblige*. It is possible that many of the poor made landless by the Acts of Enclosure joined the 'Gypsy bands' (Okely, 1983).

John McMullan (1998a) connects the measures taken against vagabonds in the 18th Century to the formation of the modern nation state as a system of social practice. There was an extension of social surveillance in response to an upsurge in the number of bodies out of place, the wandering bands and individuals threatening to the moral-spatial hierarchy. The early modern state applied the science of social order to society through a set of pastoral-state techniques. In pre-modern Britain policing functions had been carried out on a communal level, through communal rituals of moral regulation in a society characterized by face to face contact (Thompson, 1993). Social upheavals from 1600 onwards resulted in mass displacement, creating classes of 'sturdy vagabonds' and 'wandering beggars', and so on. The state practices formed in response to these upheavals involved the formulation of criminal categories, both categories of behaviour and of people. In a sense, it was out of this state development process that 'crime' as it is understood today was created (Emsley, 1997).

Mutual, communal sanctions were inadequate to deal with a population which included people who were not bound by the old social obligations. The peripatetic population of England created widespread communal anxiety at the same time as its very existence signalled the obsolescence of traditional methods of resolving that anxiety (McMullan, 1987). The developing state techniques of social surveillance transformed that communal anxiety into social anxiety. Social surveillance required the ordering and enumerating of the population according to social categories, the lowest of which included 'paupers and their families, vagrants, gypsies, vagabonds and idle and disorderly persons' (Colquhoun, 1806). The practices of governmentality and the practices of the self combined to produce the ordered social life of modernity (Garland, 1997). The order of modernity produced by it is a govern*mentality*, an ordering of the mind and the social self, mapping British society to underpin moral and administrative authority (McMullan, 1998b).

There was another progressive exclusion of Gypsies over the course of the 19th Century. A succession of measures followed the Vagrancy Act 1822, which consolidated previous laws concerning vagrants into the one Act. A series of Acts restricting movement followed (Vagrancy

Act 1824, Highway Act 1835). Later in the century the focus of legislation moved to regulating lifestyle (Public Health Act 1875, Housing of the Working Classes Act 1885), and giving public bodies the power to delimit and control space (Local Government Act 1894, Commons (Inclosure) Act 1899). Reflecting and structuring social change, the law had been given some paternalist functions, such as the establishment of compulsory education. Alongside the intervention of the state into society went increased regulation of open space and the active creation of 'governable spaces' (Rose and Valverde, 1998). Victorian intellectuals built up a racial classification of Gypsy-Travellers, with the romantic, but disappearing 'true Gypsies' at the top, and the despised, deracinated 'Tinkers' at the bottom. See Jarman and Jarman (1991) for a more recent example of this kind of distinction being made.

It was the social measures of the late Victorian era which had set the scene for legislation in the 20th Century, which has been by any measure the regulative century. The Town and Country Planning Act 1947 introduced the principle of universal spatial zoning. The Gypsies Bill (Northern Ireland) 1950 ended unauthorized camping by Travellers in Northern Ireland. The Highways Act 1959 (henceforth the 1959 Act) made camping on the verge of a highway by Gypsies and others a crime in England and Wales. The Caravan Sites and Control of Development Act 1960 (henceforth the 1960 Act) and the Caravan Sites (Northern Ireland) Act 1963 imposed regulations on privately owned caravan sites which meant that many private Gypsy-Traveller sites were closed. Many Gypsy-Travellers were rendered homeless overnight and had to take to the roadside. These measures took the situation to the point where it was impossible to live as a Gypsy and stay within the law.

Some accommodation between Travellers and the British state was reached in the 1968 Caravan Sites Act, which incorporated both rights and assimilative measures (Adams et al., 1975). It required councils to provide accommodation for Gypsy-Travellers. Special powers were reserved for 'designated' councils who were considered to have achieved their pitch targets (Brand, 1986). It seems that things have now come full circle with the 1994 Act, returning to the *status quo ante* of the 18th Century law as defender of fixed property, with no countervailing claims on the part of the propertyless admitted. It abolished the requirement to build sites contained in the 1968 Act and extended designation powers to all local authorities in England and Wales. Since then, the government has acknowledged the right of Gypsy-Travellers to live a nomadic life (Lord Evans, *Hansard*, 2003, Vol. 648, Col. 1580). A review of Gypsy-Traveller site provision by the Office of the Deputy Prime Minister is due to report in 2004. However, a conflict remains between this acknowledged right and the state of site provision and planning law, which continues to make a travelling life very difficult.

The Development of the 1968 Act

> I think the House will agree that the gipsy problem varies from locality to locality. It is up to the local authorities to deal with it (J. R. Bevins MP, Ministry of Housing and Local Government, *Hansard*, 1958, Vol. 595, Col. 139).

Through the 1950s the British government had a *laissez faire* attitude towards 'the gipsy problem'. However, as is often the case, *laissez faire* was not benign. Local authorities were able to progressively encroach on Gypsy sites, a process which sped up after they were granted extra powers under the 1960 Caravans Act. The 1960 Act and the general post-war spatial settlement had led to escalating clashes between local authorities and Travellers who were being pushed off campsites and traditional stopping places without being able to find anywhere else to go (Millward, 1986). In an attempt to resolve the situation the Ministry of Housing and Local Government in 1962 released a circular encouraging local authorities to carry out surveys of the accommodation requirements of Gypsy-Travellers in their area with a view to providing sites. As is often the case with the well meant actions of central government, in many cases the effect was the opposite of what was intended. Local authorities took the circular as encouragement to evict Gypsy-Travellers so as to be able to claim that they had no need to make provision for them. It was increasingly clear that some sort of national legislative framework was needed.

> [A] Bill to restrict the eviction from caravan sites of occupiers of caravans and make other provision for the benefit of such occupiers; to secure the establishment of such sites by local authorities for the use of gipsies and other persons of nomadic habit, and to control in certain areas the unauthorized occupation of land by such persons (Eric Lubbock MP, first reading of the Caravan Sites Bill, *Hansard*, 1967, Vol. 755, Col. 447).

The 1968 Act can be read in two ways. It can be seen as an interruption in a train of coercive and assimilative legislation, in the context of a flowering of a radical, rights based agenda under a liberal Labour government, which lasted until the 1994 Act (Home, 1993), and then returned in a limited and contradictory way under the Labour government elected in 1997. An alternative viewpoint is that the 1968

Act followed in a train of socially authoritarian legislation, intending to convert Gypsies and Travellers from their way of life by encouraging them into 'reservations', isolated from the rest of society, where they would gradually become a settled underclass (Gmelch, 1982). Neither is completely the case. The Act did not in fact reflect one overarching legal or social philosophy. As a Private Member's Bill, albeit one which had government support, it was a trade off between competing demands represented by different MPs and interest groups. Some wanted extra powers for local authorities so that there could be an 'end to the problem' of the Gypsies, while others sought to develop a framework for mutual tolerance. Most MPs who intervened in the debates, whether conservative or liberal, saw a decline in nomadism as inevitable and desirable. The following remark is fairly representative of the general mood of Parliament:

> I hope that much will be done to enable [the Gypsies'] children to move away from this nomadic life and lead a more normal one (Allan Lee Williams MP, *Hansard*, 1968, Vol. 759, Col. 1933).

That the 1968 Act did not make the majority of Gypsy-Travellers give up a nomadic lifestyle and become settled was one of the reasons given by the Conservative Government for bringing forward its abolition in the form of the 1994 Act (Conservative Party Press Release, 1992).

Conflicting Rationalities in the 1968 Act

As well as being the product of competing interests in society, and the rule-book on how those interests are legitimately able to compete, the form of law can be viewed as the outcome of different forms of rationality or irrationality. This perspective is found in the work of Max Weber (1966). He related the production of law to a mixture of competing rationalities and irrationalities pertaining to the form of authority and domination existing in society (Shamir, 1993). Leaving aside those pre-modern laws which are substantively or formally irrational – being those which rely on open bribery, or some test outside of human agency such as the oracle – law in the modern world can be divided into that which is substantively rational and that which is formally rational. In the former legal judgements spring from generalized abstract principles rather than detailed texts or case precedent. In the latter, decisions flow from reference to a dense body of rules which are intended to cover all situations, and precedent where they do not do so. Modern law includes aspects of both, but, Weber suggests, in a society characterized to a large extent by bureaucratic authority and domination the latter is more prevalent.

Beale and Geary (1994) examine the 1968 Act in these terms, applying the division between laws which are rational in form and those which are rational in substance – between the law in writing and the law in force – to explain the contradictions in the operation of the Act and its eventual failure. The crisis which led to the creation of the 1968 Act was caused by the pressures created by post-war development, including planning laws and specifically two Acts of Parliament. The 1959 Highways Act made it illegal for Gypsies – amongst others – to camp on the verge of a highway. It made a lot of temporary encampments unlawful. The targeting of the Act at a specific ethnic group appears to be unique in recent British law. The House of Lords in a subsequent (1967) ruling decided that the definition of Gypsy was not ethnically or racially based, but gave a 'lifestyle' definition of the word, covering anyone pursuing a nomadic way of life. It gave its judgement the grounds that Parliament could not have intended the definition to be racial in character.

The 1959 Act led to the clearing of many marginal encampments. The 1960 Act closed many privately owned sites. Many Gypsy-Travellers were deprived of legal places to stay. The two Acts led to escalating clashes with the police throughout the 1960s. Gypsy-Travellers tended to group together for protection and a spiral of evictions and violence developed. It was clear that Gypsy-Travellers could not both live as normal and stay within the law. There were two possible reactions on the part of the state. Further assimilation into housing could be encouraged, backed by continued legal harassment, or a framework of rights could be created which allowed them some freedom to live as nomads. In the event the 1968 Act, in attempting to answer to competing constituencies, had to combine both measures.

Beale and Geary state that the 1968 Act was a unique development. Legislation had up until that time had the effect of criminalizing large parts of Gypsy-Traveller life, making their lifestyle untenable, or had the intention of assimilating them into society. The 1968 Act was the first piece of legislation that to some extent recognized their right to a distinct cultural and social space. It was based on generalized moral principles regarding a people's right to some societal leeway. But its implementation took place in a very different atmosphere to its conception. The cultural liberalism of the 1960s was slowly displaced by a very different set of values throughout the 1970s and into the 1980s.

The authors argue that the 1968 Act was substantively rational in its design, relying on the principle that a group of citizens had the right to maintain their way of life even when it was at variance with that of the majority. However, it was a failure in practice because of the partial and contradictory application of powers held by the Secretary of State for the Environment. Succeeding Secretaries of State had the power to direct councils to build sites when they had not done so, and also the power to grant designation when a council had reached an agreed pitch target, the latter giving them rights to speedily evict Gypsy-Travellers not on an approved site. In addition, Secretaries of State possessed powers under planning law to decide on appeals against decisions of local Planning Authorities. It is suggested that the Act failed in its aim due to a clash of ideologies to do with the implementation of these powers. In practice the power of designation was overused and that of direction was hardly used at all.

The power of direction was included in the Act partly as a political escape route for local councils, a way of getting around local hostility to sites. Councils could point to the legal obligation imposed by the national government and so avoid facing negative political consequences at a local level. However, the power was almost entirely unused for the duration in which the Act was in force. By contrast the capacity the Secretary of State had under the planning regime to strike down council and private applications to build sites was used extensively in this period. The result was an institutional paralysis. The logjam did not derive from the fact that Gypsy-Travellers adhere to a varying set of principles to those of settled society, but rather from the contradictions within the legal system which were represented in these competing rationalities.

The number of designations made illustrates the uneven application of the law. In 1993, the last year the Act was in force, 106 designations had been made. Such a figure implies that a large proportion of local councils had achieved their pitch target as set by the Department of the Environment. Yet central government conceded that the Act had in the main failed to provide sufficient accommodation (Webberly, 1986; Department of the Environment, 1992). The contrast is starker in light of the fact that in the two decades of its operation only five directions had been given to councils to build sites. The problem did not solely lie with the Secretary of State. Judges have shown reluctance to force the Secretary of State for the Environment to direct councils to build sites, or to allow Travellers prosecuted for illegal camping to use the councils' failure to comply with the act as a defence. In general a combination of local hostility and central government apathy led to far less sites being built than were needed (Hawes, 1986).

Beale and Geary's opinion is that the intentions contained in the Act disappeared because it was implemented under a very different social-political atmosphere from its conception. Labour's combination of technocratic interventionism and social liberalism came to an end in the 1970s, to be replaced by the ideology of the free economy and the strong state – aggressively monocultural and individualistic. The Act came to grief not through its internal assumptions but because of the uneven way in which it was implemented, and the reliance by Judges on formal rational precepts when cases came to court. This is true to some extent, but it has to be modified. The introduction of a site building grant introduced in the light of the 1976 Cripps Report (Cripps, 1976) and its maintenance – with some restrictions – during the Thatcher government show that central government was still concerned to hold up at least part of its end of the bargain until the 1990s.

The 1994 Act and the Political Uses of Danger

The law is ideologically constituted as a value free system operating neutrally (Box, 1996). Legal transactions are conducted in this 'cold' manner. Of course, the forces that shape law making and implementation are seldom value free, substantively rational or disinterested. In addition to the broad social power relations which structure law making and implementation, there are aspects of political expediency, horse-trading, outflanking or smoking out of other political parties, all of which may be reflected in some way in the final Act of Parliament. Most of these processes can be identified in the production of the 1994 Act.

Laws are texts which produce a rational description of a non-rational set of circumstances or measures. The Conservative government represented the parts of the 1994 Act affecting the planning regime as producing a planning system that was fairer all round. It sought to present the Act as a means whereby Gypsy-Travellers and the rest of the general public would compete on an equal footing within the planning system. The 1994 Act was also the result of various social and political forces, some of them to do with the short-term interests of the Major government, some to do with the foundering of the liberal consensus which had governed crime and punishment throughout the second half of the 20th Century. Some of the measures contained in it had been flagged prior to the 1992 election by Conservative Party, receiving added impetus from the socially authoritarian philosophy of the Home Secretary Michael Howard. The perceived need of the Conservatives to outflank the Labour party on crime, and Labour's desire to prevent such an outflanking manoeuvre, led to effective opposition being largely conducted by Liberal Democrat and

Conservative peers in the House of Lords (Klug, Stamer, and Wier 1996), and by extra-parliamentary pressure groups. In the House of Lords, the part of the 1994 Act taking away the obligation on local authorities to build sites was removed, after lobbying by, among others, the National Farmer's Union, several local authorities, the Association of Local Authorities, and the Landowners Association. This was an unusual coalition who focused on the practical implications of the change. They were unsuccessful in the end, as that section of the Act was reinstated in the House of Commons.

Submissions to the Home Office on changing the 1968 Act were overwhelmingly against removing councils' duty on site provision (National Gypsy Council, 1997). There emerged two odd 'Grand Coalitions'. Inside the House of Commons the Conservative government favoured it, and the Labour opposition acquiesced, while outside Parliament an unusual combination of groups, some by no means traditionally pro-Gypsy, opposed it.

The 1994 Act specifies that six vehicles travelling together can be considered a convoy and broken up, a measure intended to prevent large convoys of New Traveller trailers. Since Gypsy-Traveller families can easily own three trailers between them, two or three families travelling together can be enough to constitute a convoy and cause an offence under the Act. Making it harder to travel together has meant that networks of family and friends which are central to the organization of Gypsy-Traveller society have been made more difficult to sustain (O'Nions, 1995).

In addition to its planning implications the Act removes all rights for Gypsy-Travellers to stop anywhere but on an authorized site. When moved on by police it is an offence to return to the same area within three months. Refusing to follow a direct order to leave can lead to vehicles being impounded and confiscated. As a result of the Act, Gypsy-Travellers were forced to move around more frequently, being moved on more often by the authorities. Overall, it had an uneven impact, which brought to mind the anti-Gypsy, anti-vagabond measures of the 1550s, which were likewise not effective in forcing Gypsies to settle. However, Gypsy-Travellers perceived that there was a new instrument in force which could, and would, be used against them.

The 1994 Act was at the time presented by both its supporters and detractors as being aimed at New Travellers, hunt saboteurs and anti-roads protestors. It is assumed that mainly by accident or omission it got Gypsy-Travellers in its sights. In fact, the first stirrings of demand for tougher legislation on the Travelling population were made in response to an unauthorized Gypsy-Traveller encampment in Surrey (*The Times*, 23 July 1990). In 1990 the District Planning Officers' Society put forward a proposal that breaches of planning law be made a criminal, instead of a civil, offence. The Chief Planning Officer of Mole Valley District Council was reported as saying that current procedures were slow and ineffective. The Society stated its desire that tougher measures be included in the Conservative Party manifesto. They achieved some success as far as unauthorized sites go, with heavy restrictions now included in the criminal law. The result was that a planning issue was conflated with crime and deviance. As several informants commented, this has meant that the Act has dealt with planning issues in a wholly inappropriate manner:

> You have to see it as a social issue, it's not a criminal issue, and the police are being used as sort of bailiffs. I think it was the biggest mistake ever that they included Gypsy legislation within a Criminal Justice bill. It was just panicking, a knee jerk reaction to raves and whatever, and they had no time in Parliament so they stuck it in with a Home Office bill, when it wasn't a criminal issue. By virtue of going for a [civil injunction] you are not criminalizing the Travelling community ('Liam', Gypsy Liaison Officer, interview March 1998).

The collapsing together of a series of criminal offences with what were at the time the civil offences of unauthorized stopping and trespass was a part of discourse around the Act. The then Home Secretary, Kenneth Baker, made a speech in 1992 promising a more punitive stance on crime. 'Bail bandits' – people who re-offend while on bail – and Travellers who were illegally camped were taken together to represent the same respectable fears. The two were placed together in a discourse of danger and containment failure.

The 1994 Act was one example of what Mary Douglas called the 'political use of danger' (Douglas, 1992; Garland, 1996). Here, the politics of anxiety focused on the violation of 'clean' rural space. Anxiety was created not just by the simple fact of boundary violation, but by the general loss of faith in the political order. It was after all the politically weak Major government of 1992-7 that established and then (sometimes merely rhetorically) attacked the folk devils of New Travellers, single mothers, and, in a speech by Michael Portillo notable for its verbal fulmination, European metrication. The far more politically confident Thatcher government also set up and then destroyed its folk devils, such as the National Union of Mineworkers. However these were far stronger targets, and arguably were a significant threat to the social and moral order that Thatcher was seeking to impose (Milne, 1994; McCabe and Wallington, 1988). In contrast, the removal of Travellers' rights was not inspired by an active attempt to create a new social order, but by the general loss of faith in the establishment, and the Conservative Party's own identity crisis following Margaret Thatcher's departure as leader.

> Since the removal of the grant, we're back in the situation where [local] politicians are needing to justify the allocation of funds to Gypsy sites on the one hand and the other justify welfare cuts and social services cuts and all the other things that are coming in with restricted budgets. It was always easier when it was a duty placed on local authorities by central government and there were funds available. Then they could tell the local population, 'well we've got to do it'. So a politician need not campaign for Gypsy issues, since there are no votes in it, it's definitely a vote loser ('Liam', Gypsy Liaison Officer, interview March 1998).

In removing the rights of Gypsy-Travellers under the 1968 Act the Major government attacked the politically weakest section of British society. Council site building ground to a halt at the same time as it became much more difficult for Travellers to get planning permission for private sites. The Act became unworkable in practice because there was often quite literally nowhere for them to go. Again, the 1994 Act often did not work, even within its own terms. It led to greater numbers of roadside sites (Local Government Association, 2004).

Forced Movement and Forced Settlement

Forced movement due to eviction and harassment makes it more difficult for Travellers to take up their rights to education, health care and other statutory services (Liégeois, 1987; Bunce, 1996; Pahl and Vaile, 1987). Those who lived on roadside sites who had to come off them after the 1994 Act and move tended to have the worst problems. On the other hand, being pushed into housing can be detrimental to Gypsy-Travellers' health as well, many reporting depression as a result of having to take up housing. Official sites tend to sedentarize Gypsy-Travellers and the movements of those who are not on official sites tends to be forced or involuntary (Todd, 1984). Local authorities have developed different policies to deal with the aftermath of the 1994 Act. Some simply choose not to use its powers of eviction, feeling it to be both unworkable in practice and unnecessarily divisive.

In contrast, other local authorities have chosen to use the powers of the 1994 Act. There is a similarly patchy approach to the Department of the Environment's Circular 1/94, which gives councils advice on Gypsy-Traveller site planning (Wilson, 1998; Home, 1995). It recommends that Travellers' accommodation requirements are met through locational and/or criteria based policies in councils' development plans. It was intended that this would allow greater opportunity for private site development, but has as often been used to prevent such developments happening (Advisory Council for the Education of Romany and Other Travellers, 1994; Commission for Racial Equality, 2004).

Northern Ireland

The Traveller population of Northern Ireland is mostly made up of Irish Travellers. The law relating to Travellers in Northern Ireland was under the control of the Stormont Parliament until its abolition. Two NI government reports were delivered on the problem of 'Gypsies and like itinerants', in 1948 and 1954 (Ministry of Home Affairs, 1948; 1955). Both were negative in the extreme with regard to Travellers, who were explicitly treated as a nuisance population (Noonan, 1997). For example, the second of the reports made the offhand comment that attempts to solve the problem in other countries had included the use of the death penalty. It concluded that the fact that Gypsies and Travellers have continued their way of life in the face of such extreme measures showed the 'there was no easy solution to the problem' (Ministry of Home Affairs, 1955).

In response to the 1948 report the then Home Affairs Minister concluded that legislation was necessary to control Travellers. The Gypsies Bill (Northern Ireland) was put to the Senate in 1950. It was a severe and punitive piece of legislation, threatening fines and prison for a Traveller encamped on land without the owner's consent. The Senate allowed the legislation through, but it was abandoned in the face of local councils' opposition. The councils objected to the inclusion in the Bill of a defence for Travellers against prosecution. Travellers would not be liable for prosecution if the local council had omitted to provide a certain level of accommodation. Throughout the Fifties and Sixties comments from the Northern Ireland government, and politicians at both local authority and Stormont level, were highly anti-Traveller (Noonan, 1997). There appeared to be no advocates for Travellers among Northern Irish politicians in the way that there were in the Westminster Parliament.

In the light of the attitude of Northern Ireland politicians it is not surprising that there was no attempt at creating site provision or forming a comprehensive policy on the issue until the 1980s. The change came about partly through the introduction of direct rule from

Whitehall, and the formation of a pro-Traveller lobby around the Traveller Support Movement. The latter found itself in a much better position when dealing with the Department of the Environment than it had with the Stormont politicians. As a result a situation with some similarities to that in Scotland was established. Councils were given full grant aid to build sites, and in recompense they were allowed enhanced powers of eviction when an agreed number of pitches had been built. In 1986 an Advisory Committee on Travellers was created, along the lines of the Scottish Non-Departmental Public Body. As in Scotland, the encouragement to local councils in Northern Ireland is based largely around carrot rather than stick. Local councils are encouraged, rather than required, to provide accommodation (Chartered Institute of Environmental Health, 1995).

The Northern Irish toleration policy is only endorsed by the Department of the Environment and not by local councils who are in favour of greater powers of eviction for themselves. Evictions of Travellers on unauthorized encampments continue, under various statutes. Extra-legal evictions are also a fact of life. Travellers move on in response both to threats from police and the paramilitary organizations. The negative response to Travellers in Northern Ireland crosses the sectarian divide and the gulf between paramilitary and state organizations. It could be argued that this experience shows the concept of 'toleration' is a flawed one. Travellers continue to be regarded as deserving only of limited tolerance, which hampers the emergence of a rights based framework. In 1999 a new policy on Accommodation for Travellers was introduced. Traveller sites were transferred to the Housing Executive in 2003.

Private Sites and the Planning Process

Council site building ceased following the 1994 Act, apart from proposed sites that were already in the pipeline. The number of applications by Gypsy-Travellers for private sites increased markedly, but the success rate of their planning applications did not. Gypsy-Travellers have enormous trouble finding private sites for themselves (Home, 1982). There is not direct legal discrimination as such, but rather a series of structural factors which combine to push them out of the planning system:

> Nationally if you look at it, out of ten applicants from the settled community for planning permission, eight will be positive and two will fail. Ten applicants from the Gypsy community, eight or nine will fail

and one will get through at the local authority stage. Of the ones which then move on to public enquiries only ten or twenty percent will get through. Compared with settled applicants, it's a disgrace, but like anything else it's politically motivated. You sit down and its local politicians on planning committees. Their seats are under pressure, so they tend to refuse planning permission and sit back and let the inspector grant it or not, and they can then point the finger at somebody else if it's allowed through ('Liam', Gypsy Liaison Officer, interview March 1998).

There is conflict between the locality and national government over the rights of Gypsy-Travellers. Local politicians and people oppose Traveller sites (Samuels, 1985), though their fears commonly prove to be unfounded when the sites are up and running (Planning Exchange, 1997). Given the difficulty that Gypsy-Travellers have within the planning system, the then Conservative government's assertion that the 1994 Act would create a level playing field rings hollow.

I think there is the case for Gypsy planning applications to be taken out of the system maybe referred to a national task force instead of going to planning inspectors ('Liam', Gypsy Liaison Officer, interview March 1998).

The above informant is suggesting that applications for private Gypsy-Traveller sites be seen in a national context. Without it, planning decisions and the ending of council site building in England and Wales will continue to push Gypsy-Travellers into unsuitable accommodation. Many submissions to the 2004 review of Gypsy accommodation by the UK Office of the Deputy Prime Minister suggested the same.

The structure of British society and the thrust of the legal system forces Gypsy-Travellers into housing (Ellerly, 1996; Franklin, 1993; Thomas and Campbell, 1992). This may seem a rather bald assertion but it appears overwhelmingly to be the case. There have been quite conscious efforts to do this:

The fact remains that these people have not been integrated and I congratulate [Eric Lubbock] for seeking to get them integrated (John Wells MP, second reading of the Caravan Sites Bill, *Hansard*, 1968, Vol. 759, Col. 1950).

These conscious attempts to settled Travellers have been assisted by a failure, deliberate or by omission, to take into account and provide for growth in the Traveller population:

> 15 years ago we had about 5 or 6 Travellers in housing and now there's 50 or 60, and that's discounting families that we didn't know about then. That's because there aren't enough sites. The family growth survey predicted that we needed another 40 pitches just because of family growth, not including roadside. And there has been no provision for them. A lot of families have to move into housing simply because of the lack of choice ('Mark', Voluntary Sector Worker, interview June 1998).

No provision is made for population growth among Gypsy-Travellers in the way that population growth, or growth in housing demand, in the settled community is projected and planned for. Increased demand among the Traveller community is neither projected nor provided for (Holgate, 1991). Effectively, the planning system operates as an agent of social control of Travellers allowing them neither the choice nor the room for manoeuvre that settled society now takes for granted (Henderson, 1993).

Categorizations of 'Gypsy Crime'

> The gipsies are not so much addicted to stealing ... as is generally supposed. They are assisted in gaining a livelihood by their wives and other women going over the district telling fortunes (Mayhew, 1861: 376).

In mid-1996 a Romany woman living in Llanelli was prosecuted under the Fraudulent Mediums Act 1951 (*The Guardian* 22 August 1996). The Act intends to punish:

> ... any person who -
> (a) with intent to deceive purports to act as a spiritualistic medium or to exercise any powers of telepathy, clairvoyance or other similar powers ...

Punishment is a fine and/or up to four months in gaol. The Act allows exceptions for the purposes of entertainment, which is why astrologers are not prosecuted for fraud. It does beg the question of whether the law recognizes 'genuine' mediums, and how. There are a couple of other Acts which ban certain forms of fortune telling: the Justice Commitment Act 1793 and the Fortune Telling Acts of 1864. Fortune telling was an important source of income for many Romany and Traveller families, and remains so for many, despite competition from gauje 'Gypsy Rose Lees'. Interestingly it seems more prevalent as a 'Gypsy' profession in Western Europe and North America, and less so in Central and Eastern Europe. Perhaps the romanticization of the

Gypsy is more ingrained in the culture of the former societies, allowing an opportunity for this sort of profession to exist.

Defining fortune telling as criminal is one example of the creation of a category of 'Gypsy Crime' in legal discourse. Over the past five years or so there has been an active attempt in the United States by a network of law enforcement officials and journalists to create and institutionalize this category (Olsen, 1998; *Vanity Fair*, May 1998; *The New York Times*, 31 May 1998). A number of articles in the American press have concerned 'Gypsy crime'. The term seems to be widespread among a number of police officers who have made it their speciality.

A report in the journal *Phactum* in 1996 concerns a talk given by a Philadelphia policeman. He was over the years a member of several police task forces concerning confidence crimes so it can be assumed that he was not a rogue voice. It is similar to many uncritical reports from law enforcement officials in the USA which specifically mention the category of 'Gypsy crime'. They define it as a specific set of crimes which Roma are skilled at, further that the main orientation of their culture is towards crime-work rather than legal labour, and that their family and kin networks sustain this mode of crime.

It would be tedious to run through the specific errors and contradictions in the media references to 'Gypsy crime' – such as references to the 'Tinkerers' from the 'Northern UK'. They reproduce some of the worst prejudices about Roma and Travellers. The Gypsies are a race 'thousands of years old', they move around, they speak a secret language, they are bred from the cradle to steal (Caffrey and Mundy, 1997; Sutherland, 1997; Weyrauch, 1997).

The media plays a part in reinforcing stereotypes of 'Gypsy' crime (Project on Ethnic Relations, 1997b; c). In both East and Western Europe they have no qualms about identifying the alleged perpetrator of a crime as a 'Gypsy' (*The Daily Mail*, 1 and 2 August 1997; *Itar Tass*, 14 February 1999). It is alleged that in many CEE countries police and the media will conspire to blame a crime on 'Gypsies' when they have no evidence as to who committed it. On a smaller scale, the same displacement of blame has gone on in Britain. The Guardian relates that a gang of casual labourers was recently paid to dump asbestos – a highly poisonous substance – that they had cleared from a building site. They left the asbestos at a number of sites around Birmingham. They had instructions to blame local Gypsies for the dumping (*The Guardian*, 1 October 1997). There are countless similar incidents, in which 'the Gypsies' provide a convenient outlet for the misdemeanours of settled society. In Britain, where they are less visible than in Central and Eastern Europe, they have become a strangely elusive pariah group.

In 1990 a woman who stationed her caravan in an abandoned quarry was subject to an enforcement order by South Shropshire District

Council. She had attempted to appeal to the Secretary of State for the Environment against the order. However, the court ruled that she could only do so under the terms of the relevant statues if she had 'an interest' in the land, a term which usually means having long term occupancy. By definition, Travellers may not have had long term continuous occupation of a piece of land, yet still may possess an interest in it that goes back many years or generations. Further evidence in the woman's disfavour was that she had made no attempt to enclose the land, which the courts would take as a sign of holding an interest in the land, or being in adverse possession of it. The principle of enclosure still operates in British law and serves to exclude nomadic Gypsy-Travellers (Forrester, 1985). The legal system has problems coping with people who demand intermittent access to land and tends to end up criminalizing them.

Conclusion

This chapter has indicated that there are a number of legal imbalances in the rights of British Gypsy-Travellers and settled people. It is tempting to put a lot of the imbalance down to the nomadic life of Gypsy-Travellers: it seems obvious that they will have more difficulties than settled people in a society overwhelmingly designed around the needs and wants of a sedentary majority . However, the issues and problems outlined in this chapter are not due simply to conflicting lifestyles of the two communities. They result from crises and contradictions within the dominant settled society, anxieties over the maintenance of the moral and social order, which led in Britain to the conflation of social and penal policies (Gilliom, 1997) and the collapsing together of criminal justice and planning law in the 1994 Act.

Chapter 6

A Panic in Perspective

Introduction

Looking to escape persecution in their home countries, several hundred Roma from the Czech Republic, Slovakia, Hungary, and later Poland, Romania and other Central and East European countries, attempted to claim asylum in Canada and Britain during 1997 and 1998. Their arrival was the catalyst for a media panic in each country. In Britain, this continued in various forms up to the time of writing (2004). This chapter explores the combination of forces which turned the Roma into refugees, and considers the reactions of media, public and politicians to the events, who rushed to label the Roma as 'economic migrants' and parasitical scroungers. The British government moved quickly to 'stem the tide' by imposing visa restrictions on Czech and Slovak citizens. The process by which the Roma were defined and constructed as solely economic migrants illustrates some structural problems with the definition of 'refugee' considered acceptable by European Union (EU) states. The government's reaction is set in the context of an EU wide attempt to control regional migration. Immigration policy under Thatcher was governed by a rhetoric of ethnic culturalism. In contrast the Blair government's policy is one of technocratic populism. It adheres to the broad EU policy of regional containment of both economic and non-economic migration for the purposes of resource protection and labour market management. With this aim the EU had created a *cordon sanitaire* of Central European states like the Czech Republic who guarantee to control immigration on their Eastern borders. This appeared to become redundant when these countries joined the EU in 2004.

In the first half of the 1990s, with the Iron Curtain now a sieve, scare stories abounded in the Western European press about the huddled masses poised to flood the richer countries of the world. The nations of Western Europe had little need to control their borders to the East when the Communist states did the job for them. With the collapse of totalitarianism, and of some of these states, control of land borders became a pressing institutional need almost overnight, and European Union states took co-ordinated action to ensure it. Some of the predictions appeared to be proved right by the displacement caused by the fragmentation of Yugoslavia. A lesser, but also significant, exodus, was that of Roma in four countries of Central and Eastern Europe: Romania, Poland, the Czech Republic and Slovakia. Wherever they arrived they were the focus of a reaction out of proportion to their numbers, which will be examined in this chapter. It concerns the narration and discourse of space, place and subject in Europe.

Race and Politics: Roma Refugees in Germany

In mid-1991 the Romanian government employed miners to violently break up anti-government demonstrations in Bucharest. After they had dispersed the demonstrators, groups of miners went to Roma areas of the city. While police looked on, they terrorized the residents, administering violent beatings and destroying possessions. This incident was one of many, involving official complicity in the violent actions of 'respectable mobs' of Romanians. Their actions included burning families out of their houses (European Roma Rights Center, 1995). The police have tacitly tolerated the anti-Roma violence (European Roma Rights Center, *Letter To Chief Of Police Of Mures Country, Romania*, 23 March 1998). Such extreme violence, with no hope of protection from legal authorities, combined with poverty and day to day discrimination persuaded many Romanian Roma to head West, along with many other CEE nationals. The first port of call for many was the new united Germany (Thranhardt, 1995).

From mid-1991 Romanian refugees featured as a particular problem for the New Europe (*The Sunday Times*, 28 July 1991). The issue then dropped out of the media spotlight outside countries immediately affected until mid-1992. A number of Romanian Roma asylum seekers in Germany had been housed in a hostel in the former East German town of Rostock. Towards the end of August of that year a demonstration of 1,000 neo-Nazis took place at the hostel. The demonstration became a violent protest over five days and nights which eventually forced the authorities to move the Roma out of the hostel, in which they had been subject to a virtual siege (*The Times*, 27 August 1992). The neo-Nazis were given the support of local citizens and councillors. Local people cheered the neo-Nazis on in their attacks on the hostel (*The Times*, 26 August 1992). The interior minister for the *Land* of Mecklenburg-Vorpommern spoke of having a 'certain understanding' for their actions, suggesting that the Roma were responsible for having 'released aggression in their German neighbours' (*The Times*, 26 August 1992). The actions of the neo-Nazis achieved their aim of making their locality *auslanderfrei*: the regional government was forced to evacuate asylum seekers from the area (Husbands, 1995).

That the violent actions of the neo-Nazis appeared to be the instrument of popular feeling also appeared to be the case with regard to anti-Roma violence in the Czech Republic and other European countries. The neo-Nazis were seen as being able and willing to do what the national government was constrained from doing. As one resident of Rostock put it, 'It's all very well for these politicians and trade unionists to criticize us but they don't have to live next to them [Romanian Roma]' (*The Times*, 26 August 1992). In the words of a British journalist present at Rostock, 'It is not the malevolent energies of the 300 pasty-faced neo-Nazis which turned a night of protest into a five-day orgy of violence, but the active support of several thousand spectators of all ages' (*The Times*, 28 August 1992). One of the myths created in both the German and the international media was that the violence was wholly perpetrated by 'skinheads' when in fact it had the full support of a swathe of ordinary Germans (Willems, 1995). Another myth was that the violence could be understood as the result of socio-economic alienation in the backward, run down and alienated old East Germany (Stock, 1994). This was belied by the repetition of events similar to those in Rostock in the Western *Land* of Brandenburg some weeks later (*The Times*, 6 September 1992), and past hostility to 'non-German people in Germany' that was articulated in the pre-unification Federal Republic (Wilpert, 1991).

The conclusion was that the actions of the German government boosted the far right electorally (*The Times*, 30 January 1993). A common process, and one reproduced in this instance, was that the mainstream political parties reacted to an outburst of racial tension by attempting to take the far right viewpoint on board. Declaring themselves to be tough on bogus asylum seekers, they adopted and legitimated the language of the far right. The mainstream parties attempt to defuse the far right by adopting, at least verbally, some of its aims. The effect is often, as it was in this case, to legitimate the extreme right and give it a leg of respectability to stand on (Harris, 1994).

The German government ended up paying the Romanian government a substantial amount to accept its citizens back. Under an agreement signed in November 1992 the German government could return unsuccessful asylum seekers to Romania with or without the correct documentation (*The Times*, 14 October; 12 December 1992).

About £30 million was given by the German government on condition that the Romanian government used some of it to rebuild the homes of those Roma who had been burnt out of their houses by local mobs. There is substantial evidence that it was not used for that purpose (European Roma Rights Center, 1996). The appearance of Central and Eastern Europe's Roma population in the headlines did not last for long, and little more was heard about them until 1997, when groups of Czech and Sovak Roma began applying for asylum in Canada, and then the UK.

Refugees in Canada: With Your Own Eyes

On August 5th 1997, the TV Station Nova in the Czech Republic broadcast 'With Your Own Eyes'. This programme was purportedly a documentary showing Czech Roma enjoying life in Canada. Among other things they mentioned the generosity of the Canadian state and the lack of discrimination and racism on the part of the general population. From the second week of August to the first week of September 1997 several hundred Roma asylum seekers arrived in Canada. The number of arrivals for that period was estimated at five hundred individuals (*Inter Press Service*, 9 September 1997). Some of them applied for refugee status, some for residency status (*Associated Press*, 13 May 1997). Immigration officials, it is alleged, pressured some into returning immediately to the Czech Republic. This matter was investigated by the Canadian Immigration Department as it would have involved the immigration officials over-stepping their powers (*Inter Press Service*, 9 September 1997).

The Czech and Canadian governments issued statements to discourage the Roma from leaving the Czech Republic (*Associated Press*, 16 May 1997). Czech premier Vaclav Klaus stated that it was 'wrong for citizens of a free and democratic country to seek asylum abroad'. In the same press report Canadian Immigration Minster Lucienne Robillard had sent an official to the Czech Republic to 'turn back a wave of thousands of thousands of Roma'. It is doubtful that their efforts had a great effect, and the size of the possible out-migration was exaggerated from the start. However it did stir some action at national government level on rights of Roma within the Czech Republic itself (*The Toronto Globe & Mail*, 15 May 1997; *The New York Times*, 11 September 1997).

> So far we've learnt 'all-right' and 'hello' but we've seen the documentary, and we know they are good people up in Canada ... they'll surely have

patience with us (Czech Roma departing for Canada, *Associated Press*, 13 May 1997).

The popular response to the arrival of Roma in Canada was somewhat less measured and polite than that of the editorial column of the Toronto Globe & Mail. The would-be refugees were housed in homeless hostels in Toronto, the port of arrival. In addition to harassment and theft from co-residents of the hostels, the Roma were subject to violent attacks by racists, referred to as skinheads in the press (*Inter Press Service*, 9 September 1997). Intolerant stereotypes were aired in the press, one example being a story in *The Toronto Sun* headlined 'Gypsies Exist on Crime' (6 September 1997). A story in the Toronto Star reported an unnamed immigration official as claiming that half the asylum seekers possessed criminal records (5 September 1997). These stereotypes were reinforced with a Toronto city councillor's statements that the Czech Roma constituted a 'dangerous criminal element' (*The Toronto Star*, 30 October 1997). In a direct response to the refugee situation Ottawa imposed visa requirements for Czech visitors in October 1997, having lifted them in April 1996, leaving Hungary as the only Central or East European country not being subject to a visa requirement (*The Toronto Globe & Mail*, 19 October 1997).

Two myths were set up almost from day one of this 'crisis'. There was a myth of departure set up by Canadian and Czech commentators: that the Roma were leaving the country in search of an easier life, which they had seen on a TV documentary. The pressures to leave the Czech Republic were in fact far more urgent. As well as being subject to violence and hostility from their neighbours, Roma were given strong encouragement to leave on the part of their fellow countrypeople. This took the form of local authorities paying for one-way airline tickets to Canada, on condition that the Roma signed away the leases on their flats (*The Toronto Globe & Mail*, 13 May 1997). The actions of the local state in the Czech Republic rather belied the wishes of the national executive, which was concerned about its international image as stable, democratic and the most Western of the post-Communist states. There was a curious duality, with local authorities keen to use this opportunity to rid their localities of Roma, and the national government insisting that they stay where they were.

In addition stood a myth of arrival, which was that all the five hundred Roma were determined to get refugee status one way or another. Something which was only mentioned in early Associated Press reports, and rather lost in the succeeding brouhaha, was that several Roma had applied for residence permits, rather than refugee status, which was altogether different. In addition there were those that immediately returned home on discovering that entry into Canada was not, after all, automatic. Altogether these factors substantially reduced the total number of claimants out of that five hundred, in itself a fraction of the 'thousands and thousands' quoted by an unnamed Canadian immigration official (*The Toronto Globe & Mail*, 18 October 1997). It was said by one immigration official that around fifty of the Roma had decided to return to the Czech Republic. One of the asylum seekers said that most of the rest remained merely because they had nothing to return to. Many had given up their homes to make the move; others had had their flights paid for by their local councils on condition that they gave up their right to residence.

Refugees in the UK: Gypsies go to Heaven

> I was born and bred in the Czech Republic but as a gypsy felt I could never really be accepted. The British seem more welcoming and tolerant (Czech asylum seeker, Dover, *The Independent on Sunday*, 26 October 1997).

'Gypsies go to Heaven' was another programme in the series broadcast by Czech TV Nova, which included 'In Your Own Eyes'. The story broke in the media on 20th October when BBC and ITN news programmes rather dramatically reported a 'wave' of incoming migrants arriving in Dover. At that point the number of arrivals was under two hundred. The total that summer eventually peaked at between eight hundred (*The Scotsman*, 22 October 1997) and one thousand (*The Daily Mail*, 22 October 1997). Most were Czech Roma, but there were some Slovakians also. As with Canada, some immediately departed when they found that entry was going to be difficult.

The dominant theme in the British press was that there was a flood of economic migrants seeking to abuse the country's asylum laws (for example, various *Times*, *Sun* and *Daily Mail* reports quoted elsewhere here). Home Office minister Mike O'Brien took up the theme and stated that asylum laws were clearly in need of revision. The Times had a number of articles about the Roma, one of which suggested that many more were on the way (*The Times*, 21 October 1997). In a parallel with the earlier situation in Canada, Roma in the Czech Republic and Slovakia were interviewed and stated that they looked on Britain as a favourable destination because it had a reputation as multi-racial and tolerant. Like those who arrived in Canada, their later experience was to belie the image they had of the host country.

There was some attempt in the media to represent the reasons why being a Roma in the Czech Republic and Slovakia might not be very comfortable. *The Times* (21 October 1997) detailed some of the violence and discrimination that are a mundane fact of life for Roma in these countries. It also found space to spin the story for its own anti-European slant, suggesting that Britain was obliged to accept the asylum seekers because of the recent Dublin Convention on migration. The Dublin Convention prevents asylum seekers who have already passed through one EU country being sent back to it, on the grounds that they should have lodged in the first safe country. The leading article went as far as to suggest that Austrian and German border officials 'are evidently waving through cars and coachloads from Central Europe *en route* to Britain, knowing that they cannot be held liable to take them back' (*The Times*, 21 October 1997).

The opinion of the Times was that Britain was being used as a dumping ground for migrants coming into the European Union from Central Europe. The Dublin Convention mentioned in the article was the *Convention For Determining The Member State Responsible For Examining Applications For Asylum Lodged In One Of The Member States Of The European Communities, Dublin 1990* (reproduced in Wallace, 1996). In actual fact it was designed to prevent what EU governments saw as a larger problem on the part of controlling refugee movements, that of limiting multiple applications, whereby a person refused asylum in one EU state could apply for asylum in another. The Convention limits applicants to one EU state. *The Times*, *The Daily Telegraph* and Euro-sceptic Conservatives spun the story as being one of Britain bearing the asylum burden for the rest of the EU. The liberal Guardian and the British left represented it as an instance of Britain failing to live up to international obligations that other EU states manage to comply with. Both failed to emphasize the EU wide process that had been going on since the establishment of the Terrorism, Racism, Extremism, Violence and Immigration (TREVI) group in 1976, and exaggerated the distinctiveness of British asylum law in this regard. In fact the harsh provisions of the Asylum and Immigration Appeals Act 1993 are broadly in line with the co-ordinated movement at an EU level to establish a 'fortress Europe' (Kostakopoulou 1998). Fortress Europe represents an exclusionary zone in which there are minimal controls on internal borders but stringent controls on the borders of the EU as a whole (Tuitt, 1996).

Among the press, the liberal papers (*The Guardian*, *The Observer*, *The Independent* and *The Independent on Sunday*) emphasized the reasons why the Roma were leaving their countries and making the difficult trek across Europe on the basis of a TV documentary. In general the media slant was that, whatever they had endured at home, the asylum seekers were false claimants; that the system was especially open to such false claims; and that they were costing the community in which they were resident a great deal. There were some stark examples of panic reporting that cropped up, particularly in the regional press (*Newcastle Journal*, 31 October 1997), but also in the national tabloid press. The media are freer in using the word 'Gypsy' than they have been in using other ethnic labels (for example: 'Gypsy Scam Grows'; 'The Gypsy Flood that may sink £10m'; 'Warning over new influx of Gypsies', *The Daily Mail*, 23 October 1997).

In another parallel with the experience of the would-be refugees in Canada was the mobilization of far right organizations against the Roma. The extreme right National Front organized a demonstration on 15th November, just under a month after the first arrivals. It rallied about fifty of its members to demonstrate on the sea front at Dover, where they clashed with a larger number of activists of the Anti-Nazi League. During this confrontation the Roma themselves kept largely out of sight. Their reticence was not surprising since the actions of the National Front and the British National Party must have seemed to confirm what must be the worst fear of the refugee: that his or her experience in the country of arrival will turn out to be much the same as that they have left.

As with Canada and Germany the government acted quickly to make sure it was giving the appearance of toughness, and dealing with the problem. Home Secretary Jack Straw announced on 27th October that the period asylum seekers would have to prove that they had suffered discrimination at home was to be reduced from twenty-eight to five days. In his statement to Parliament he was quite clear that he thought that the asylum seekers in Dover were 'abusive asylum seekers', and had no chance of gaining entry. Many of the Roma certainly thought they had no hope of entry, since on the same day Mike O'Brien reported that half of them had returned to France (*CTK News*, 17 October 1997). France itself seemed to have suffered no such panic at the prospect of the would-be refugees returning.

> We have reports that Czech and Slovak Roma are on the move in Eastern Europe. Britain is taking a firm line and will not be a soft touch for illegal immigrants with no right to asylum. My message is, "Do not think you will get through" (Jack Straw, *The Guardian*, 9 April 1998).

The issue went to ground for a while, and then revived six months after the initial panic. *Scotland on Sunday* (29 March 1998) claimed that hundreds of Roma were leaving the Czech Republic for Britain following another series of racial attacks by skinheads (not, in this instance, as the result of a television documentary). *Reuters* (9 April

1998) reported the pre-emptive warning by the Home Secretary, who informed Eurostar – the company that runs trains through the Channel Tunnel – that it would be subject to the same carrier liability that affects airlines. The report received little coverage in the national press, apart from the two sources already mentioned. A National Front demonstration in early March 1998 received little publicity outside Dover and the anti-Nazi press. 'Street' action faded as the far right parties began to focus on the more generalized bogeyman of the 'asylum seeker', a cause taken up by the media and mainstream politicians.

> We get up to ten gipsy families a day flying out to London ... to help the British immigration authorities, we put a little 'g' by their names on the flight list, so that they can know what to expect (Czech Airlines employee, Prague, *The Daily Mail*, 13 October 1999).

In 2000 the Romanian foreign minister Peter Roman stated that Roma, by emigrating, damaged his country's image abroad. Other Central and East European countries also expressed some sense of being 'shamed' by the presence of 'their' Roma as asylum seekers in Britain and other Western European countries. The shame, however, was attached to the Roma themselves, rather than to the set of conditions which created strong 'push' factors for them.

The accession to the EU of the Czech Republic, Slovakia, Poland, Hungary and seven other countries in 2004 created a renewed flurry of concern in some British newspapers. *The Sun* expressed fears of an influx of Roma following those countries' accession to the EU, picturing hordes waiting to cross what it said was an 'open border' (30 April 2004). At the same time there was some crowing on its part that the Roma asylum seekers from those states who were having their claims processed in the UK would automatically lose their right to social security support. The government deemed those countries that joined the EU as being no longer capable of persecuting their citizens.

Immigrants and Aliens: Migration and the British State

> Criminals who suffer from loathsome diseases, who are turned out in disgrace by their fellow countrymen ... who fill our streets with profligacy and disorder (Conservative Party pamphlet, 1905).

> [Resolves] that the Labour Representation Committee be instructed to promote legislation to stop the landing of pauper aliens in this country (Resolution of Stockton Trades Council, 1905).

The 'Alien' is the disordering Stranger who violates protected social space (Swyngedouw, 1995). Legislation to restrict the entry of such aliens was largely non-existent in Europe until the beginning of the 20th Century. From then on Western Europe ceased to be a space of unrestricted migration, and began to be a space bounded by the legislative imperative to control certain categories of mobile subject (Bovenkirk, Miles, and Verbunt, 1990).

> The truth is that we get the floating scum – those who would go anywhere and do anybody and who are a burden on their community (H. Lawson MP, *Hansard*, 1905, Vol. 145, Col. 773).

The UK Aliens Act of 1905 was the beginning of a series of legislative enclosures of national space. It is thought to have been the result of agitation over the entry of Central and Eastern European immigrants into Britain, especially Jewish migrants who were often escaping from a rising tide of anti-Semitism (Gainer, 1972). The forces behind the production of the Act were a complex product of anti-Semitism, anti-Alienism and economic protectionism coming together to set up barriers against 'out' groups. Roma played a barely visible, but present, role in the production of the Act:

> A little while ago a large number of gipsies were taken over to America, but were refused admittance and brought back to this country ... and were sent about from county to county – a most disgraceful state of affairs (Howard Vincent MP, second reading of the Aliens Bill, *Hansard*, 1905, Vol. 145, Col. 777).

There are pictures of German Roma taken in the 1900s in the Scottish Ethnographic Archive. These were probably the German Lovari who were referred to the Parliamentary Debate on the Aliens Act of 1905. Panic over incoming Roma surfaced again in the 1920s, with moral panics over Romanian Coppersmiths, possibly Kalderash.

> It is our duty as Britons to keep our race pure (W. Greene MP, *Hansard*, 1925, Vol. 180, Col. 285).

From 1963 onwards immigration has been increasingly complexified and bureaucratized. The Immigration Act 1971, British Nationality Act 1981, Immigration Act 1988, Asylum and Immigration Appeals Act 1993 (Richmond, 1994), have each progressively added more restrictions as to who may enter the UK and who may claim certain rights. The normal pattern of legislation from the 1960s to the 1990s has been for an immigration panic to be followed by legislation. One example is the mass arrival of Ugandan Asians in the UK being followed by the 1971

Act. In contrast, with the Roma refugees of 1997 and 1998 the dominant discourse used was one of crime and fraudulence, rather than a cultural or racial threat. It was not British culture or identity, nor harmonistic race relations, which had to be protected, but British bank accounts. Although there was a secondary discourse which addressed the perceived contamination of cultural space by the Roma, the orthodox argument was that they were a threat to spatial order.

During the 1990s and into the 21st Century concern with crime and the criminalization of refugees has become more dominant in the UK than concern with race and the racialization of refugees (Morris, 1997a). The potential refugee became subject to criminalization in many ways. The Asylum Act 1993, in common with the legislation of many EU states, requires the compulsory fingerprinting of asylum claimants. Many can expect to be subject to long-term detention while their claims are considered, the use of which has also increased since the introduction of the 1993 Act. The intended refugee is as a matter of course made the subject of measures normally reserved for suspected criminals.

Up until 1989 intra-European migration was locked in a Cold War stasis. Since the beginning of the Cold War Western governments had quoted the restrictions on internal and external travel practised by the Communist states of Eastern Europe as evidence of their camp-like totalitarian nature. In respect of this, it was normal practice to accept people claiming asylum in Western Europe as defectors and political refugees (Fassman and Munz, 1995). To a degree, the conflict between East and West around the issues of unrestricted travel was mythology. For most of the Cold War governments of West and East operated a *realpolitik* in this regard, and it was notable how little population movement took place. Since the end of the Cold War, EU governments have explicitly sought ways to restrict inter- and intra-regional population flows. European wide action was co-ordinated through the TREVI group of the European Community Ministers for Justice and Home Affairs, established in 1976, and the EC Ad Hoc Group on Immigration (Collinson, 1993). Both were later subsumed into the K4 Commission (Wallace, 1996) as part of the Treaty on European Union in 1993. The EU was establishing a trans-national system of migration control aimed at the exclusion of excluding most potential mobile subjects (Morris, 1997b), in contrast to its aim of creating a regime of free movement for objects, capital and services within the EU (Lahav, 1998).

As a result, there is a widening gap between those who are able to move freely between states and those who can expect to be subject to harassment or internment at every border. Being able to walk through the Blue Channel at the customs barrier in any EU airport keeps one in complete ignorance of the experiences of those who are unable to do so. It is something of a revelation to actually be the subject of an interrogation by immigration officials on arrival into a country, to have the photo on one's passport minutely examined, to have one's motives questioned in depth. Yet this extremely rare experience for the Western traveller is commonplace and everyday for a whole class of individuals, the untouchable caste in a global system of apartheid held in place in part by the actions of EU states.

A Cool Reception for 'Giro Czechs'

> Invasion Of The Giro Czechs (*The Sun*, 21 October 1997).

An important question for considerations of the interplay of race and power is the process by which the refugee group's ethnicity was constructed. Were they thought of as Czechs and Slovaks first, or as Roma first? Czech and Slovak popular opinion rejected them on the grounds that they were Roma. Many Czechs and Slovaks were happy to get rid of them. They were seen as an embarrassment to the majority, a reminder of backwardness, and so on, and local councils were even prepared to pay for their departure. This mood was represented at local government level, with local authorities in Czech Republic and Slovakia actively encouraging the Roma to leave (*The Toronto Globe & Mail*, 13 May 1997).

In contrast to the perception of Roma in their home country the British government and popular opinion appeared to be as concerned about the fact that the Roma were from Central and Eastern Europe, rather than their being Roma as such. This perception of individuals from the CEE states is common in both elite and popular opinion in Western Europe. Central and East Europeans of any sort are felt inherently likely to be a threat to Western Europe's high resource status. The British press and public tended to speak about resource competition on the part of residents of Central and Eastern Europe, an area which over the years since 1989 seems to have mutated from being part of the halved European soul to a perilously close outpost of the Third World. The very distinction of Central from Eastern European is a bone of contention for residents of CEE countries. Popular British terminology categorizes all of the former Communist states as 'Eastern Europe' with connotations of backwardness and underdevelopment. However, the peoples of these states frequently prefer to be thought of as Central, if not West, European. The Czech Republic in particular was keen to differentiate itself in the minds of the selectors for EU and NATO membership from other CEE countries.

The concern to be seen as 'Western' was captured in a letter sent by the Czech-Slovak Association to the Canadian Minster of Immigration. Non-Roma Czech residents in Canada were somewhat embarrassed to see their mother country thought of as a place from which people might be fleeing persecution. The Czech-Slovak Association was moved to write a letter to the Minister of Citizenship and Immigration, arguing that the Czech Republic was 'an environment not distinctly different from that of Canada's, and possessed a credible record of support for human rights. Though the letter was later presented as arguing that Canada should not accept the asylum seekers (*The Toronto Globe & Mail*, 23 September 1997), its tone is more one of defensiveness. It presents the Czech nation-state as sufficiently modern to be put alongside Canada. It was embarrassed at the possibility of Czech nationals being accepted as refugees.

> The prejudiced Englishman is apt to call 'dirty' whatever is foreign (Canon Barnett, Russell and Lewis, 1900: xxv).

> The *mobile vulgus* – the inferior kind of people on the move, dribbling or gushing into places where only the right kind of people should have the right to be (Bauman, 2000: 93).

The rejection of the demanding other was verbalized by one Dover resident as 'we've got enough problems of our own' (*World in Action*, 15 December 1998), and rather more explicitly by parents in Dover who objected to the hundred or so Roma children being schooled alongside their children. They spoke explicitly in terms of competition for limited resources, 'all the attention is being given to them and all this money is being spent and they could just say goodbye and disappear in a year' (*The Times*, 21 October 1997). This is not to deny that some element of straightforward prejudice against 'foreign kids', or 'Gypsy kids' was present. This prejudice is at least reinforced by, or finds expression in terms of, resource competition between social groups. The new arrivals included at least one lecturer, who may not have been likely to be competing in the labour market with working class people for scarce resources. As with most migration, it is often the better off who are the ones to attempt the journey.

This indicates that the panic over Roma asylum seekers is not a moral panic in the classic sense – a signifier of a crisis in the moral order. Central and East European Roma migrants in Britain and other Western European countries became objects on to which pent up frustration and anger are released. The question then is, anger about what? Frustration with what? There seemed to be a feeling among many of the local people in Britain who objected so strongly to the presence of Roma and other asylum seekers that these people were being 'dumped' on them. They articulated a sense that their locales were being rendered as 'empty space', that their places were valueless and meaningless in the eyes of those in power, and that this was symbolized by the presence among them of those with no place. This alienation stems from a sense among many in Britain and elsewhere that the 'state' is no longer 'on their side,' that the welfare community has been deserted by a globalized, privatized state that no longer represents the nation – or rather, a nation that they feel a part of.

The Refugee and the State

The response to forced population movement has always been embroiled in political agendas and economic interests. States began to acquire an increasing concern with controlling migration during the 20th century, particularly after the First World War, with various restrictions put in place in the UK and USA for example. Two processes coincided: the increasing insistence, in Europe, that nation-state boundaries correspond with ethno-national boundaries meant a large number of displaced persons whose nationality or ethnicity was not welcome in the nation-state of origin. Complementing this was an increasing concern within already established states with maintaining their national wholeness. So the same process that was producing refugees in various parts of Europe was also slamming doors that previously might have been open.

After the Second World War, West European states were happy to allow for de facto limits on population movement to avoid any refugee problems. During the Cold War era refugees were often used as pawns in a power game between Soviet and Western blocs. The latter bloc maintained its commitment to the 1951 Convention as demonstrating its commitment to universal individual rights (Chimni, 1998). The existence of the Iron Curtain on one hand, and the difficulty of long distance travel on the other, kept intra- and inter-continental migration low (Hopkinson, 1992). The explosion in cheap air travel from the late 1960s caused the nations of Western Europe to take a more active stance in the control of refugee numbers. The end of Cold War divisions hastened action on a European wide level. In response to the increase in refugee flows during the 1990s Britain participated enthusiastically in the European Union wide harmonization of asylum policies (Kaye, 1992).

The collapse – 'end' is a word which suggests far too much closure – of the Cold War has led Western nations to shift to a policy of regional containment. The 1951 Convention has been undermined by the actions of these states, which have sought to limit the entry of 'new asylum seekers' who are not seeking refuge from Communism and do not conform to the image of the ideal refugee. The activities of the UN High Commission for Refugees have increased hugely during the 1990s, and perhaps the Western nations are keen to see it do its job of regional containment (Joly, 1996). The UNHCR in the former Yugoslavia had a primary policy of restricting large-scale refugee flows. There were suspicions that was serving the needs of donor governments rather than of the refugees (Cunliffe and Pugh, 1998; Hathaway, 1995). The refugee crisis resulting from the Yugoslavian conflict was contained under a policy of 'temporary protection', in which the emphasis was placed on returning refugees to their places of origin as soon as possible (Roberts, 1998). It was a spur to the EU-wide harmonization of refugee regimes (Brochmann, 1997). Not without potential merit, the regional containment policy creates some practical problems. Roma, who have no place in the ethnic order created by the Dayton peace agreement, have found many difficulties in returning to their homes, persecution by neighbours being one. The EU was active in creating a myth of return as the necessary adjunct of its favoured policy of providing temporary sanctuary.

The Construction and Criminalization of 'Refugee'

In recent years, successive refugee crises have shown a conflict between the demands and precepts of national law and those of international law.

> Refugee hearings are a peculiar hybrid of courtroom-style interrogation, loosely-structured story-telling and inter-cultural discussions involving bureaucrats (who rarely exhibit an understanding of the Third World countries from which most refugees come) and claimants (who generally exhibit as little understanding of the host country) (Barsky, 1994: 66).

Robert Barsky designs an interpretative account of refugee hearings in Canada under the UN Refugee Convention. He describes this as the process of constructing a productive other. The discursive process by which a claim for asylum is processed is in part one of constructing the refugee other, but is mainly one in which the experience of the claimant is reduced to fit in with bureaucratic requirements and procedures. Both parties to the process have to operate within this reduction, since the refugees' advocate also has to squeeze his or her experience, a product of economics and politics as well as (direct) violence (Ferris, 1993), into the category of 'well founded fear of persecution'. Hence, the story produced is one that can describe only a small part of the refugee experience. The bureaucratic and legal filters that are applied remove most of the complex of reasons that may force a person to leave their home country. On the one hand the definition of persecution is drawn tightly and excludes a lot of harassment, and on the claimant's side the presentation of their client as having a well founded fear also requires leaving out a lot of other factors from the equation.

The image of the suitable refugee is rather a saintly one. He or she must have done nothing illegal in the country they are departing, and not participated in violent anti-regime activity. The complexities of living under a persecutory regime or as a marginalized outsider often render illegal activity a necessity of survival. The refugee hearing process is does not allow for the messiness of life in such a regime. Claimants are advised explicitly and implicitly to shape their experience to fit that demanded by the bureaucratic process of the hearing (Barsky, 1994). Success in the hearing process demands success in a specific form of narrative construction. The refugee is a constructed and defined identity, labelled within a bureaucratic process which makes and remakes the individuals who are fed through it (Zetter, 1991). Often there is a mismatch between the refugee's experience and the way he or she must narrate it to obtain asylum status. Many refugees are aware of this, and object to the abstract and standardized categories into which their experience is expected to fit (Frederico, 1991).

To receive assistance from their hosts, would-be asylum seekers have to perform as helpless, persecuted (and grateful) subjects. Rather like the 'sick-role', there are a set of expected behaviours which will lead to one either fitting the role as defined by the bureaucratic process, or failing to fill it and being rejected (Parsons, 1980). The CEE Roma have had problems with precisely this definition. They did not fit the expected role of 'refugee': they came from what appeared to be fairly stable, fairly liberal capitalist states in the near-West of Europe. They were not displaced by war or famine. For many commentators they did not qualify as an ethnic minority who could have been subject to racial persecution (*Daily Telegraph*, 20 September 1998). There was no place for them in the categories of the asylum system.

The asylum process officially exists to determine whether the would-be refugee has a well-founded fear of persecution. It is ironic, then, that the experience of the asylum seeker in the host country can cause him or her to think that if they had not had such a fear before, they certainly have one on arrival. This was the experience of the Roma asylum seekers in Canada in 1997 when their hostel was attacked by skinheads. In Rostock skinhead groups had set out to cause serious injury to the Roma. This experience is not represented in the refugee hearings, since it is outside their scope. In the UK, where the detention of asylum seekers is by no means a rare occurrence (Cohen, 1989), the migrant may feel that his experience in the host country is worse than that in his home country. Many of the Czech Roma seeking asylum at Dover in 1998 were detained in Rochester Prison. They might ruefully have reflected that at least their home government did not practice detention without trial. The use of detention centres and prisons to hold asylum claimants is one aspect of the increasing criminalization of the refugee in Europe (Rudge, 1989). It contributes to the trauma they have already experienced. The increased application of detention by default to asylum seekers draws into question the status of universal human rights in European liberal democracies (Bhabha, 1998; Caloz-Tschopp, 1997). In particular, it undermines the concept of citizenship based on voluntary membership of the nation, instead locating it the principle of cultural or ethnic belonging to a territory bounded in time and space (Kurthen, 1995).

As with the view of the rise of the far-right in Europe, liberal opinion in Western Europe assumes ethnic fundamentalism to be a feature of the Eastern states, the former Communist republics which have not progressed to recognizing the value of multi-culturalism. Yet well before the Czech Republic introduced its ethnic citizenship law which excluded many Roma, discussed elsewhere, the British government prepared for the increase in global migration by enshrining in law the relationship between blood and citizenship, in the 1981 Nationality Act. Though not overtly excluding one group or another, its intention was to put certain ethnic groups at a disadvantage. The Act pioneered the EU wide policies on immigration enshrined in the 1990s which co-ordinated selection and exclusion criteria across the EU. Refugee recognition procedures in EU states are constructs, with their own internal institutional dynamics. For example, it is the case that as the numbers of asylum seekers from a certain country rises, the proportion granted asylum falls (Bocker and Havinga, 1998a). The decrease does not necessarily correspond to a rise in the number of bogus applications (Hov, 1993), rather it is more likely to be an institutional response whereby the system is increasing in severity towards that group, reasserting the overall balance. The institutional imperative is to control the number of applicants receiving asylum (Collinson, 1993).

Europe as a Restricted Space

The Roma refugee panics of 1997-1998 emerged at the tail end of a sustained crisis in the approach taken to refugees and asylum seekers (Landgren, 1998). The USA and Western European states throughout the 1980s and 1990s remoulded their refugee policies to create a much harsher regime. Innovations such as criminalizing illegal departure, introduced in the USA in 1997, tipped the balance towards a presumption that the would-be refugee is a false claimant. Those who travel without documents are defined as criminal, rather than as – potentially – persecuted.

Most Western countries encourage refugees to stay in the region where they came from. In 1992 the immigration ministers of the then European Community collectively proposed the concept of Safe Country of Origin lists. SCOs are countries which are considered to have adequate human rights records. Human rights organizations have queried the inclusion of certain countries on this list, as not having in fact an ideal human rights record. Being from a country on an SCO list raises the standard of proof needed to gain asylum status. Roma from the Czech Republic and Slovakia face very different situation to Kurds from Turkey, despite both groups being stateless and suffering persecution by dint of their group membership. The existence of SCO lists violates a deeper principle, which is that of the right of any individual to be considered for refugee status. It automatically excludes a large number of people from the process, and defines them as bogus asylum seekers. Although the lists are mostly harmonized, this is not by design, as EU co-operation on drawing them up has been non-existent. Given the continued concern with limiting refugee flows into (Western) Europe, however, it is likely that this will be an area of greater – though not unproblematic – co-operation in coming years (Brochmann 1993).

The first barrier a refugee faces to have any chance of being successful is that of removing him/herself from the country of origin. Action on a European wide level has been taken to make this extremely difficult. In the UK the Immigration (Carriers' Liability) Act 1987, as amended by the Asylum and Immigration Appeals Act 1993, ensures that carriers – ship and aircraft – are now fined if they deliver people to the UK without the correct documentation. This provision was the direct result of an EC wide initiative of the TREVI group (Tuitt, 1996: 74). Amnesty International (1991) has reported that airlines are now being used as policing agents, preventing those who have inadequate documentation but from ever being considered by the system. Almost by definition refugees are unlikely to have the correct documentation, and often have to bribe their way out of their home country. The implementation of carrier liability was part of an overall EU agenda, aiming to restrict movement between European and non-European states, and contain humanitarian crises on a regional basis (Tuitt, 1996).

Czech Roma as a whole are unlikely to hold valid passports, one reason being that many were deprived of citizenship rights by the 1993 Citizenship Law. For many of them, not having the correct documentation is a normal part of life. Unfortunately for those seeking to prove they have a well founded fear of persecution, this class action on the part of the state does not count in their favour, since it is on an individual basis that the would-be refugee must have a well founded fear of persecution. Being deprived of a certain right on the basis of being a member of one group – unless the state does so explicitly – is insufficient proof, and may not even be admitted into the hearing process. Research has indicated that it is generalized violence, rather than specific human rights abuses, which are the major cause of refugee flows (Schmeidl, 1997). Yet it is precisely this factor which falls through the net of the asylum hearing.

Changes in asylum procedure in Canada and the UK have been aimed at reducing the length of time the process of approval or rejection takes. However, a judgement in Canada still takes on average fourteen months to be delivered (*The Toronto Globe & Mail*, 15 May 1996), only slightly longer than it takes in Britain. The length of time taken for a refugee claim to be processed has some bearing on the snap judgements made in the British press and by British politicians, including government Ministers, that the Roma were bogus asylum seekers. Such a judgement takes in practice at least a year. This became apparent from some reports that appeared in the Canadian press some time after the panic had died down, when the claimants who had stood by their claims began to tell their stories in the refugee hearings. One young student gave a moving account of being attacked by a 'gang of five or six skinheads' who had severely beaten her with a baseball bat (*The Toronto Globe & Mail*, 28 December 1997). It was her story, broadcast in the original TV Nova documentary in August, which was held responsible for the original rush of asylum seekers towards Canada.

Since then, a number of rulings went in favour of the Roma applicants. In January 1998 a British court granted asylum to three Roma, all of one family, who had left the Czech Republic and arrived in Dover that Autumn (*Radio Free Europe/Radio Liberty Newsline*, 27 February 1998). In April of the same year a Czech Roma family of 20 individuals were given asylum in Canada on the grounds that they faced racial persecution in the Czech Republic (*Radio Free Europe/Radio Liberty Newsline*, 14 April 1998). Throughout April there was a steady trickle of successful application for refugee status in both countries. One typical judgement of the Canadian Immigration and Refugee Board ruled that Roma from the Czech Republic faced cumulative harassment and discrimination. Roma, the Board found, were unable to appeal to their home authorities for protection, the police and judiciary consistently failing to take seriously incidences of racial violence (*The Toronto Globe & Mail*, 24 April 1998). Again in Britain in May of 1998, a family from Slovakia were awarded asylum by the Immigration Appellate Authority (*Independent*, 21 May 1998). *Radio Prague* reported (15 July 1998) that of the one thousand and five hundred Romanies who sought asylum in Canada in the previous year six hundred had returned to the Czech Republic. The Canadian Immigration authorities to suggest that it indicated that they were economic rather than political migrants. However many cited the fact that relatives were not able to join them as reasons for returning (*Roma Advocacy Centre*, Toronto, 16 July 1998). The fact that less than half had returned does not indicate that they were not refugees. Reasons for returning are as complex and contradictory as reasons for departing in the first place, a cold welcome not least among them.

The attempts of West European states to exclude migrants from the South and the East derive from a number of imperatives (Robinson, 1995). It is easy to assume that racism is one of them. However there seems to be a more complex interplay of institutional forces at work. Politicians in Britain, Canada and Germany emphasized the feeling that the refugees were not genuine asylum seekers. Only a few fringe politicians in Britain and Canada articulated a sense that they were culturally incompatible. It is not acceptable amongst the European elites to talk in these terms, so the objection to the asylum seekers was articulated in bureaucratic language of fairness and fraudulence (European Commission, 1994). Liberal democracies justify their stringent immigration controls according to an image of themselves they portray as being a soft-touch, unable to control large scale immigration because of their open nature. For the most part this is not the case (Freeman, 1994). They are able to control immigration quite stringently and in any case there is no evidence that strength or laxity of existing asylum regimes affects country choice (Bocker and Havinga, 1998b). Yet West European states remain nervous at the prospect of being overwhelmed by an invasion of uncontrollable subjects (Hamilton, 1997).

Looking into the construction of Western modernity, one might point to the intense spatial management and control that go into state formation. As was pointed out in Chapter 4, few spaces are left alone or unmanaged. There is a mind-set strongly oriented against people who appear and then disappear into the background. There is in place across the EU a complex of restrictive policies aimed at protecting resources, and also keeping out those who may represent a cultural threat (Stasiulis, 1997). What is shown by the experience of the Roma asylum seekers is that the distinction between economic and non-economic migrant is a bureaucratic construction that fails to encapsulate the complex and contradictory motives that produce migrants. The process of deciding which individuals qualify as the ideal refugee also operates to support a certain idea of the recipient country, as in a way possessing some of the characteristics of the ideal refugee: long suffering and just, and charitable. Refugees are often the direct results of First World policies in the Second and Third World, a case of chickens coming home to roost. In the case of Roma asylum seekers there is a slightly different dynamic at work, underpinning the nature of European modernity. This is a unique case of asylum seekers arriving from one ostensibly Westernized country (the Czech Republic) to others (the UK and Canada).

Mobile Objects, Restricted Subjects

Roma and Gypsy-Travellers have been subject to more continuous forced movement and forced settlement than any other group in the history of Europe apart from the Jews. This chapter examined the experience of Central and East European Roma as would-be refugees during the 1990s and into the 21st Century. It considered the way in which the EU has become concerned with spatial population management as part of the process of nascent state formation it is undergoing. It reflected on the way in which Roma have become a recurrent 'problem' because they are perceived as violating this spatial control system: for the politicians of Europe they are matter out of place. This chapter concludes with some points placing the experience of the Roma within the globalized system of mobile objects and restricted subjects.

Robin Cohen (1987) identifies three classes of individuals in contemporary Europe. There is the citizen, a privileged individual with increasing rights and the ability to move to and work in any country of Europe. Then there is the denizen, the relatively privileged resident alien who has work in a country but no rights of citizenship. The denizen is in a different situation from the past because his or her children will not now automatically be able to assume citizenship by virtue of *ius soli* (Hammar, 1990). Last and most problematic in the eyes of policy makers is the helot. Helots are individuals who are illegal entrants, failed asylum seekers, overstayers on visas and so on. They are almost completely lacking in rights, such as the right to due process.

Cohen concludes his tour of the 'frontiers of identity' (Cohen 1994) by contrasting the position of the immigrant or refugee – then there was not such a great distinction – before the Second World War to the situation currently. Despite recurrent restrictions, deportations and panics the position of the refugee in the pre-war Anglo-Saxon world was more often than not an optimistic one. Immigrants to America, Australia and Canada could reasonable hope to start up a new life, whatever the circumstances of their arrival in the country (Cohen, 1991). The crucial change is that now individuals are accorded a legal and bureaucratic status of increasing permanence, a status which dictates the position of the individual in the division of labour, in society, and that governs his or her relation to the state and freedom of movement. The status of citizen, denizen or helot are increasingly fixed – even from generation to generation – and the actions of the EU are concerned to keep things that way, fixing people in their 'home' regions if nothing else. There is increasing co-ordination within and outwith the EU over citizenship/refugee policy, with CEE states now increasingly drawn into the migration regime, creating a Russian Doll of migration zones.

Bauman identifies two classes of mobile individuals within the global order. The first 'travel at will, get much fun from their travel ... are cajoled and bribed to travel and welcomed with open arms when they do'. By way of contrast, the second 'travel surreptitiously, often illegally, sometimes paying more for the crowded steerage of a stinking, unseaworthy boat than others pay for business-class gilded luxuries' (Bauman, 1998a: 89). On arrival the latter can face a battery of carceral measures, such as summary arrest, detention and deportation (Simon, 1998). The members of the first class are universally present, and the members of the second universally foreign. Foreign-ness is not tied to place of origin but to the ability to manipulate space, or rather to the ability to be freed from space, from the constraints of spatiality. It is something Roma and Gypsy-Travellers have perhaps always been aware of. Bauman labels the divide one between 'tourists and vagabonds'. However, his division leaves out a crucial third element, that of forced movement, and the coming into being of the refugee nation. What it does capture is the interconnectedness of the two classes. The marginalized are said to inhabit a different world, the Third World. Yet this is a globalized Third World, created, sustained and penetrated by the same forces that produce huge global inequality.

A recent (1998) proposal by the EU is to move from permanent asylum rights to temporary refugee rights (Black, Koser, and Walsh, 1998). The plan is intended to allow EU states to cope with sudden influxes of refugees, such as those resulting from the Bosnian war. The plan is for a four-stage response to a refugee situation. The first stage is to deal with a refugee crisis at source, by creating 'safe zones'. The next is to contain it in the region, using EU funded refugee camps and so on. The third would be to allow temporary asylum in the EU in the event of the first two failing, and the final stage would be mandatory repatriation of refugees as soon as it is judged safe. The plan fits in with the European Union's desire to offer only temporary refuge, in place of a permanent or extended stay, and to contain population movements on a regional basis (Rogers, 1992). Like the measures already in place to contain migration, which have been examined in this chapter, it assumes that 'the refugee' is something foreign to Europe. The experience of Roma has been a stark reminder that this is not the case.

Chapter 7

Closed Spaces, Restricted Places

Introduction

This chapter returns to the earlier sociological perspectives with which to interpret the exclusion and marginalization of Roma and Gypsy-Travellers. It argues that the treatment of outsiders in post-modernity has both similarities with and differences to that of classical modernity. For example, the Roma of Central and Eastern Europe have been outsiders in both modernity and post-modernity. Under the Nazis, they were subject to genocidal extermination, in which a large part of the intellectual and physical resources of a highly industrialized state were turned to the purpose of eliminating them with murderous efficiency. The new exclusions affecting them are more local and spatial in form. For instance, there is the creation of light zones and dark zones, in which marginalized populations are pushed into dark zones, where they are left to their own devices. In the Czech Republic, Roma are pushed into ghettos or encouraged to leave the country. Local councils pay for one-way airline tickets for Roma on condition that they give up their houses. I argue that, in Europe, Gypsies either have to stop being Gypsies (spatial control) or go and be Gypsies somewhere else (spatial exclusion).

This chapter examines the forces of regionalization, globalization and localization as they affect Roma and Gypsy-Travellers. It is argued that various developments in the society and the economy are creating and institutionalizing a separation between a network of globalized metropolitan centres, and non-metropolitan localities and peripheries which are unable (or, occasionally, unwilling) to participate as global actors. New forms of regionalism and spatial zoning are affecting Roma and Gypsy-Travellers. Examples of this include the creation in the Czech Republic and Britain of 'ungovernable spaces', separated from the rest of society, and the spatial cleansing demanded by conservative-national politicians in both countries. The chapter concludes that the emerging globalized European order creates a series of tensions between localities and nation-states, such that we can speak of the emergence of 'post-national states', which are concerned with controlling the mobility of individuals in the interests of maintaining their place in the global economy.

One of the central concerns of this book has been the experience of Roma and Gypsy-Travellers within European modernity and the system of nation-states, and the construction of 'Gypsies' as objects of a regulatory discourse associated with nation-state modernity. Given that, it is worth considering that the emergence of post-modernity and increasing levels of globalization could offer some relief, since they would suggest the weakening of the institutional underpinnings of that regulatory discourse. Roma and Gypsy-Travellers have had a specific place in the interstices between micro-localities, in which the concrete relations of society are enacted, and macro-structures, such as the nation state or supra-national system, which delimit and define those localities. This involves the relations between Gypsy-Travellers and the state, on a national and local level, and looks at some recent conflicts between those two state formations in terms of their relationship to Gypsy-Travellers in the UK and Roma in the Czech Republic. This illuminates the restructuring of the relationship between localities and the nation-states which increasingly seek to operate within a global economy and society, and the new challenges which face Gypsy-Traveller society within an increasingly globalized European modernity. There are several aspects to globalization which affect Roma and other Gypsy-Travellers in Europe: the development of ungovernable spaces, of private law enforcement, and the re-making of the local within a global context.

Globalization, Nation and Ethnicity

Globalization has become a global concept in sociology. Yet not all sociologists have found it to their taste, suggesting as it does the abandonment of many a cherished sociological assumption. In particular it forces us to rethink our understanding of 'society' as meaning a nation-state bounded society (Taylor, 1996; Waters, 1995; Wood, 1997a; b). Of those who have attempted to assimilate the concept, there are two competing perspectives on globalization. Anthony Giddens takes it as the result of the disembedding and time-space distanciation processes of modernity, which means that it is a relatively recent development and one that is intimately associated with modernity. Roland Robertson (1995) understands it as something that predates modernity, and has merely been accelerated by it. It is important to understand the concept as implying some deep qualitative changes in the structure of social life.

Daniel Bell (1987) understands globalization to mean the end of geography, predating the end of history announced after the Revolutions of 1989 (Fukuyama, 1992). Many other commentators (Toffler, 1980) have taken this up in the context of the information revolution, arguing that the development of virtual workforces, teleworking and so on will lead to the death of geography as an independent variable in human life. Human understanding of space is bounded by time: the time taken to cross it, and to communicate across it. As that time is reduced towards the infinitesimal, so our sense of space is compacted. As this chapter will illustrate however, globalization may have freed some individuals from constraints of time and space, but for many the opposite is the case. The local has not been discarded, and in Europe of the 21st Century geography has bitten back with as much of a vengeance as history has. The shrinking of space by communications technology does not render it meaningless: the opposite if anything. Rather, spaces and subjectivities are transformed, although not always in terms of a 'reactionary politics of an aestheticized spatiality' (Harvey, 1989: 305).

The rise of nationalism and a renewed ethnic politics in Europe since the late 1980s, and the continued strength of Islamic fundamentalism, is often used to refute arguments about globalization and the emergence of a global society. Certainly it overturns the assumption that globalization equates with a McDonaldized homogenization of society, in which global corporations turn people into undifferentiated consumers. However, theories of globalization were never really about the levelling of societies into all encompassing sameness. Rather, the concept describes the implication of every locality in a globalized system of economic, political and cultural exchange, an exchange which as often creates and reinforces inequalities between various localities and classes of individual as the opposite (Kayatekin and Ruccio, 1998). These inequalities are both material and cultural. The idea that globalization might lead to increased differentiation between localities and groups of people is a counterintuitive one, but no less the case for that. It will be illustrated in this chapter with regard to some developments concerned Roma and Gypsy-Travellers in 1990s Europe.

The interpretation of globalization employed in this chapter is that a set of processes – economic and institutional – are producing a division between a network of globalized metropoles and non-metropolitan localities. The term 'metropole' here denotes cities which are able to participate fully in the global economy and polity – such as Prague, or London. There are also cities which are more excluded from the global system, such as Belgrade, and those which are on its periphery, such as Moscow. The price of exclusion from the global nexus is high. Belgrade has certainly declined hugely since it was the capital of a unified federal Yugoslavia, when it was a holiday destination and home to Soviet Europe's most open and stimulating intellectual life (Glenny, 1993). As well as the metropoles, there are the 'hinterlands', areas which are likewise in an ambivalent relationship with their own national capitals. Viewed from the hinterlands, metropolitan capitals are ambivalent, being both sources of pride as the centre of the nation and yet often mistrusted, as being out of touch with the rest of the country. It is this aspect of globalization which problematises the prevalent model of democracy and citizenship within modernity, in which citizens are members of sovereign nation states answering to no higher authority (Urry, 1996). The mismatch between the effective globalization of many aspects of sovereignty, and its formal retention in the nation-state creates a series of tensions and conflicts between metropoles and localities, one of which concerns attempts to re-nationalize the nation.

There is what seems to be a bifurcation between two forms of regionalism – the 'atavistic' regionalism exemplified by the re-ethnicization of Kosovo by the Serbian state prior to the 1999 conflict, and the 'modernizing' regionalism of the Czech Republic. In either case the region is seen as the basis from which to respond to globalization, either as a carrier of nationhood or of future prosperity. In the former case international institutions mostly follow, rather than oppose, these forces of ethnic localization. The European Union and the United Nations were forced into legitimating ethnic cleansing both in their actions during the Yugoslavian civil war and in the electoral system set up in Bosnia, which accepts a form of 'ethnic cantonization'. The application of an ethnic *realpolitik* by the UN and EU in the former Yugoslavia excluded the many Roma who were unable to lay claim to membership any of its constituent ethnic groups (*Radio Bosnia-Hercegovina*, 21 December 1998; European Roma Rights Center, 2004b). In the latter, national governments keenly endorse the regional development model to attract global capital. Both are responses to globalization, and it is not intended to suggest that the first is 'bad regionalism' and the second 'good regionalism'. There are criticisms of both, which will be discussed later on in this chapter.

In much of the former Communist bloc, populism combines with the exclusion of members of powerless ethnic groups. It is no surprise that those on the receiving end consistently happened to be Roma. In much of Central and Eastern Europe Roma are often negatively associated with the departing Communist regimes, often described as having been the teachers' pets of the communists, pampered and privileged. Roma returning to the former Communist countries after 1989 were resented and felt to be exploiting their fellow nationals. In contrast other returning nationals were generally welcomed back. It was far easier for people to express resentment against returning Roma citizens than the former nomenklatura, who are more often than not a part of the new elite, and are everywhere to be found doing well out of the new frontier capitalism. An extreme example was the retrospective labelling of executed Romanian dictator Ceausescu as a Gypsy. Indeed, there was and is a popular myth in Romania that the Securitate secret police were members of another race, whose origins were obscure but who were physically distinct from Romanians (Verdery, 1993).

To some extent the ease with which these ideas have taken root is due to the form of social organization under Communism. Lacking a strong civil society, citizens often need recourse to the black market for necessities, and the use of bribery and coercion was a common factor in day to day life. Career, house, access to health care and basic services, was often linked with one's workplace and the personage of the boss. The weakness of civil society in Communist societies, and the penetration of what would normally be considered private institutions by the state, meant a peculiar place for national-ethnic identification. It was both used by the Communist governments to legitimate their power, but also was one of the few forms of identification which people could hold onto that was not wholly tainted by Communism. National identity was and is used to legitimate the state, but paradoxically it was and is also held onto by individuals as something separate from the state. The exclusion of Roma from the discourse of nation and ethnicity has meant that they were doubly excluded after the fall of Communism. In the minds of many in Central and Eastern Europe they were associated with Communism (Crowe, 1995: 57), and were not considered to be a legitimate part of the nations and polities which replaced it.

Private Security, Private Justice and Ungovernable Spaces

There are two broad themes in this chapter: the remaking of spatial divisions and zones within the globalized nation-state; and the interaction of the local with the global and its effect on constructions of ethnicity and identity. The first theme is examined in this part; the changed forms of state authority and state action that have come about as nation-states have rushed to be a part of the global economy, and the impact of these new spatial-state formations on Gypsy-Travellers. One of the effects of globalization and the weakening of the state has been the increased use of private or quasi-state forms of power (Johnston,

1993; Newburn and Jones, 1997). Roma and Gypsy-Travellers have throughout European history been subjects of the most coercive forms of state power (Fraser, 1992: 131). Modernity has placed them as the objects of a regulatory discourse which at various times has forced them to settle (Milton, 1998), split up families (Tebbutt, 1998), and deprived them of traditional stopping places (Campbell, 1995). As such, changes in the structure of the modern nation-state, and the forms of state power in particular, have a profound effect on Gypsy-Traveller society:

> Privatization [means] the loss of market share by the public police in providing defense against crime. There is a growing dualism in policing in all developed nations, with the public police providing security for the poor and private police providing security for the rich (Bayley, 1998).

Bayley points to the danger that affluent classes will come increasingly to rely on privatized law (or rather, order) enforcement and object to paying taxes to provided police services to the poor and marginalized. Or rather, they will demand a different form of policing of the poor, with policing more concerned with protecting the well off from the poorest and not maintaining the universal rule of law. Marginalized groups have always been 'over-policed and under protected' (Reiner, 1997). What is changing here is the explicit restructuring of policing practices to effect this, and the reification of the marginalized as an 'outlaw group', living in a walled 'dark zone'. In parts of Central and Eastern Europe there is an inverted form of this phenomenon. Rather than there being simply greater reliance on private policing, the public police are coming to behave like the private police, only protecting parts of the community, specifically those that have affluence or influence. Roma are in many areas of Central and Eastern Europe excluded from police protection (Project on Ethnic Relations, 1997a; European Roma Rights Center, 1996). The Roma are policed, rather than being provided with policing services.

In Britain the police are no longer regarded by many sections of society, not just the marginalized, as an omnipotent or omnipresent representative of the universal and fair rule of law. The crisis of popular trust in national state authority has been one motivating factor behind the rise of private or quasi-state forms of policing and surveillance in Britain. These forms of policing and surveillance are in increasing use by local authorities. City and town councils have employed private security forces to patrol housing estates and town centres, and residents have been encouraged to do the same. One instance of the employment of private force by a public authority can be seen in the way some councils in Wales have used it to control Gypsy-Travellers' horses.

Horses have an important place in Gypsy-Traveller culture. Judith Okely (1983) claims that they are seen as a particularly clean form of animal, in contrast to cats and dogs, which are capable of violating the mochadi regulations. Horses do not violate the inside/outside distinction which she regards as the central boundary of Gypsy-Traveller identity. However, horses have other associations among Gypsy-Travellers as well as that of cleanliness. They are felt to be reserved and sociable, similar to the ideal Gypsy-Traveller lifestyle. They are intimately associated with travelling itself, and though travelling using horses is now largely impractical in the UK, they remain a symbol of Gypsy-Traveller culture. It is no surprise that Gypsy-Traveller horses have a large emotional investment made in them, an investment that extends far beyond notional monetary worth (Stewart, 1997).

Horses are one of the many points on which Gypsy-Travellers have managed to accommodate to modernity whilst maintaining the valued possessions of their culture. As well as being an economic asset and a carrier of social values, horses are also a frequent point of conflict between Gypsy-Travellers and the local state. Recently in South Wales, one local council has employed a bailiff's company to clear the Gypsy-Travellers horses from council owned land. In the past, the council has generally been happy to allow the horses to graze on unused and marginal public land, as still happens in several places in England and Wales. The bailiffs have employed some very dubious tactics to capture the horses, which commonly involves chasing them with a motorbike, which terrifies them, then stunning them with a dart gun. Gypsy-Travellers are upset not only at having their horses confiscated but at it being done in such a manner.

When horses are confiscated and the fines not paid by the owner, they are then put up for auction by the local authority. In the past, Gypsy-Travellers were able to use this sale to get their horses back for minimal financial expenditure. If possible, they would pack the auction room with friends and family, who would then bid deliberately low, so that the horses' original owner would be able to buy their horse back for as little as a pound or two. From the Gypsy-Travellers' point of view they were simply restoring the horse to its rightful owner, and in so doing reinforcing the strong kin and friendship networks which are so vital to Gypsy-Traveller society. They used their strong social network to minimise the loss engendered by this conflict with institutional modernity. Local authorities became aware of this over the years, and some attempted to get round what the Gypsy-Travellers were doing by moving the auctions out of the immediate area. Until recently the Gypsy-Travellers have been able to keep up with them, so that the actions of the local authorities merely required that the owner travelled further afield to get their horse back. However, with horses confiscated recently in the case quoted above, the Gypsy-Traveller network has been at a loss to find out where they are being taken for auction. It was suspected that the horses were being taken to somewhere in the Midlands, but nothing is known for sure. For local Gypsy-Travellers this was unprecedented.

The local authority was going to some extremes to ensure that the horses were kept out of the hands of the original owners, keeping even the location of the auction a secret. There seems to have been a trend away from the broad tolerance of their horses which Gypsy-Travellers could have enjoyed in the recent past. They are being subject to new form of enclosure. The equivalent of communal grazing rights are removed, not by private landlords in pursuit of agricultural improvement and profit, as happened in the enclosures of the 18th and 19th Centuries (Yelling, 1977), but by the local state in pursuit of social stability and tidiness. Part of the incentive for the local state to do this is to establish its locality in the global system, to make it into a desirable commodity. Attracting inward investment requires the council to actively sell its locality and its citizens to investors, to engage in the active commodification of place (Urry, 1995). One of the areas in which Gypsy-Travellers had left their horses grazing was earmarked as part of a potential greenfield business site. It was felt by local Gypsy-Travellers that they were being 'cleaned out' in preparation for new business developments. It is somewhat ironic, since Gypsy-Traveller sites were commonly built on what was at the time 'out of the way' land, which has now been redesignated as valuable. The local state's revaluation of the land signals yet another struggle over the meaning of the locality, a struggle instituted in this instance by the need to attract global capital to the locality.

The conflict between Gypsy-Travellers and councils over the control of horses was indicative of the changed way in which thestate operates in Britain. The increasing use of non-state power both by the state and non-state institutions modifies Weber's definition of the state as the institution with a monopoly on the use of violence within a given territory. The globalized state increasingly seeks to operate through proxies, as in the introduction of private prisons, the contracting out of prisoner holding and transportation services, and so on. The proxy state is somewhat similar in form to the state of the 19th Century. It has taken on a moral, proselytizing role regarding society whilst attempting to be *laissez faire* with the economy . Its economic disengagement is combined with strong social engagement in certain areas, with some highly interventionist practices backed up with surveillance technology. Many of the innovations of the Labour government elected in 1997 – such as on welfare reform, health or prisoner sentencing – have been statements of the state's moral role in re-making its citizens. It has been characterized as moral authoritarianism, with the state seeing its primary purpose as guaranteeing an ordered yet flexible labour force imbued with the work ethic which can perform in the global labour market. Officially the Labour government has a more positive attitude to Travellers than its predecessor did. However, since the 1994 Criminal Justice Act the relationship between Gypsy-Traveller and settled communities has become more frictional in many areas of the country, turning previously tolerated points of contact between Gypsy-Traveller and settled society into ungovernable spaces.

Council Sites as 'Dark Zones'

> The first thing that happened when we came on site was that the police turned up in one of their vans, which was about the most inauspicious start to the occasion. It immediately set everyone on edge ... The police first said that they had been called to [a specific pitch] because of a fight: the wardens replied that they hadn't heard anything, to which the policeman said that if the police got any more hoax calls they wouldn't be coming back. Then he asked where [the pitch] was. He clearly hadn't actually checked the pitch itself. Further investigation [on our part] showed it was a case of domestic violence – a man had attacked his wife and then cleared off. The police showed no inclination to hang around and do anything – although I was under the impression that they were required to investigate complaints of domestic violence. Off they went (Fieldwork Notes, September 1998).

These slightly irritated fieldnotes describe an experience when carrying out work on a council owned site. They illustrate the difficult relationship that often pertains between police and Gypsy-Travellers. One of aspect of globalization is the emergence of ungovernable spaces or 'dark zones'. These are areas which are policed with neither consent nor mutual trust. In a sense, the police were treating that South Wales council site as the classic ungovernable space. They would only visit it in fairly large numbers. They were not prepared to ask any of the other residents the location of the pitch they were looking for. Neither were they prepared to speak to the individual who had called them on to the site. Gypsy-Travellers living on the site were not being extended the standards of treatment that other members of British society would normally expect from the police. They were automatically under suspicion. When the police realised that there had been an instance of domestic violence, rather than a fight between Gypsy-Traveller men, they simply left abruptly, without following up the complaint. It was left to one charity worker who had gone to the site for an entirely different purpose to question the victim and to deal with the aftermath.

There was a clear sense that Gypsy-Travellers as a whole constituted a law and order problem for the police, rather than citizens with rights and entitled to their protection as individuals. The final warning one of the policemen gave was that if they received any further 'hoax' calls they would simply not come out to the site, a warning given despite that fact that the call was not a hoax. It was made for a definite reason, in that there had been an instance of domestic violence. The threat of withdrawing police protection altogether was quite a serious one, considering that the particular site had seen much conflict between two family groupings who had a long history of hostility to one another. The police officer's statement could be seen as a declaration that the site would become a no-go area, a dark zone. The Travellers were being defined and treated as an ungovernable or unmanageable class.

Part of the problem that some council sites have arose from a legacy of the implementation of the 1968 Act where the building of council owned sites was combined with the 'designation' of areas in which councils were judged to have fulfilled the accommodation needs of Gypsy-Travellers (Millward, 1986). Designation conferred powers on a council to evict Travellers who were illegally camped. The system meant that Gypsy-Travellers tended to end up being forced into accommodation which was not always suitable. In particular families with long running feuds were frequently unable to avoid living on the same site. As described elsewhere one effect was to push a lot of people onto welfare dependence. The 1994 Act hastened this process, with official sites becoming more overcrowded as a result of the effective extension of designation to the whole country .

It has often been stated that Gypsy-Travellers view public institutions with some hostility and suspicion. The reverse could equally be said to be the case. With the introduction of the Criminal Justice Act 1994, and the powers of eviction and confiscation it allows police to use, Gypsy-Travellers are being defined as an ungovernable class of people, occupying an ungovernable space. By ungovernable it is meant that they are being treated as objects of a coercive law enforcement strategy, rather than consumers of a policing service. Of course, relations with Gypsy-Travellers vary from police force to police force, and from individual to individual. It does however appear that the semi-truce which prevailed after the introduction of the 1968 Act has been brought to an end in many parts of the country.

Despite its problems, the period between the 1968 and 1994 Acts was one where national policy was concerned with extending some measure of universal rights to a socially excluded group. The 1994 Act pulled Gypsy-Travellers into the emerging discourse of surveillance and control, where marginalization is turned into criminalization. The new Labour government has signalled some changes in attitude with regard to Gypsy-Travellers. Its policy on their legal status and the Criminal Justice Act 1994 remained broadly the same as that of the previous government, and it took until 2003 before significant movement towards a change in policy began to be manifested. The outcome of the consultation by the Office of the Deputy Prime Minister currently underway has yet to be seen, however.

The result of the general shift to post-social democratic policing has been the creation on the one hand of ungovernable spaces containing ungovernable populations, as above, and on the other hand of pressure to create hygienic spaces for the containment of ordered labour forces, as seen in the treatment of Gypsy-Travellers' horses. One the other hand some local authorities are still able to maintain what they see as a fair balance between the two, and do not use the 1994 Act at all, seeing it as unworkable.

As can be seen, globalization is not about the universal homogenization of localities, but rather it frequently creates and reinforces differences between certain forms of locality. These differences are partly a matter of 'resistance' by locals, but more often they are actively created by forces of globalization. The differences enforced by heterogenizing globalization are both ideological and material, and they have important consequences for individuals who occupy the various forms of locality.

The Locality and the 'True Country'

In Greek Antiquity, the city – the polis – was the ideal social organization. In the modern European nation state the nation is commonly organized around a single metropole which contains the main organs of the state and the economy. Despite being the locus of material power, the city is seldom ideologically constructed as the carrier of national identity. The 'true country' is more often taken to be the rural countryside, in which national values are symbolically rooted. National values are created and then symbolically rooted in the countryside, the rural space playing a central role in the symbolic imagination of place. The battle over Kosovo was an acute instance of the symbolic rooting of nationalism. Serbia claimed Kosovo as fundamentally Serbian, although 90% of the population is Albanian (Garton-Ash, 1999). To Serbs Kosovo is the fountain of their civilization, whatever the actual history of it might be. They see the 1389 Battle of Kosovo as a clash between European civilization and Eastern barbarism, and it is in these terms that the current struggle is being played out.

Rural spaces have a disproportionate role in the national imagination. Hence the conflict between Gypsy-Travellers and settled people that takes place in the countryside is situated in terms of the meaning those rural areas are imbued with. The rural locale, though having been mostly emptied out of people since the advent of industrial society, is paradoxically seen as the container of the roots of the nation. It is in actuality a site of struggle and conflict over meaning.

Ireland is a good case in point for illustrating the relationship between an idealized vision of the countryside and the formation of the nation. In the construction of Irish nationhood, Travellers have been excluded as aliens and destructive of the ideal nation. MacLaughlin (1996) describes the evolution of Irish national identity and the exclusion of Irish Travellers from it. He associates anti-Traveller racism with the rise of 19th Century bourgeois nationalism, which linked 'the people' with 'the homeland' and which was militantly sedentarist. Travellers, like the itinerant or landless poor, were not citizens of the new nation, but were more like wards of the state, a state which gave itself the power to remove their children or to force them into housing. Helleiner (1995) examines in greater depth the pre-independence antecedents of anti-Traveller racism in Ireland, in which she places more recent discourses about the place of Travellers in the Irish nation.

Despite the evidence that Travellers have formed a distinct part of the Irish population since Celtic times (Meyer, 1891), the popular understanding of their origin was set by the Republic of Ireland's Commission on Itinerancy (Commission on Itinerancy, 1963). In it, they were described as the descendants of the rural poor made homeless during the Potato Famine, who were then forced into itinerancy as a way of life. In constructing the origins of Travellers in this way the Commission was performing a double exclusion. During the 1950s and 1960s the Famine was not very much discussed in Ireland (Dodd, 1996; Davis, 1997; Toibin, 1998), being viewed with some shame and embarrassment if anything. Associating Travellers with the famine confirmed the un-Irish nature of both, and removed from Travellers any claim to ethnic identity. If their way of life was merely the product of Ireland's greatest historical calamity then the programme of settlement proposed by the Commission on Itinerancy would have greater legitimacy. It would be removing a stain produced by colonial history.

In contrast to the representation of the countryside in national mythology, the city is commonly envisioned in mainstream discourse as a dangerous place, the source of decadence and decaying national values, and of problems for respectable country dwellers (*The Times*, 25 November 1995). The metropole is the place to which immigrants, outsiders and deviants gravitate. Something like this point of view is reproduced in the current relationship between the locality and the globalized European city. The values of the metropole are commonly felt to be hopelessly out of kilter with those of the rest of the nation, and it is seen as being populated by a distant and out of touch political class. Some level of alienation may be inevitable given the material relationship between the centre and the periphery, but the re-making of the nation under globalism has given these feelings a sharp edge, especially as it is increasingly hard to maintain many of the boundaries between 'city' and 'country'. Bauman (1998a) describes how people focus their concern on the perceived local disorder of the underclass, ignoring the global order imposed by the elite. What is seen here is similar, in the sense that members of the underclass are interpreted as threats to the order of the locality. However, the locality is also the site of dissatisfaction with this division of order.

'Liberals who don't Know the Score': Metropole and Countryside

> I once met a Gypsy who behaved like a human being. Maybe it's strange, but he behaved like a human. But the rest, they behave like animals. They steal, kill, don't pay their rent. They're unpleasant and we don't like them (Resident of Czeskaly Liba, 'Refugees From Democracy', *Canadian Broadcasting Corporation*, 1997).

There was quite a strong feeling in many parts of the Czech Republic outside Prague that the capital had a different mindset to the rest of the country, and in particular that it failed to understand or appreciate the 'Gypsy Problem'. Time and time again local politicians and people spoke of a national government out of touch with the less developed rural areas, obsessed with pleasing the European Union and international opinion:

> They're not persecuted. They just make trouble here. And they steal ('Refugees From Democracy').

The many non-Roma Czechs who made comments like the ones above were concerned that conflict with the Roma was being narrated by outside observers as a story of persecution and racism, with the

Roma as the victims of discrimination. They sought to re-narrate the story with themselves as the victims of a recalcitrant minority. The Czech Republic is the point at which the two regionalisms clash – it seeing itself as Western, Western Europe defining it as Eastern, partly on the basis of the situation of Roma in the country. Some Czech people were keen to describe the Roma as a bar to regional modernization, whereas the derided liberals posited anti-Roma feeling as an instance of regional atavism. They were resisting a globalizing narrative of their localities.

Most persecution of Czech Roma, in the form of racial attacks and so on, occurs outside Prague itself. Perhaps the anonymity of the city offers some protection to them. Despite this, there is socio-spatial segregation in Prague – very few Roma are visible in the town centre, or in any of the tourist areas. Before visiting the Czech Republic one hypothesis that was going to be examined in this book was that there was a large economic gulf between Prague and the rest of the country, and that this would go some way toward explaining the different levels of conflict between Roma and non-Roma in various parts of the Czech Republic. There were certainly some parts of the country which were far worse off Prague, although without a doubt the Roma areas were in a perilous economic state compared to even the poorest 'white' Czech areas. However, anti-Roma violence has been recorded in both affluent and depressed areas of the countryside (*CTK News Agency*, 18 January 1998). Instances of it were observed in one very depressed post-industrial town, and in one affluent town. It is not sufficient to explain anti-Roma violence in Central and Eastern Europe as the product of an alienated post-industrial underclass. The town of Czeskaly Liba, whose resident was quoted above, is in a relatively affluent area of the country, north of Prague. Likewise, conflicts between localities and metropoles over the treatment of Roma and Gypsy-Travellers are not confined to countries that have recently experienced the shock of free-market transition:

> Claude Balland [Mayor of Tonnoy] has watched Gypsies come and Gypsies go, helping themselves to land, water, sanitation facilities and occasionally private property. He has listened to the complaints of the 650 townspeople, and likewise to the assurances of indifferent bureaucrats far from the problem (*Toronto Star*, 24 July 1998).

Conflict over Roma and Gypsy-Travellers' place in the rural locale could be see in Tonnoy, a small town in France. The French Roma and Sinti had traditionally camped on an area of common land next to the river. In the summer of 1998 the mayor decided that their presence was detrimental to the town and hired a mechanical digger to dig a trench around the encampment. They could still enter and leave the site, so the mayor's action was less about literally restricting their movement than symbolically hemming them in. The mayor was contemptuous of the response of the Parisian press, and of the Parisian government:

> I wanted to rap on the table. I'm a little mayor, but when I do a . . . bold stroke like that it gets the attention of the powers that be. It brought the TV cameras.

The mayor claimed that his intention was to have the law regarding the responsibility of small towns to provide services for Gypsies changed. At the moment French law places certain obligations on towns of a certain size to provide limited facilities for 'Gens du Voyage' as they are termed legally. However, this can not have been the case with regard to Tonnoy, since it is far too small to come under this requirement. It would seem that the mayor was using conflict with Gypsies to establish his personal political profile, not an uncommon practice in Europe. One mayor in Northern Bohemia acknowledged that there was a political payoff in raising the 'Gypsy problem', in instant publicity and notoriety (*Reuters*, 3 July 1998). Likewise, Balland was not shy of appreciating the visibility that can be gained from some generated controversy.

It is often the case that residents of a locality could be rather proud when some controversy had forced their national government and media to 'sit up and take notice' of them, after years of feeling ignored or isolated. That sort of emotion was in evidence during the anti-foreigner violence that swept the former East Germany in 1992. The statements of East Germans after the attacks on refugee hostels in Rostock and other towns reflected a degree of pride in having attracted the attention of the world. This resident of Dresden couched his feelings in terms of reassertion of the integrity of the nation where it was being degraded on a local level:

> We are no Nazis, we are simply patriotic Germans, but we do not want our cities taken over by blacks [Roma] and foreigners (*The Times*, 24 November 1992).

In statements like this there was a sense that the actions of the national government had excluded these forgotten localities from a say in what was happening to them. There is some similarity with the sentiments expressed by supporters of Enoch Powell in the 1960s, who opposed Black and Asian immigration to Britain. They objected to the social fabric of their communities being changed, a change which they had not been asked about and over which they had no control (Schoen, 1977). Immigrants and refugees who are perceived as socially or racially different, and hence radically challenging to the meaning of the locality, are a reminder of the impotence lurking behind every assertion of power. The German government's refugee policy had meant that towns in the former East Germany had a large influx of asylum seekers. The racist violence of 1992 was viewed sympathetically by many Germans, if not supported outright (*The Sunday Times*, 6 December 1992). The violence was a vehicle for expressing dissatisfaction with a number of developments, not least the feeling of many that they were without a political voice within the nation. Again, many local politicians used the media attention to reassert the place of their locality in national politics. The anti-foreigner violence and its narration were concerned with reasserting the integrity of the locality, and the belonging of the locality to the nation. It could be argued that it was a specific response to developments associated with a globalized polity and economy, almost of a piece with the vaunted new protest politics. Like their left-wing counterparts, new racists have learnt to think global and act local.

'Dumping Gypsies': Gypsy-Travellers' Place in the British Locality

> Gypsies, however, suffered most from the fact that, especially after the sixteenth century, the European world was increasingly divided along immutable axes of binary and self-excluding differences (MacLaughlin, 1999a: 41).

Two of the axes MacLaughlin refers to were settled versus nomadic and civilized versus wild. Part of the establishment of these axial divisions involved the taming of the landscape, which meant taming and ordering those within it. This specifically affected those Gypsy-Travellers who occupied the Celtic fringes – the romantically savage Highland landscape imagined by the Victorians might have been spoiled by the existence of actual 'savages' among the windswept heather. However to focus wholly on this is to ignore the urban and peri-urban nature of Roma and Gypsy-Traveller settlement. It seems to have been the case that urban and peri-urban 'Gypsies' were more problematic as they were not part of the rural landscape, and perhaps are therefore doubly out of place. It is necessary to balance the characterization of Gypsies as existing 'at the peripheries' or 'on the margins' with the fact that wherever the may conceptually exist, they actually live all over.

There is another sense in which Gypsies are 'out of place' – McLaughlin identifies the way they are perceived as having an a-historical nature. There is confusion over where they come from in the past – Egypt, India or the Moon? There has been little attention paid to historical development and change, except that of decline. Their values of resignation and fatalism are celebrated (van de Port 1998). Their lives were a circle of suffering and privation (MacLaughlin 1995). For themselves, Gypsies have sometimes played on this for outsiders. Being out of time and out of history can be a way of being invisible.

During the 1990s there were concerns expressed by Conservative Party politicians to reassert the integrity of the rural locality, claiming that it was under threat from an influx of Gypsies. Throughout the period leading up to the introduction of the 1994 Criminal Justice and Public Order Act Conservative MPs representing rural seats complained that urban dominated Labour councils were failing to take their constituents' interests into account. Specifically, it was alleged that they were 'dumping Gypsies' in rural areas with no regard for local feeling.

Throughout the remainder of the Major government's period in office Conservative MPs and Peers used the issue of sites for Gypsy-Travellers to attack Labour or Liberal controlled local councils, and to attack the Gypsy-Travellers themselves. In an adjournment debate in the House of Commons in January 1997 Jerry Wiggin, MP for Weston-Super-Mare, brought up the issue of the use of a temporary caravan site to house Gypsy-Travellers in the South West of England:

> In March 1992, some hard-core arrived on the site. By the time of the general election [in May 1992], the gipsies had arrived on the site; they are still there in 1997 (Jerry Wiggin MP, *Hansard*, 1997, Vol. 1746, Col. 262).

The county council had been forced by a local landowner to evict the Gypsy-Travellers from another unauthorized camp in a quarry. It had no places on official sites and decided to allow them to stay on a site which had been earmarked for a relief road. It then applied for emergency planning permission. The parish council objected, as did 10,000 local residents who signed a petition against the placing of the Gypsy-Travellers there. However, the county council was able to gain planning permission for three years, claiming to be waiting until official site in the same area was ready:

> The council is considering spending between £350,000 and £400,000 to provide pitches on these 13 sites. It has selected two sites: one in Sandford and one in Hutton Moor road, both of which are entirely

> unsuitable. The latter is next to a large residential park of elderly people, who have suffered for many years because of trouble with itinerant gipsies; and the former is in a quiet backwater between two nice villages where gipsies have never been and have no business to be (Jerry Wiggin MP).

The MP's complaint was that councils were using their powers to accommodate Gypsy-Travellers in areas where they were not wanted, although he admitted in another part of his speech that they were not wanted anywhere. Popular mythology has Gypsy-Travellers as country dwellers, but the MP was re-narrating them as an urban problem being exported to rural areas by urban dominated councils. The rural idyll was being violated by troublesome Travellers. In Parliamentary debates on the 1994 Act Conservative politicians drew on the imagination of the rural idyll, which New Travellers in particular were seen as violating. Traditionally, Gypsy-Travellers were in contrast accorded a marginal but nonetheless accepted place in the countryside (Halfacree, 1996). Here we see traditional Gypsy-Travellers having even that marginal place delegitimated. The MP also objected to what he claimed were the disproportionate resources set aside for Gypsy-Travellers:

> The traveller who clearly is not prepared to confine himself to the social customs of the rest of the population now seems to be treated infinitely better than the ordinary citizen (Jerry Wiggin MP).

His feeling was that firstly, the national government was happy to pass the buck on to local authorities. Second, that urban dominated local authorities were happy to push Gypsy-Travellers out into rural areas where there were least voters to offend, and that neither the national Conservative government nor local Labour authorities had any real appreciation of the rural countryside.

The Conservative Minister responding to the debate, Robert Jones, took the time to sympathize with local (non-Gypsy-Traveller) residents, and to point out that the then Conservative Government had ended statutory provision, replacing it with the following policy:

> Our land use planning policy on gipsy sites is set out in Department of the Environment circular 1/94, entitled 'Gypsy Sites and Planning'. We encourage gipsies to provide their own accommodation, applying for planning permission when that is necessary, like everyone else (Robert Jones MP, *Hansard*, 1997, Vol. 1746, Col. 265).

His assertion that Gypsy-Travellers could provide their own accommodation ignored the many difficulties they have in creating private sites. Everything in the Minister's preceding statement had made it clear that Gypsy-Travellers are almost never welcome in any part of the countryside. It is the case that any proposal for a Gypsy-Traveller site, whether private or council, receives enormous and heartfelt local opposition. Hence it was somewhat disingenuous of the government to assert that Gypsy-Travellers were welcome to apply for private sites on the same footing as any other member of the public. It must have been clear to ministers in the Conservative government that the weight of evidence was that even local authorities, with all their resources, found it extremely difficult to gain approval for sites that they had been legally required to build under the 1968 Act. The difficulty Gypsy-Travellers have had in exercising the most basic right – to own one's own home – raises the question of the place they have in the British locality, the space of everyday communities such as those spoken for by Jerry Wiggin.

The locality is the point at which the forces of globalization and the structures of the nation state come into contact with the actual lived experience of individuals. It is the locus of material forces and the focus of ideological struggles over meaning and identity, a few of which were quoted above. Globalization has meant for many localities an emptying out of a lot of the material forces it had previously under their control. Like the hyperghetto, which is one form of locality, it has lost much autonomy, both to global forces and to the national state, the latter being particularly marked in Britain during the 1980s. Local authorities in Britain are shadows of the powers they once were; town centres are subsumed into national shopping chains; local networks become part of global networks.

As these processes have continued, globalization has produced heterogeneous localities. The locality has become increasingly a source of meaning and identity with which to resist or engage with globalization. The locality is, or has the potential to be, constantly recreated in response to global developments in a process of 'glocalization' (Robertson, 1995). All localities are increasingly drawn into the process and even created by it. The extent to which they are active or passive participants in this process marks the boundaries of social inclusion and exclusion in the global society. Just as there are hierarchies of individuals according to their ability to participate as active agents in the global economy so also there are hierarchies of localities arranged according to the same measure. The locality is a space of contested meaning and purpose, a contest which takes place against an increasingly global backdrop.

Citizenship, Mobility and the European State

There are some historical parallels and continuities in the experience of Roma and Gypsy-Travellers throughout Europe in the way that they have undergone waves of persecution or exclusion at broadly similar times in different parts of the continent. In 17th and 18th century Scotland 'Egyptians' were deported to the New World, probably the West Indies or Virginia (*Edinburgh Tollbooth Books of Warding And Liberation*, 1663; 1698). The law operated to exclude them on the grounds that they had no place in the feudal order. Like the 'vagabonds and wandering beggars' they were without access to land, they had no set place in the social environment. Across Europe anti-Gypsy persecution seemed to be coming to head during this period, with 'Gypsy Hunts' in the Netherlands, and a round of laws in German states which made it illegal to be a Gypsy.

In the Europe of the 17th Century most individuals were defined by their place in the feudal-patriarchal order. In 21st Century Europe it is citizenship that is the defining quality of an individual. Citizenship confers rights of movement, work, access to services and so on. Gypsies have found themselves effectively excluded from citizenship in many parts of Europe. Following the 'Velvet Divorce' of the component parts of Czechoslovakia in 1993, the Czech Republic introduced a new citizenship law which initially excluded many Roma who had been born in the Czech lands from citizenship.

State incorporation and hypertrophy under Communism has been replaced by its social disengagement and, in some instances, its social atrophy. Its collapse is understandably much to the relief of many. However, the freedom for Roma has meant freedom to be the victim of what might be called 'citizenry mobs'. An unfortunate fact of the press reporting of the situation in Eastern Europe is that is has tended to report attacks on Roma as being carried out by 'skinheads'. This serves the purpose of producing a 'skinhead other', reassuring Western observers that racism is something other to a tolerant and civilized Europe. It would appear that where there are skinhead groups they have often the passive and sometimes the active support of most citizens, including judicial authorities. Often the violence is not carried out by skinheads but by groups of 'ordinary people'. The deployment of citizenship structures the forms of mobility that an individual can employ. In particular it defines the extent to which their mobility is forced or voluntary.

The European Union and Mobility

The movement of Roma from the Czech Republic, Slovakia and other Central and East European countries illustrated the way in which processes operating at a European and global level interact with those of nations and localities. The outright anti-Roma prejudice of some Czech and Slovak citizens was reproduced in startlingly similar terms in Britain upon the arrival of the refugees. The representatives of national entities were more coy in their language than the press and the public. Concerned with efficient resource management and seeking to prevent large-scale population flows across borders, governments continued to operate according to a set of assumptions established in the aftermath of the Second World War and the establishment of international conventions on the treatment of refugees. The trend is for Western nation states to consistently undermine the universalist provisions of these conventions, and in the case of EU states to do so with increasingly co-ordinated collective action that has united politically disparate governments from Spanish and French Socialists to British Conservatives.

Up until the revolutions of 1989 the system of grand apartheid developed in Cold War Europe had heavily restricted the movement of individuals within the European continent. Devoid of a voice in the globalized nation-state, the poorest are now using the only form of protest they have, and are voting with their feet. The conflict between East and West Europe is not longer one of ideological confrontation, but is about control over the movement of people between the two. The agreement the Bonn government came to with the governments of Poland and the then Czechoslovakia in 1991 was that the latter two countries would strengthen the controls along their Eastern borders and so provide Germany with a shield against migrants from further East (*The Times*, 3 December 1991). This is typical of most of the agreements between governments of West Europe and those on the border of the EU. They have often included requirements that the Eastern countries act as a *cordon sanitaire* against unregulated migration into the EU. Along with such legal provisions as the introduction of carrier liability these countries form a system of pre-migration selection for EU states. The EU is able to offer the prospect of favourable trading conditions, aid, or eventual EU membership, in exchange for a three-hundred mile wide border zone for the whole region.

Capital moves with increasing speed and almost complete freedom across borders, and the global economy has developed as an economy which is capable of acting as a single unit in real time (Castells, 1996).

It is something of a truism that well off individuals are becoming increasingly mobile, with the total number of tourists predicted soon to be larger than the population of any individual nation (Waters, 1995). Increasing value is placed in information and services, and objects are increasingly informationalized, increasingly mobile in form, to the extent where they are much more freely mobile than many individuals. The most advanced sectors of the economy deal in products that can instantly be transferred down phone lines. Governments are responding to developments in the global economy by trying to adapt their economies to deal in and with these highly mobile objects, while also increasing their efforts to sort and select mobile subjects (Lash and Urry, 1994). Mobile subjects can be anyone from highly valued 'symbolic analysts' (Reich, 1997) to the Roma migrants at the other end of the scale.

Related to attempts to increase bureaucratic filtering of individuals, there is a new international class system developing, consisting of three sets of relatively mobile individuals. The two largest classes might be characterized as the core and periphery of the global economy – without necessarily referring to their geographical location. There are on the one hand the 'flexible specialists', who are in great demand. They possess the transferable skills required to operate in any nation, skills corresponding to the 'flexible paradigm' of the labour market (Brown, 1997). They operate within the real-time units of the global economy, within nodes that are linked in with each other across large spatial distances. On the other hand, there are the 'new helots' (Cohen, 1987). This term was originally applied to African and Asian migrants in the West European labour market. It fits also the cheap labour supplied by workers from Central and Eastern Europe, fulfilling the low paid jobs that still need to be done in the post-modern economies of advanced industrial societies.

These migrants are screened and chosen, and can be asked to leave when their usefulness is over. The increasing mobility of objects within the global economy means that the market for the new helots in Western Europe is shrinking, despite the concerns expressed in the British popular press, leading to increasing emphasis being placed on ensuring that they remain where they are and service the global economy from outside the borders of Europe. The structural requirement for migrant labour in Western economies may be decreasing, after several decades of continuous increase. It might be the case that information rich mobile objects are increasingly substituting for this second class of information poor mobile subjects. Less deterministically, there are also ideological and socio-political factors involved in the shutting off of non-EU migration. In the post-

Cold War era a structure of control is being created, rendering certain individuals static and others mobile (Chimni, 1995).

The Post-Nation State

European societies are undergoing horizontal and vertical fragmentation while at they same time they develop a functional unity within the global economy. Areas of former Soviet states are divided along ethnically homogenous lines, and often run by mafias rather than a civic elite. The Yugoslavian wars saw the re-emergence in Europe of the warlord, exemplified by the Serbian general Arkan. They were able to employ all the paraphernalia of modernity – the Internet, mobile phones and so on – in what seemed at times to be an almost surreal recreation of a pre-modern Europe. Of course, to assign the violence of the warlords to a barbaric, pre-modern era is in fact to mistake the nature and extent of institutional violence within modernity. Exclusionary, excising violence has been a part of modernity through and through: it has merely taken a different form in Bosnia. Europe has since 1945 generated a myth about itself, that it is the most civilized and peaceful part of the world, a myth which was only sustainable when the continent was divided between two far larger powers and which collapsed along with that system. Globalization has meant the challenging of this myth. Just as the meaning of local spaces are contested, so is the meaning of the space marked 'Europe'.

Globalization is the supreme achievement of modernity, but it also marks the decline of some of the most important carriers of the modern project (Albrow, 1996). The nation-state in particular is increasingly lost within the global system. From the age of imperialism in the 19th Century nation-states have been able to be part of larger enterprises, enterprises which professed a moral purpose, be it the British Empire and the White Man's Burden or NATO and the protection of the free world. Since the end of the Cold War there are no grand moral projects to be allied with, the most on offer being a technocratic economic convergence within the EU (Pelagidis, 1997). To a large extent the role of the nation-state has been reduced to servicing the global economy and regulating the movement of individuals within the global system.

There are two general hypotheses put forward to describe the fate of the project of modernity in the global age. One is that globalization is a further extension and development of the project, though this project is increasingly moving beyond the prediction or control of individuals, nation-states or political movements. The iron cage is now a juggernaut. Since the material forces of modernity are expanding at an exponential rate, then there is some evidence for this thesis. The alternative interpretation (Albrow, 1996) merely points to the lack of control as evidence of the end of the modern project, since its central purpose was the ever greater extension of human control over the environment and society. Indeed one of the major theorists of modernity defined the human condition as the ability to consciously control the social and material environment. However, both theses seem to put too much faith in the path of modernity in the first place, underestimating its contingent nature. In 20th Century Europe three major systems competed for dominance: Communism; Fascism; and liberal democratic capitalism (Mazower, 1998). It was not historically inevitable that the latter should emerge victorious, indeed it has often done so by the skin of its teeth. Contingency remains as part of the experience of every individual in a globalized society, and with it continuous and seemingly insurmountable conflict over the meaning that globalization has for states, societies and localities.

Conclusion

This chapter has tried to illustrate how globalization has instituted new conflicts between localities and their metropoles, and between competing interpretations of the meaning of those localities. Globalization has changed the ways in which the European nation-state relates to individuals both within its territory and outside the immediate region. It has profoundly affected Roma and Gypsy-Travellers, making the Roma of Central and Eastern Europe into an international issue, and making the place of Travellers in the British countryside a contested one. It is this contestation of the meaning of places that connects the experience of British Travellers to that of Czech Roma and French Roma and Sinti. They find themselves constructed as ungovernable populations, and the places where they live become ungovernable spaces. Roma and Gypsy-Travellers in the Europe are subject to exclusion from the dominant idea of locality, as well as from actual localities. As localities are increasingly coming to compete against each other in a global marketplace they seek to actively exclude groups who might impact on their competitive ability. For Roma and Gypsy-Travellers this is just the latest episode in a long history of regulatory discourses to which they have been subject.

Chapter 8

A '21st Century Racism'?

Introduction

The exclusion of Gypsies draws on some long-standing prejudices. However, the fact that there is such a long history of anti-Gypsy feeling in Europe should not distract us from the new forms of exclusion that have emerged. This chapter concludes the book by considering what the new forms of exclusion indicate about European society. There is the establishment of spatial segregation and control of movement on a Continental level, the process of spatial cleansing and ghettoization on a local level, and the formation of a European identity and a European model of citizenship with which many excluded groups find themselves in an ambivalent relationship. In the light of this some uncritical assumptions of the value of 'Europe' as an idea and a set of institutions are challenged.

Summarizing the main findings of the research and drawing out the wider significance of some of the findings this chapter argues that there has been an increasing encroachment on the lives of Roma and Gypsy-Travellers within Europe. The rejection of Roma and Gypsy-Travellers, particularly at a local level, can be placed in a far reaching historical context that shapes contemporary landscapes of memory in Europe. Yet there are particular forms of exclusion characteristic of modern European societies, East and West. There is the establishment of spatial segregation and control of movement on a Continental level, the process of spatial cleansing and ghettoization on a local level, and the formation of a European identity and a European model of citizenship with which Roma and Gypsy-Travellers find themselves in an ambivalent relationship. In the light of this some uncritical assumptions of the value of 'Europe' as an idea and a set of institutions are challenged. The chapter raises some questions about competing forms of reason and rationality. It is argued that the problems European modernity creates for Roma and Gypsy-Travellers demands the remaking of a self-critical, open and reflexive modernity which will avoid both the ethnic fundamentalism and cultural essentialism of post-modern neo-tribalism, as well as the bureaucratic and universalist exclusions of classical modernity.

It was the privilege of the European countries that began colonizing the globe from 1542 to present themselves as bringing Christianity to the sinful. At a later date, the imperialism of European modernity was presented as letting the light of civilization in on barbarous 'dark continents'. Fifty years of peace since the end of the Second World War allowed for a less invasive, more insular myth to develop, that of a common European home, peaceful and prosperous, to be built up in and by Western European states. The history of the last decade of the 20th Century has reasserted the truth that the real dark continent is Europe itself. The idea of Europe is the veil pulled across the messy, violent, painful history of the existing, historical Europe. This book has explored the experience of one outsider minority within this dark and often closed continent, detailing various forces contributing to their exclusion in Europe of the 1990s. It has attempted at each point to draw out the connections and relationships between these forces, and this chapter will conclude by situating these forces as forming a topology of identity and exclusion which impacts on Roma and Travellers.

The Main Findings

Roma and Travellers consist of a large number of distinct and diverse groups, spread across many continents. There are Irish Travellers, English Romanichels, and so forth in the USA. There are Roma in South America and North Africa. Doubtless there are many other groups scattered around the world and known only to themselves. This book has focused on Roma and Gypsy-Travellers within Europe, attempting to highlight some developments in social exclusion affecting outsider minorities in Europe. It has taken Britain and the Czech Republic as two sites of study, comparing and contrasting the different experiences of Roma in the latter and Gypsy-Travellers in the former.

A number of themes have emerged from the research. The first was the processes of race and racialization occurring across the continent, in which the resurgence of anti-Roma racial violence in Central and Eastern Europe was examined. The second was the development of socio-spatial segregation, considering the experience of Roma in the Czech Republic and Gypsy-Travellers in Britain. The third was legal exclusion: the impact of the Criminal Justice Act 1994 on Gypsy-

Travellers in the UK was taken as a starting point, but its deleterious effects were placed in the wider context of planning law, zoning and the historical criminalization of activities associated with Gypsy-Travellers. The fourth was migration, and the division between mobile objects and restricted subjects, which pertains to the treatment of asylum seekers in Britain. The final theme was the relationship between globalized space and localized place, and how out of this a network of dark and light zones are being constructed by socio-economic forces and state practices.

The book has examined the social exclusion of one outsider minority in Europe. It has placed their experience in terms of the nature of European modernity, and its specific state and institutional structures and practices. It has grounded these practices in a consideration of the spatial nature of exclusion, how identity relates to place, and how power is implicated in spatial patterning. The overarching perspective is of a topology of exclusion, a patterning of the space of Europe by legal structures, institutional forms, and practices of identity, which serve to make life difficult for outsider minorities, of which Roma and Gypsy-Travellers are one.

Key Points

- Roma and Gypsy-Travellers have to put a lot of work into sustaining their structural relationship with settled society. As well as ensuring their own economic viability, they have to police moral and social boundaries. They are constantly faced with potential loss of ontological security, in that they have to have everyday contact with gauje who may end up violating these boundaries. In a similar fashion, the ambivalence of modern life is displaced onto them by settled folk, and in doing so the moral and social boundaries of modern society are maintained.

- There has been recently the establishment and retrenchment of regulative patterns affecting Roma, Gypsy-Travellers as 'out' groups within Europe. In some ways the forms of exclusion and the purposes of regulation affecting them are new, or are newly articulated. In others they appear to be revivals of old anti-Gypsy actions, such as the pogrom. These regulative patterns take different forms in different places.

- As shown by the brief historical sketches in Chapters 3, 4 and 5, Gypsies have most often been perceived as dangerous to the unity of spatial meaning identified by Simmel. He identified it as part of the universal human condition, but this book has tried to situate it more specifically as part of European modernity.

- Roma and Gypsy-Travellers have found themselves in an ambivalent relationship to the formation of a European identity and a European model of citizenship. European Union states are constructing a landscape of mobile objects and restricted subjects, creating a topology that makes movement difficult and uncomfortable for certain classes of restricted subjects.

- The formation of new forms of exclusion in Europe challenges uncritical assumptions of the value of 'Europe' as an idea and a set of institutions. The production of mental boundaries of 'Europe' is interrelated with the production of physical boundaries on the movement of subjects and of bodies.

- One of the ways governments have historically chosen to destroy Gypsy society is to tie them to the land. Paradoxically they are also often prevented from living on their own land. The British Government in particular has adopted this contradictory policy towards Gypsy-Travellers, on the one hand encouraging them to settle, on the other making it difficult for them to halt their trailers where they would like.

- There is a complex interrelationship between economic activity and cultural identity, which creates paradoxes for the individual. The structural position of Roma and Gypsy-Travellers within European society also gives them a role in the construction of Europe identities. They play the part of 'the Stranger', the internal outsider.

- There are two approaches to the Stranger within European modernity, the assimilation of the liberal project that destroys the Stranger's strangeness, and the exclusion of the racist-national project that excises him/her altogether. Both approaches have been employed against Roma and Gypsy-Travellers, and have been described in this book. The 1990s have seen a combination of the two approaches to the Stranger. As ambivalence and uncertainty have heightened, so European nation-states and peoples employ both assimilative and exclusionary strategies against the Stranger.

- As an internal outsider group with Europe 'Gypsies' symbolize both the de-spatialization and de-temporalization of identity, and the inability of social power to keep pace with productive power. They are out of time and out of place, yet a constant presence in the European imagination.

- It has been stated and re-stated throughout the book that the institutions, structures, state practices and identity formations prevailing within European modernity create problems and challenges for Roma and Gypsy-Travellers. It is easy to point to the extreme examples of the Holocaust or racially motivated violence in Central and Eastern Europe, and to ignore the way in which these exclusions operate on a more mundane, everyday level. They restrict the movement of Gypsy-Travellers, damage their family structure and forms of social organization. They push Gypsy-Travellers in Britain into housing or onto crowded and inappropriate council sites. In the states of Central and Eastern Europe they ghettoize Roma and keep them as a disempowered underclass.

- The book has been a critique of sociological conceptualizations of outsider minorities. In both case studies – Britain and the Czech Republic – Roma and Gypsy-Travellers resist categorization. They don't fit either with theories of modernist rationalism or post-modern tribalism. They represent a moral ambiguity: they resist categorization, myths of origin, and sometimes will even deny their identity. The approach to them taken by gauje academics and state functionaries is likewise ambiguous.

Europe, Outsider Minorities and Regulative Patterns

Writing at the start of the 21st Century, it is easy to forget that the end of the Cold War and the collapse of Communism heralded an enormous wave of optimism about the future of Europe (Rittberger, 1993). The various 'Civic Forum' movements that had begun in Leipzig and spread rapidly throughout the Communist states suggested new models of politics and citizenship. Their success in toppling a set of fifty year old totalitarian regimes was not only unexpected and unpredicted by most theories of social change (Mazlish, 1990, but see also Mouzelis, 1993), they have also had great difficulty explaining it even well after the fact (Opp, 1993). The events of 1989 challenged some basic assumptions about 'where the power really lies' (Beck, 1998: 37). The regimes were not in a fundamental economic crisis, nor were they challenged militarily. To speak of a crisis of legitimacy might also be an exaggeration, as many of the people who played a part in the downfall of Communism expressed their aims as reform of the socialist system, rather than its replacement by capitalism (Bodemann and Spohn, 1990). Despite all this, the regimes fell, giving up the ghost with hardly a whimper. The events of 1989 bore out the maxim that revolutions are often made by accident (Mann, 1993).

What was less surprising and all too predictable was that the optimism about new social forms generated by the revolutions disappeared fairly rapidly (Bozoki and Sukosd, 1993). Roma were the first to feel the brunt of the problems created by the transition to capitalism. Not only did many of them lose their jobs, they were also the target of racial violence from their fellow countrypeople and, in some instances, the police. As has been shown in this book, the difficulties they have faced have not been only or largely due, as is often asserted, to the reassertion of ancient ethnic hatreds characteristic of East European countries. Rather they have been a part of these countries' modernization, their development from the institutional stasis of totalitarianism. As such, the denial and exclusion of Roma in Central and Eastern Europe is related to the forms of exclusion Travellers have faced in Britain and in Western Europe as a whole. They are both constructed in terms of the basic structures of European politic life: state, nation and citizenship (Melcic, 1994).

It is tempting amidst a process of rapid social change to look for constancies over time. At first sight, one constant of European history has been the exclusion and marginalization of Roma and Gypsy-Travellers. It appears simple to assert then that European modernity relies upon the exclusion of internal aliens, continual outsiders, of whom Roma and Travellers are supremely effective examples. However, we should not be blind to the changing nature of exclusions affecting them and other outsider minorities. There have been times and places in which Roma and Gypsy-Travellers were able to live relatively freely and unbothered. The 1990s has not been one of these times. This has seen the establishment and retrenchment of regulative patterns affecting Roma, Gypsy-Travellers and other outsider groups within Europe. In some ways the forms of exclusion and the purposes of regulation affecting them are new, or are newly articulated. In others they appear to be revivals of old anti-Gypsy actions, such as the pogrom.

These new and new-old racisms are often localized in a particular way. In 2004, *The Sun* in its British edition reported on 'Roma gipsies' planning to come to Britain from Poland, the implication being that they would be criminal scroungers. The same report appeared in its Irish edition, with the 'gipsies' renamed as 'travellers'. Was this simply changing the narrative to a local context? Or was it explicitly linking specific fears about nationally specific groups of Gypsy-Travellers with Central and Eastern European Roma?

Myth, Identity and Ontological Threat

> All unsettled tribes who live among settled peoples seem to become convenient scapegoats (Encyclopaedia Britannica, 1999).

This book has described many instances of the exclusion of Roma and Gypsy-Travellers. Their rejection and demonization in popular discourse draws on some long-standing prejudices. The myths which continue to circulate about them can seem almost timeless and placeless, having a surprising consistency in different parts of Europe and at different points in history. Of course, they only appear to be timeless and placeless, but are actually articulated in spatially and historically specific terms. For example, in ironic contrast to the reality for Roma and Gypsy-Travellers in Europe, a ubiquitous European folk myth of the Gypsies is that they steal children. This has also been attributed to Jews. The anti-Semitic myth that Jews sacrificed Christian children was used as the excuse for a number of anti-Jewish pogroms in the Middle Ages (Dundes, 1989).

It has been common in many, maybe most or all, European countries for parents to scare their children with the threat that the Gypsies will come to take them away. The myth of the child snatching Gypsy, like that of the Gypsy who leaves a child on the doorstep, projects settled folk's ontological insecurity about origins onto an outsider group. It can't be said often enough that it is the exact reverse of the actual relationship between Roma and Gypsy-Travellers and the state, their children having been forcibly removed from their families in many countries of Europe on the grounds that they were a maladapted minority (Okely, 1997). Gypsy-Traveller parents have absorbed the knowledge of what the state is capable of doing out of expressively benign intentions and unsurprisingly retain a degree of caution about allowing their children into its care.

Tales circulated in the Soviet era of dark eyed Gypsies stealing various people, and stealing people's souls. There are longstanding legends from the 19th Century and before about the strangely seductive power of the Gypsy, mildly represented in the folk song, 'the Raggle-Taggle Gypsy'. Research into a 'mytho-geography' of Europe, examining how these folk myths about Gypsies develop and the purpose they serve would be valuable for understanding the construction and maintenance of European and national identities.

Europe, Identity and Exclusion

Europe is a continent of nation-states. The much remarked upon decline of the nation-state as a carrier of social power and cultural meaning began in Europe with the Cold War, when Europe was divided between two external powers. The collapse of the Cold War has not led to a revival of the European nation-state. This has led many to ask what constitutes European identity. One answer is given by the European Union, which demands allegiance from Europeans as the carrier of Europe's historical destiny. There are in the EU the makings of a European state, certainly. Whether it will be a multinational state, or a state-nation which becomes a nation-state will only be answered in time. It is illuminating to observe the process of creating an imagined community that is at work in the EU. There is something called Europe, and there appears to be some common European heritage and identity, which all individuals who live in this continent share. The EU is concerned with enhancing knowledge of this heritage and at the same time constructing it, choosing what aspects of a country's heritage are 'in common' – such as Beethoven – and which are to remain specific to that country – such as the Nazi Holocaust.

The origin of European identity is interesting in itself, and a useful perspective from which to examine the exclusion of outsider minorities within Europe. It can be postulated that European identity developed in opposition to outsider groups, and that throughout European history Jews and Gypsies have been the constant outsider. In some countries, such as Romania, a close relationship between anti-Roma feeling and nation building has been identified (Beck, 1989). It has been said that the Roma were Europe's first 'blacks' (Puxon, 1973). Convulsive events in its history have tended to see these groups being singled out for persecution. An interesting counterpoint to this view is provided by some recent ethnographic work in Serbia that seems to indicate the converse of this process at work there. The Serb informants defined the incommensurability of their ethnic identity through the symbol of Roma 'wildness,' identifying Roma with an outsider identity opaque to cool, rational Western thought (van de Port, 1999). The image of 'Gypsy' unreason and disharmony gave the lie to the claims civilization had over humanity in general, and Balkan humanity in particular (van de Port 1998).

Durkheim (1957) took the view that nationalism should and would promulgate a social and moral order in which the individual could realise his or her self. It is not intended to suggest that nationalism is inherently progressive, rather that neither national nor pan-national identities are rarely born innocent. They are born soaked in blood. This pessimistic statement is not made out of post-modern smugness at the impossibility of progress and the totalitarian nature of meta-narratives. Issues of racism, sexism and so on cannot be dealt with without some reference to universal human rights. But this book has been concerned to tell the story of a people who have almost constantly found themselves having to deal with the underbelly of progress, a dark continent within a dark continent. So any study of Roma and Gypsy-Travellers like this one also has to be a study of Europe, of European folk identity.

If European identity is to be made an object of study, it is important to know if it should be treated as a national identity, or as something qualitatively different. It seems at first sight to be much more a construct of post-war intellectuals, bureaucrats and politicians rather than something starting from the ground up. However, pan-European institutions and politics are older than national ones. The Roman Empire was such a structure. Its successor in terms of temporal power was the Catholic Church, whose decline began not with the rise of the nation-state, a relatively recent invention, but an ideological struggle, in the form of the Protestant Reformation. Politicians who treat the development of the EU as one more step in the progressive working out of a pan-European identity miss the point. 'Europe' in some form or other has been around for far longer than they think, and, like nationalism and socialism, it is often in its most enthusiastic manifestations that it has been most destructive of peoples and cultures.

Citizenship and Exclusion

Citizenship is a form of association peculiar to modern society. Like modernity, citizenship is universal and particular at the same time (Halfmann, 1998). It is a form of inclusion and exclusion closely bound up with modernity. There are two separate processes at work here. In Western Europe economically devalued individuals are being excluded from participation in citizenship, partly through their coerced inclusion within a surveillance welfare system. On the other hand, in Central and Eastern Europe Roma are often simply being excluded from civil society altogether. The complex processes by which the meaning of place is established can be seen in the workings of the Czech citizenship law of 1993. This excluded many Czech Roma from citizenship, pushing many further to the margins of society. In response, some Roma have asserted their right to be part of the Czech nation. In contrast, many others reject this identification as unrealistic. The denial of citizenship to Czech Roma has to be placed in the context of the changing nature of citizenship in Europe, in particular the two contrasting ideas of civic and ethnic citizenship.

The French Revolution created an entirely novel concept, that of the civic citizen, who was accepted as a member of a civic entity on the grounds that he accepted the fundamental ideals of that entity, such as the Rights of Man. The civic concept of citizenship developed in the following years and centuries, and was codified in the right of *ius soli*. *Ius soli*, or right of soil, awards citizenship by dint of being born in the territory of the nation-state to which one is claiming citizenship (also known as the *jus loci*, right of place). Rights were in theory granted according to universal qualities adhering in humanity, however flawed and inconsistent this may have been in practice. Europe has also produced a competing version of citizenship, the *Volk* citizenship that inheres in rights of blood. *Volk* citizenship rests with membership of a ethnic group.

A birthright based in geography, *ius soli* was the basis for British citizenship until the introduction of the 1981 Nationality Act. That Act introduced for the first time in British law the *ius patri*, the right of blood (or *jus sanguinis*). This takes ancestry rather than place of birth as the basis for deciding citizenship. Having British grandparents allows one rights of residence in Britain. It also puts the right of citizenship in the gift of the government and government agencies, whereas previously it had been an automatic birth entitlement. Either or both concepts may be enshrined in the citizenship law of a state, in the latter case more emphasis being placed on one or the other right.

The UK Nationality Act of 1981 was an attempt to construct a *Volk* citizenship, affirming the concept of patriality in British law. It was of a piece with Thatcher's concern with protecting the cultural boundaries of her idea of Britishness. In her words, prior to the 1979 General Election:

> If we went on as we are, then by the end of the century there would be four million people of the New Commonwealth and Pakistan here. Now that is an awful lot and I think it means that people are really rather afraid that this country might be swamped by people with a different culture. And, you know, the British character has done so much for democracy, for law, and done so much throughout the world that if there is a fear that it might be swamped, people are going to react and be rather hostile to those coming in. So, if you want good race relations, you have to allay people's fears on numbers.

She was drawing an explicit connection between legal citizenship and cultural citizenship. However, the British government seems to have changed tack during the 1990s. Recent innovations like the 1999 UK Immigration and Asylum Act are much more technocratic in their identification and exclusion of undesirable subjects. Asylum is restricted on the grounds of cost, and the humiliating procedures which the asylums seeker must go through bear some resemblance to the principle of 'less eligibility' which informed the old Poor Law, making conditions in the workhouses so excruciating that only the completely destitute would endure them. They exhibit the 'chauvinism of prosperity' (Habermas, 1992).

Originally, the perspective on the Czech citizenship law that was to be taken in this book was to be that it was part and parcel of a tendency towards ethnic homogenization in European life in general and Central and East European countries in general. It does perhaps reflect this tendency to some extent. However, it appears to fit better with the general thrust of policy on citizenship and migration of West European states that became manifest during the 1990s, towards excluding those who have been made economically redundant (Beck, 1997). They appear to be establishing a set of technocratic exclusions corresponding to restrictions of entry and citizenship within the EU and its satellites, such as the Czech Republic. The form of citizenship prevailing within this area of Europe seems to be increasingly supra-ethnic and supra-national. The best hope for groups who are left out of this form of citizenship is perhaps to construct a model of post-ethnic, post-national citizenship. There is at the present time a rights deficit within the European Union, and the concept of European citizenship was created with the intention of filling it. However, this concept has not been the basis for a set of trans-national rights which can be set against state interests, but has to date effectively been used for the most part to exclude non-EU citizens (Bhabha, 1998).

Post-Ethnic, Post-National Citizenships

Given the criticisms of citizenship presented above it is worth considering some alternative models which may provide a more accommodating political and cultural space for Roma and Gypsy-Travellers. The expansion of European Union institutions in recent years has involved the notion of a supranational, European citizenship, which was put forward in the Maastricht Treaty. The form EU citizenship has taken is unusual in that it does not reside in the individual, but rather in the individual's membership of a constituent nation, yet paradoxically it is also the first form of citizenship in the modern world that does not include a direct national element. Wiener (1997) refers to it as the first post-modern citizenship. It is post-modern in as far as it is removed from national boundaries and identities, but it is still rooted in its member nations – nobody can become an EU citizen without being first of all a citizen of a member country. In that sense it might be better to call it a form of citizenship corresponding to globalized, rather than post-modernized, institutional forms.

In the extent to which it is globalized, EU citizenship provides a common platform for all EU citizens through which they can engage with the global economy. So far, European citizenship does not appear to have been an effective model of an inclusive, post-national or post-modern political community. In part this is because of the limitations mentioned above (Tiilikainen, 1995). However, despite its orientation towards the global market, the EU has created institutions through which non-national or trans-national minorities can assert their rights. This can be seen in another extant model of citizenship without boundaries – Islam – with which to compare the attempt to construct some sort of common proto-national or trans-national identity for Roma (Mirga and Gheorghe, 1997).

The Islamic population of Europe has been formed through migration and population displacement, in addition to the various Islamic communities long established in Europe, such as those in Bosnia and Kosovo. Muslim political movements in Britain and France have, often successfully, defended their cultural distinctiveness which they have often felt to be in danger of undermining by the host culture (Soysal, 1997). Although these campaigns occasionally used European institutions, such as the European Court of Human Rights, they were more successful when articulating transnational community demands in terms of national citizenship rights. This entails a form of participation in the public sphere that breaks down some assumptions about collective action, requiring political mobilization at several levels, the local, the national, and the international. This form of multi-layered mobilization may be the most effective response for a transnational minority to the emerging political structure of Europe (Vertovec, 1999).

There are strong institutional barriers in the way of the creation of such a mobilization. The institutions of the European Union remain remote from individuals, and are subject to minimal democratic control. Likewise, the effective forms of citizenship in the EU have been governed not by idealistic notions of a *homo Europeanus*, nor for the most part by ground level citizen networks. Both institutional policy and forms of citizenship have been defined by a set of policies which can be labelled 'technocratic populism' and which employ a technocratic exclusion that will be described next.

From Ethnic Exclusion to Technocratic Exclusion

The Blair government's approach to the refugee 'crisis' examined was characterized by its overall approach to social issues, which is here labelled a technocratic populism. The Labour government is technocratic on most big issues, with the exception of foreign policy, and populist on the small ones. Its behaviour contrasts quite strongly with the ideologically driven Thatcher government, and even with the lukewarm Major administration. The government uses the rhetoric of economic rationality to justify many of its policies. From welfare reform to foreign policy, government spokespeople insist that justice and economic rationality go hand in hand, and never fail to point out the economic benefits of their policies. Political debate is suffused with this terminology. It is rather ironic that a decade after the death of political Marxism political debate is conducted wholly in these terms. They allow for a measure of progressive policy where there is no argument against it in economic terms, so equal rights for gays, women, and so on, are accepted as fine and even desirable because to interfere with individual opportunity is to interfere with the logic of global capitalism.

The politics of the Blairite Third Way is a technocratic populism. It is far more concerned with 'what works' and removing barriers to individual opportunity. It is happy to accept a multi-cultural nation if multi-culturalism does not interfere with the country's ability to perform in the global economy. This affects all parties. There were no 'rivers of blood' style speeches from Conservative Party politicians in response to the Roma asylum seekers who arrived in the UK during 1997 and 1998. In contrast it is the Czech and Slovak public who are far more concerned with ethnic populist response – local authorities paying to get rid of the Gypsies, racial violence, and so on. It is this latter development that contributes to the forms of exclusion characterized as a post-modern racism, or meta-racism (Salecl, 1993).

The European Union restricts the movement of certain subjects, where those subjects violate the technocratic order. On its margins the EU seems prepared to accept the *realpolitik* of ethnic homogenization. The form of technocratic exclusion prevailing within the EU is able to live with the realities of ethnic exclusion prevailing on its borders. European wide institutions like the European Court of Human Rights seem able to offer some sort of redress for Roma and Gypsy-Travellers who are unprotected by local and national government in their own countries. However, to date few cases have been brought and fewer still won.

Theorizing 'the Other'

The concept of the other has become so ubiquitous within the sociological lexicon that it tends to be thrown around without much consideration, as a handy catch-all for the representation of marginalized and excluded groups in society. The concept has been applied so widely over the years that it is danger of becoming useless. If every study that uses the concept is taken into account it could seem that every member of society except white heterosexual middle aged urban dwelling males belongs to 'the other'. I want to redraw the boundaries of the concept a little, as well as offering some criticisms of the way in which it has been used, so that it can be applied in a more meaningful manner.

The main problem with the concept has to do with its catch all application. It tends to lump together hugely various and differing identities and cultures into one concept (Shurmer-Smith and Hannam, 1994). The same criticism has been applied to Edward Said's (1978) idea of 'the Orient' and 'Orientalism'. It homogenizes both the diverse cultures and societies of the Orient, and those of the Occident. There is a danger of taking one aspect of the Other to be dominant, to the exclusion of more mundane features of their life, and to ignore 'others within the other'. With studies involving Gypsy-Travellers there is a temptation to only focus on the exotic, ignoring or downplaying the extent to which they experience the same mundane problems and challenges which face any member of society. Following on from this, studies invoking the Other are also in danger of creating their object, disavowing the links between Gypsy-Traveller society and the rest of society, and the extent to which their concerns and needs may be shared with other sections of society. It can blind the researcher to an understanding of the ways in which Gypsy-Traveller society is affected by changes in the wider society, implying that there are two separate identities: a 'true' identity, and an identity as constructed by the wider society.

'Gypsylorist' is a term used by Roma scholars to describe a certain research standpoint adopted by gauje. It is taken from the name of the Gypsy Lore Society. It refers to a standpoint in Gypsy scholarship which romanticizes and exoticizes the 'true Gypsy' (Borrow, 1948), onto whom is projected the gauje scholar's own romantic leanings and dissatisfactions with modernity (Acton, 1979). The 19th Century Gypsylorists were engaged in reifying the object of their study. Socio-biological researchers reify their object on genetic and racial lines. Modern sociological studies of Gypsy-Travellers may be more benign, but they can fall into that trap as well when employing the concept of the Other and Orientalism. It should be possible to recognize the construction of Gypsy-Travellers and other groups as 'Other' in European thought, whilst also seeing the complexity of actually existing relations between the two societies on many levels, and the conflicts and compromises that exist between and within societies. Just as there should be scope in public policy to allow for integration without assimilation, there should be scope in social theory for appreciating the ordinariness of the other without removing its uniqueness.

Reason and Competing Forms of Rationality

Roma and Gypsy-Travellers are often represented as behaving irrationally, especially when they have difficulty engaging with bureaucracies such as the health or education systems. It is the purpose of this section to use their experience to criticize and challenge some dominant notions of rationality. The word rationality comes from the Latin for 'calculation', referring to the proportion of food doled out to soldiers in the Roman army. Rationality describes a calculating ability, but is more than merely a technique. It takes the form of a compulsion to calculate the worth of individuals and groups. A specific definition of rational behaviour, covering constructions of time, of boredom and the work ethic, characterizes the European self. The theme of rationality and reason is intertwined with how European modernity defines itself and the ways in which it describes and frames its treatment of Gypsy-Travellers.

There are two different points to this section, the discussion of economic rationality as it is used to explain certain forms of behaviour, and the discussion of bureaucratic and legal rationality, which is used to explain some of the conflict between Travellers and the bureaucratic systems of modernity. The fact that there exist competing and conflicting forms of reason and rationality ties in with the idea of the Stranger and matter out of place, and links back to the theme of identity, and the function of certain forms of reason in defining Europe identity and informing the processes of citizenship. As a competing form of rationality this section will examine nomadism as economically rational behaviour, and look into the economic basis of Travelling.

The terms 'rationality' and 'rationalism' are usually used as a synonym for 'good'. The lack of definition extends to academic usage, where the word may be used in many different senses in the same paper or book. Examining Max Weber's definition of rational, Brubaker (1991) tries to separate the word out into its component parts, finding in the process that Weber employs it in sixteen distinct senses, from describing types of organization, to aspects of behaviour, mindsets and so on. I'll be using the term in several different senses also, though thankfully not sixteen. I will differentiate them into; economic rationalism; bureaucratic rationality; substantive and formal rationalities in law; and minority counter-rationalities.

With the term economic rationality I am referring to a paradigmatic set of assumptions about the organization of systems of social relations according to a relatively narrow technocratic definition of 'efficiency'. The application of rules of economic rationality involves, among other things, introducing market principles into previously non-market areas of social life, such as education, healthcare and broadcasting. Market evangelism is a necessary part of creating monetary values for services and goods which previously were not allocated a specific price, with such things as the allocation of a cost to a hospital operation; the assessment and justification of policy in largely or solely monetary terms, and so on.

Keith and Pile (1993) relate the idea of 'the West' to 'an imagined locus of a particular form of rationality'. The West is not a physical space as such, though it often corresponds to and is rooted in a physical space, that of Europe and to a lesser extent North America. It is a concentration of power and a concatenation of objectifying rationality.

White tribes outside of the space of rationality – such as those in Australia or South Africa – take themselves to be a part of 'the West' in this sense. Recently these white tribes have become more distanced from the West. Australia has in the past two decades begun the process of remodelling itself as an Asian country, partly due to the perceived severing of cultural and economic ties with Britain, which has focused increasingly on the European Union. Afrikaaners state that they are a white tribe of Africa, and in the post-apartheid state claim the rights of separate development formerly accorded to black tribes under the system of Grand Apartheid – the right to form a self-governing Bantustan, and so on.

The idea of Europe is a more space-specific one than that of 'the West'. Though its influence extends far beyond its boundaries, the concept is usually – and I postulate, increasingly - imagined as a geographical one. It is a spatially located imagined identity, although the extent and nature of its spatial boundedness is contested. Increasingly Europe is severed from the West. There have been a number of political and economic conflicts with the USA, notably over the Kyoto Protocol and the Iraq war of 2003. The work of mimesis – the creation of memory – has been most intense in this decade with regard to the creation of the memory of Europe. Mimetic production does not exist in a vacuum. It corresponds to the production of the European super-state. The production of mental boundaries of 'Europe' is interrelated with the production of physical boundaries on the movement of subjects, of bodies. The formerly universal European West appears to have withdrawn into a regional Western-Europe, in which boundaries of identity are increasingly coterminous with the geographical boundaries of 'Europe'. Hence it might be said that the work put into the definition of 'Europe' has meant a withdrawal from universalist conceptual rationality, though there has been a large shift towards the almost universal acceptance of economic rationalism as the basic organizing principle of society.

Cultures of Rationality and Irrationality

The culture of poverty thesis is one example of the application of the concept a quantity theory of rationality to behaviour. It is conceived as a zero sum game in which the absence of long-term rational thinking prevents the individuals concerned creating sufficient cultural and material capital to keep up with the game. It comes as no surprise that the culture of poverty thesis has been applied to Gypsy-Travellers especially, but also to Roma. Research in this framework has been carried out in both the UK and Ireland and despite the recantations of some researchers and the discrediting of other work it still provides quite a popular framework for thinking about disadvantage and social exclusion, especially in Central and Eastern Europe (Bereczkei, 1993; 1998).

There are several alternative explanations for behaviour defined as irrational. It is possible to look at it in terms of restricted rationality. Rational behaviour is limited by material, social and other constraints, forcing the group into adopting apparently irrational ways of behaving. Though sympathetic to the position of the subject group, the perspective of restricted rationality still places their behaviour on a hierarchy of rationalities. They are forced into adopting a lesser form of behaviour when ideally they would not have to. Effectively this is a form of the culture of poverty thesis, taken from a materialist perspective. Another explanation, that of 'rationality from below,' goes a bit further to suggest that there are simply different and incommensurable rationalities depending on one's position in the social structure. What seems impenetrable or perverse from one standpoint is simple common sense from another (Kornblum and Lichter, 1972). It is the case that Roma and Gypsy-Travellers often describe gauje behaviour in precisely these terms, as impenetrable and irrational.

Moving away from the dominant concept of rationality altogether, the problem for sociology and anthropology is how far to pursue functionalist explanations for group behaviour, which despite the lip service paid to post-structuralism most researchers still instinctively do. Every identifiable human behaviour tends to be divided into 'functional' and 'residual' by sociologists. The functional serves some purpose, in maintaining cultural coherence, expanding economic prosperity. For some, culture functions to propagate genetic information in the form of 'memes' (Blackmore 1999). Behaviour which can't be explained as functional is termed residual, something that was once functional but changes in society or group structure have rendered it obsolete and it perseveres through habit. Super-functionalists will of course re-incorporate residual behaviours as actually functional in the long term – tying the group together through habitual adherence to the past, and so on. There is a conflict here between the need for sociology to find the 'explanation' for behaviour, which usually involves an explanation other than that provided by the research subjects, and its expressed desire to take those research subjects at face value and to allow them to 'speak for themselves'.

Perhaps the problem lies in part in sociology's unspoken adherence to rationality and its keenness to find rational explanations. Challenging that adherence puts us in danger of sinking into the postmodernist quagmire, and in denying the primacy of rationality as an explanation making the assumption that therefore there can be no explanation at all, rational or otherwise, for social behaviour outside the limited local narrative provided by the participants. Hopefully this nihilistic stance can be avoided. Ending the dominance of instrumental-rational explanations should not mean that all possible explanations are tipped into the deconstructionist swamp. It should however evince a degree of openness to explanations that allow for some blurring of the distinction between the functional and the residual.

The culture of poverty thesis is one way of imposing a reasoned framework to actions which may seem mystifying to the outsider. It has often been employed by sociologists and policy makers who have benign intentions, but it is impossible to get away from the conclusion it offers, which is that poverty is the fault of the poor, and that therefore the way to fight poverty is to break up the culture of poverty. In actual fact the poor have developed numerous collective networks for sustaining themselves in the midst of material poverty. Policies based on the culture of poverty generally serve to break up these networks too, and end up disempowering people and leaving them less able to deal with material deprivation without relying on the state. A cycle of dependence ensues, with state 'intervention from above' being worse than useless when it does not reflect the needs and realities of the poor and marginalized.

It is my argument that the application of rationalism in general and bureaucratic rationalism in particular has during this century led to a decline in the romantic mythology of Gypsies that was created in the 18th and 19th Centuries. The romanticized culture of exoticism has been replaced in the representation of Gypsies by the culture of poverty. George Borrow has been replaced by Charles Murray. As bureaucratic control over the lives of Gypsies has increased, so their presence in the anthropological imagination has been eclipsed by a growing presence in the bureaucratic imagination as irrational and out of place. There is not a strict dichotomy between the two. Anthropology has in the past been fully in the service of the bureaucratic control of Roma and Travellers, for example during the Holocaust. It would seem however that bureaucratic rationality has denatured romanticism. Paradoxically, the withdrawal of faith in scientific rationality and the re-enchantment of nature has not caused a revival of Gypsy romanticism, just the opposite in fact. Gypsies are ever-present reminders of the necessity of nature, the fact that it is only in the urban European imagination that it exists as an escape from the social relations of capitalist modernity.

An assumption that the behaviour of marginalized groups in modernity is governed by self-interested reason might be a fairly good working hypothesis. That this reason might be long term and neither irrational nor based on instant gratification would also be a fair assumption. The reader has to bear in mind the normality of day to day life, the way decisions are cobbled together from a variety of pressures and needs. Some of these decisions are to do with community norms, true enough, but many are to do with fulfilling basic needs, maintaining a peaceful family life, and so on. What might seem opaque to an outsider can often be put down to an inability to see what is right in front of one's face, and the best academic work on 'the other' is that which appreciates the everyday as well as the exotic, or rather the exoticized. Fundamentally a work of this kind has to appreciate how the structures of modernity outlined in this book define themselves against outsiders like Gypsy-Travellers; how in doing so they construct an imaginary 'Gypsy'; and how Gypsy-Travellers themselves engage with the reality of being subjects of the flux of modernity. The different meanings of rationality can be seen in an examination of the meaning certain economic judgements have for British Gypsy-Travellers.

The Stranger and the Borders of Identity in Europe

One of the paradoxes of European life during the 1990s has been that the collapse of universalizing, totalizing ideologies has not created a society in which 'difference' or 'the other' can reside undisturbed. Globalized conditions of consumption and production were supposed to have rendered racial, national, ethnic and regional differences moot. As outlined in this book, in many instances the opposite has happened. In Europe, struggles over identity have brought to the fore processes whereby those who violate the map of identity are excluded, symbolically and practically. An examination of European modernity in terms of the concepts of 'the scapegoat', 'the Stranger' and 'the *unheimliche*' will serve to demonstrate that these developments are not so paradoxical.

The Frankfurt School applied psychology to the creation of scapegoat groups in modern society, specifically pre-war Germany and the Jews (Adorno et al., 1969; Reich, 1972). Adorno *et al* associate racial prejudice with a personality inclined towards authoritarianism. Recent research from Hungary (Todosijevic, 1998) has indicated that anti-Gypsy attitudes are more closely associated with authoritarianism than are anti-Semitic attitudes. In the *Dialectic of Enlightenment* Horkheimer and Adorno (1973) use psychoanalysis to explain hatred of Jews as a projection of fear and repressed desire. A psychologically based explanation of anti-Gypsy sentiment, also drawing on work on anti-Semitism, is provided by Maciejewski (1994). He uses Freud's definition of 'the uncanny' (*unheimliche*) to draw some parallels and contrasts with anti-Semitism. The 'uncanny' is defined in part as the perception that the uncanny object is both familiar and unfamiliar. It is what is both known and not known. Hence it is dangerous to the borders and integrity of the ego (Freud 1955), frightening because of its connection with what is known and familiar. The uncanny is that about which the ego is uncertain. The original German word, *unheimliche* translates directly as 'the unhomely'. The word *heimlich* means what is homely, comfortable and close, but also what is hidden, buried and concealed with conspiratorial intent. Like anti-Semitism, anti-Gypsy feeling is generated from projection. The anti-Semite projects onto the Jew his own self-loathing. Maciejewski argues that the anti-Semite is engaged in projecting repressed Oedipal father-hatred, the father being representative of the ambivalence of civilization. Hatred of Gypsies however stems from the fear of the mother, the past origin, the repression of the pleasure principle and the apparent freedom Gypsies have from the constraints of the sedentary individual.

Moving towards a more sociological perspective, Marlene Sway (1981) applies Simmel's use of the concept of the Stranger to the relationship between Gypsies and settled society. This is a good beginning at understanding how settled society constitutes boundaries between it and Roma or Gypsy-Traveller society, most academic work stopping at the way Roma and Gypsy-Travellers maintain social boundaries, and at appreciating the way European modernity seems to *need* outsider groups.

> The Stranger is thus being discussed here, not in the sense often touched upon in the past, as the wanderer who comes today and goes tomorrow, but rather as the person who comes today and stays tomorrow. He is, so to speak, the potential wanderer: although he has not moved on, he has not quite overcome the freedom of coming and going. He is fixed within a particular spatial group, or within a group whose boundaries are similar to spatial boundaries. But his position in this group is determined, essentially, by the fact that he has not belonged to it from the beginning, that he imports qualities into it, which do not and cannot stem from the group itself ... He is near and far at the same time (Simmel, 1950: 402).

Simmel defines the Stranger as the potential wanderer. The Stranger is a fixed member of a spatially located group, but is not of it. Strangers represent a combination of proximity and apartness, closeness and distance. European Jewry is the archetype of the Stranger, and Simmel lists several characteristics pertaining to perceived strangeness.

First and foremost the minority possesses a strangeness of origin. This is certainly true of Roma and Gypsy-Travellers, perhaps more than any other group. Their origin was for a long time in doubt, partly because of the many myths about it that sprang up, some spread and encouraged by themselves as useful to maintain their exotic image. It was said variously that they were Egyptians, Papist spies, 'Minions of the Moon,' one of the lost tribes of Israel, the survivors of Atlantis, or a people condemned to wander the earth for having made the nails for the Jesus' cross. The Stranger is also 'no owner of soil', both in the literal sense of not owning land and in not being part of the spatially fixed hierarchy. They are always at least potentially mobile, lacking any permanent claim on the land. This is not in fact true of Gypsies everywhere. The Spanish *Gitanos* have permanent and long term dwellings, and are most certainly a fixed feature of Spanish society (Quintana and Floyd, 1986). It does apply to most of Europe's Roma and Travellers in that they have often been prevented from owning land, or have chosen not to. One of the ways governments have historically chosen to destroy Gypsy society is to tie them to the land. Paradoxically they are also often prevented from living on their own land. Governments have adopted this contradictory policy towards Gypsy-Travellers in particular, on the one hand encouraging them to settle, on the other making it difficult for them to halt their trailers where they would like.

The Stranger is an objective outsider. In this sense they view the group, its values, habits, mores, conventions, from the perspective of a disinterested outsider. Objectivity stems from this combination of being close yet distant. It may explain why Roma and Gypsy-Travellers have been and are so popular as fortune-tellers. During the Middle Ages they were seen as being able to cross the division between magical and material spaces (Soulis, 1961). Being viewed as both within and without society they are able to make unencumbered judgements and evaluations, and can be an oubliette, a receptacle for things one wishes to forget about. In the Middle Ages the Church provided a total, yet dissatisfactory narrative, for social life. Similarly in modernity the nation-state and its associated institutions provides a totalizing but incomplete meta-narrative. Stranger minorities, because of their social position, can provide both more satisfactory counter-narratives for individuals and a focus for the ambivalence and uncertainty created by this dissatisfaction.

The Stranger is a true economic rationalist, and lacks the primordial emotional commitment to the host society that its members like to think overrides self-interest. It means they are both free and uncommitted, and hence dangerous to the group, as it is assumed that the Stranger's objective rationality could be turned against the group at a time of crisis or external threat. It follows from this that members of the host society do not share what they feel is their ethnic specificity with the Stranger. So it is that the relationship with the Stranger is always contingent. They are a potential fifth column, and are easily transformed into the representatives of organized crime, racial degeneracy or international conspiracies.

> The human being is the connecting creature who must always separate and cannot connect without separating ... and the human being is likewise the bordering creature who has no border (Simmel, 1994a: 10).

Aleksandra Alund (1995) examines the spread of new social movements based primarily on identity as a mobilizing factor, these being strongly Western, and the mobilization of ethno-fundamental consciousness in both East and West are facets of a similar process. The end of the meta-narratives which had dominated intellectual life in Europe, the decline in power of the nation-state over national life, and the general divergence between globalization on the one hand and neo-tribalist social fragmentation on the other, have created numerous collective and individual identity crises. At the same time new and 'new-old' identities are being constructed, often in terms which are exclusionary and heterophobic. The resurgence of identity politics within Europe has produced numerous Strangers (Dessewffy, 1996).

Simmel's use of the word refers to a dialogic process, a unique form of interaction between the Stranger and the majority group, which relies largely on the Stranger not attempting to assimilate, to abnegate their identity. The Stranger represents what Simmel said about humanity being bordering and able to transgress borders, and the Stranger is disturbing through proximity. Simmel says that 'the distance of a being from us signifies in everything the psychological unity of that being' (Simmel, 1994b). It is the proximate other which is disturbing, threatening to overthrow that psychological unity. Increasingly, however, there is within Europe no single narrative of strangeness, no single scapegoat or enemy. Rather:

> Individual, social and national insecurity, the preoccupation with law and order, jobs and the nation are ... combined into one complex syndrome in which external threats and internal doubts are hard to disentangle (Hassner, 1991: 147).

Jennifer Welsh (1994) expands the focus beyond modernity, seeing a long-term logic in the establishment of a cultural and social space of Europe stretching as far back as the 9th Century. The internal enemy, the resident outsider, has had a central function in defining and affirming a European identity (Zukier 1996; Tabboni 1995). These internal enemies included at different times Communists, Jews, Turks and Gypsies. She identifies one particular development that is central to the findings of this book. More and more, unwanted population movement is being seen as a problem for the whole of Europe rather than any one nation-state within it, and action is being taken on a European level to restrict that movement. As ambivalence and uncertainty have heightened, so European nation-states and peoples employ both assimilative and exclusionary strategies against the Stranger.

Ambivalence and Uncertainty, Tradition and Time

We are constantly told that we live in a post-traditional world. The site clearing operation of post-modernism was supposed to have denatured, defoundationalized, deconstructed and demolished everything in its path. Both belief in the past (the authenticity of tradition) and in the future (the inevitability of progress) have been undone (Diken, 1998). Post-modernity collapses some of prevailing divisions between time and place, between high and low culture, and between historical periods. Yet it does not render time(s) and place(s) unimportant, often the exact opposite. What it does do is insert ambivalence and uncertainty into time and place, rendering linear notions of temporality and causality less than useful.

The ambivalence of post-modern European life is centred on this collapsing certainty. Society's productive power has now far outstripped its social power. The one certainty is that this process is likely to continue. Marx, along with many others, assumed that massive increases in economic productivity would go along with massive increases in the power of humanity to control the lifeworld, to take charge of itself. All the working class would have to do is take control of the instruments of the state and of productive power and they would have control over social power. If anything, the reverse has been the case. As new work practices revolutionize production, people, both as individuals and as collectivities such as trades unions, have less control over the production process. The Internet creates information saturation, and people have more and more difficulty trying to filter out the information they want from that which they don't want. In some ways the confounding of social power is a positive development. It makes an event like the Holocaust far less likely to be repeated (Bauman, 1991b). Yet is also brings forth new dangers, in the unintended consequences of technological development, and in the post-modern forms of surveillance and control of outsider minorities that have been detailed in this book.

The Yugoslavian wars of the 1990s put to bed the once fashionable idea that holocausts are products of, or always require the technology and social organisation of, modernity. There was not much rigorous, distanced or bureaucratic about the violence unleashed then. It is in fact easier, at least for sociologists who have invested so much in the concept of modernity, to understand racism, ethnic cleansing, and various forms of exclusionary action as yet another dismaying product of that all encompassing juggernaut, or to see it as another instance of Foucauldian surveillance and control. It is not so easy to fit the medieval flaunting of viciousness and bloody, protracted and painful retribution that swept much of the former Yugoslavia into this schema, which may be why so many sociologists ignore it.

These paradoxes are not failures of the system, although they may represent failures of our understanding. Rather they inhere in the forms of production and the practices of social power which characterize this period of modernity. It might be a little trite to say that in the midst of a combination of uncertainty and globalized homogenization people cling to the narcissism of minor differences, and 'identity' becomes the focus of individual and collective action. We also need to go beyond the rather easy conclusion that outsider minorities become the scapegoats for uncertainties experienced during rapid or bewildering social change, although both these statements are the case to an extent. In my view, the resurgence of ethnic nationalism in Europe is just one phenomenon resulting from this collapsing of time and space, and the way social power lags further and further behind productive power. De-spatialization and de-temporalization produce a threat to meaning, which will not be resolved as long as historically constituted nation-states remain as the carriers of meaning and collective identity.

What has this got to do with Roma and Gypsy-Travellers? It is my hypothesis that as an internal outsider group with Europe they symbolize both the de-spatialization and de-temporalization of identity, and the inability of social power to keep pace with productive power. They are out of time and out of place, yet a constant presence in the European imagination. It has been stated and re-stated throughout the book that the institutions, structures, state practices and identity formations prevailing within European modernity create problems and challenges for Roma and Travellers. It is easy to point to the extreme examples of the Holocaust or racially motivated violence in Central and Eastern Europe, and to ignore the way in which these exclusions operate on a more mundane, everyday level. They restrict the movement of Gypsy-Travellers, damage their family structure and forms of social organization. They push Gypsy-Travellers in Britain into housing or onto crowded and inappropriate council sites. In the countries of Central and Eastern Europe they ghettoize Roma and keep them as a disempowered underclass.

In a sense, the exclusions faced by Roma and Gypsy-Travellers are an attempt to deal with ambivalence. Those minorities who are perceived as violating the neat social and spatial ordering of modernity are subject to rejection and exclusion. They are 'Stranger' minorities. Ambivalence is built into the relationship between modernity and the individual. The greater the ambivalence created by rapid social change and the globalization of local spaces, the more outsider minorities become the focus of the fears generated by it. The experience of Roma and Gypsy-Travellers demands the remaking of modernity as self-critical, open and reflexive. This book has demonstrated that Roma and Gypsy-Travellers have been on the receiving end of the ethnic fundamentalism and cultural essentialism of post-modern neo-tribalism, as well as the bureaucratic and hegemonic exclusions of classical modernity. Only a project which both accepts the value of universal rights and liberties, whilst also being able to cope with difference, will avoid both (Goldberg, 1994).

Given the extent of the exclusion of Roma and Gypsy-Travellers examined here, it is important for sociological research to focus on the damaging effect of the identification practices of powerful actors on outsider minorities. At the start of this chapter I referred to Europe as a dark continent. On reflection it may be more correct to state that for the majority of individuals living in Europe it is the centres of power and decision making of governments and corporations which are the dark continents. They are never so dark than when it comes to subjecting them to the extent of scrutiny and surveillance which the powerless and marginalized are often unable to avoid. If sociology is to make any claims to being a science of progress it should want to reverse this relationship of scrutiny. Perhaps therein would lie the true service to Roma and Gypsy-Travellers, and to all people who have been at one time or another pushed to the edge of society.

Bibliography

Newspapers and Newsletters

Christian Science Monitor.
The Daily Mail.
The Guardian.
The Independent.
Phactum, newsletter of The Philadelphia Association for Critical Thinking.
Radio Free Europe/Radio Liberty.
Roma Rights, newsletter of the European Roma Rights Center.
The Scotsman.
The Sunday Times.
The Sun.
The Times.
The Toronto Globe & Mail.
The Toronto Star.
The Toronto Sun.

Texts

Acton, T. (1979), 'Academic Success and Political Failure: A Review of Modern Social Science Writing in English on Gypsies', *Ethnic and Racial Studies*, Vol. 2(2), pp. 231-241.

Acton, T. (1991), 'Defining The Limits of Tolerance: UK Government Policy on Gypsies', *Roma*, Vol. 35, pp. 20-33.

Acton, T. (1994), 'Categorising Irish Travellers', in M. McCann, S. O'Siochain, and J Ruane (eds). *Irish Travellers: Culture and Ethnicity*, Queen's University Press, Belfast, pp. 36-53.

Adams, B., Okely, J., Morgan, D. and Smith, D. (1975), 'Gypsies: Current Policies and Practices', *Journal of Social Policy*, Vol. 4(2), pp. 129-150.

Adorno, T., Frenkel-Brunswick, E., Levinson, D. J., and Sanford, R. N. (1969), *The Authoritarian Personality*, Harper & Row, New York.

Advisory Committee on the Framework Convention for the Protection of National Minorities (2002), *Opinion on the United Kingdom*, Council of Europe, Brussels.

Advisory Council for the Education of Romany and Other Travellers (1994), *Directory of Planning Policies For Gypsy Site Provision In England*, ACERT, London.

Agassi, J. (1996), 'The Contemporary Role of Historians of Science and Technology', *Protosoziologie*, Vol. 8, pp. 385-401.

Agnew, J. (1996), 'Time Into Space: The Myth of "Backward" Italy In Modern Europe', *Time & Society*, Vol. 5(1), pp. 27-45.

Albrow, M. (1996), *The Global Age: State and Society Beyond Modernity*, Polity, Cambridge.

Amnesty International (1991), *Les Sanctions aux Transporteurs: Des Difficultes d'Access au Territoire*, Amnesty International, Paris.

Anthias, F. (1995), 'Cultural Racism or Racist Culture? Rethinking Racist Exclusions', *Economy and Society*, Vol. 24(2), pp. 279-301.

Ashworth, A. (1997), 'Sentencing', in M. Maguire, R. Morgan, and R. Reiner (eds)., *The Oxford Handbook of Criminology*, Oxford University Press, Oxford, pp. 1095-1135.

Ballard, R. (1997), 'The Construction of a Conceptual Vision: "Ethnic Groups" and the 1991 UK Census', *Ethnic and Racial Studies* Vol. 20(1), pp. 182-194.

Bancroft, A. (1999), 'Gypsies to the Camps!: Exclusion and Marginalization of Roma in the Czech Republic', *Sociological Research Online*, Vol. 4 (3), http://www.socresonline.org.uk/socresonline/4/3/bancroft.html.

Bancroft, A., Lloyd, M. and Morran, R. (1996), *The Right to Roam: Scotland's Travelling People*, Save the Children, Edinburgh.

Bantjes, R. (1997), 'Benthamism in the Countryside: The Architecture of Rural Space 1900-1930', *Journal of Historical Sociology*, Vol. 10(3), pp. 249-269.

Banton, M. (1980), 'The Idiom of Race: A Critique of Presentism', *Research in Race and Ethnic Relations*, Vol. 2, pp. 21-42.

Banton, M. (1983), *Racial And Ethnic Competition*, Gregg Revivals, Aldershot.

Banton, M. (1988), *Racial Consciousness*, Longman, London.

Barany, Z. (1995), 'The Roma in Macedonia: Ethnic Politics and the Marginal Condition in a Balkan State', *Ethnic and Racial Studies*, Vol. 18(3), pp. 515-531.

Barany, Z. (2002), *The East European Gypsies: Regime Change, Marginality and Ethnopolitics*, Cambridge University Press, Cambridge.

Barondess, J. (1998), 'Care of the Medical Ethos: Reflections on Social Darwinism, Racial Hygiene, and the Holocaust', *Annals of Internal Medicine*, Vol. 128(11), pp. 891-898.

Barsky, R. (1994), *Constructing A Productive Other: Discourse Theory And The Convention Refugee Hearing*, John Benjamins, Amsterdam.

Barth, F. (1969), 'Introduction', in F. Barth (ed.), *Ethnic Groups and Boundaries: The Social Organization of Culture Difference*, George Allen & Unwin, London, pp. 9-38.

Barth, F. (1974), 'The Social Organization of a Pariah Group in Norway', in F. Rehfisch (ed.), *Gypsies, Tinkers and Other Travellers*, Academic , London, pp. 285-299.

Bass, W. (1998), 'The Triage of Dayton', *Foreign Affairs*, Vol. 77(5), pp. 95-112.

Bauer, Y. (1994), 'Gypsies', in Y. Gutman (ed.), *Anatomy of the Auschwitz Death Camp*, Indiana University Press, Bloomington, pp. 441-455.

Bauman, Z. (1989), *Modernity and the Holocaust*, Polity, Cambridge.
Bauman, Z. (1991a), *Modernity and Ambivalence*, Polity, Cambridge.
Bauman, Z. (1991b), 'The Social Manipulation of Morality: Moralizing Actors, Adiaphorizing Action', *Theory Culture & Society*, Vol. 8(1), pp. 137-151.
Bauman, Z. (1992), *Intimations of Postmodernity*, Routledge, London.
Bauman, Z. (1997), *Postmodernity and its Discontents*, Polity, Cambridge.
Bauman, Z. (1998a), *Globalization: The Human Consequences*, Polity, Cambridge.
Bauman, Z. (1998b), *Work, Consumerism and the New Poor*, Open University Press, Buckingham.
Bauman, Z. (2000), *Liquid Modernity*, Polity, Cambridge.
Bayley, D. (1998), 'Policing in America', *Society*, Vol. 36, pp. 16-19.
Beale, A. and Geary, R. (1994), 'Gypsies, Judges and the State: A Review of the Caravan Sites Act 1968', *Cambrian Law Review*, Vol. 25, pp. 89-101.
Beck, J. (1997), 'From Citizens to Criminals: The Loss of Citizenship of Czech Gypsies in the Transition From Communism', Conference of the Society for the Study of Social Problems.
Beck, S. (1989), 'The Origins of Gypsy Slavery in Romania', *Dialectical Anthropology*, Vol. 14(1), pp. 53-61.
Beck, U. (1987), 'The Anthropological Shock: Chernobyl and the Contours of the Risk Society', *Berkeley Journal of Sociology*, Vol. 32, pp. 153-159.
Beck, U. (1998), *Democracy Without Enemies*, Polity, Cambridge.
Beier, A. L. (1974), 'Vagrants and the Social Order in Elizabethan England', *Past and Present*, Vol. 64, pp. 3-29.
Beier, A. L. (1985), *Masterless Men: The Vagrancy Problem in England 1560-1640*, Methuen, London.
Bell, D. (1987), 'The World and the United States in 2013', *Daedalus*, Vol. 116(3), pp. 1-30.
Bereczkei, T. (1993), 'r-Selected Reproductive Strategies Among Hungarian Gypsies: A Preliminary Analysis', *Ethology and Sociobiology*, Vol. 14(2), pp. 71-88.
Bereczkei, T. (1998), 'Kinship Network, Direct Childcare, and Fertility Among Hungarians and Gypsies', *Evolution and Human Behavior*, Vol. 19(5), pp. 283-298.
Bernasovsky, I., Jurickova, J. and Ferak, V. (1994), 'Population Genetic-Study in Gypsies (Roms) From Slovakia: Distribution of Blood-Group Genetic Markers', *Anthropological Science*, Vol. 102, pp. 409-419.
Bhabha, J. (1998), 'Enforcing the Human Rights of Citizens and Non-Citizens in the Era of Maastricht: Some Reflections on the Importance of States', *Development and Change*, Vol. 29(4), pp. 697-724.
Black, R., K. Koser, and Walsh, M. (1998), *Conditions for the Return of Displaced Persons from the European Union*, office for the official Publications of the European Union, Luxembourg.
Blackmore, S. (1999), *The Meme Machine*, Oxford University Press, Oxford.
Bocker, A. and T. Havinga (1998a), 'Asylum Applications in the European Union', *Journal of Refugee Studies*, Vol. 11(3), pp. 245-266.

Bocker, A. and Havinga, T. (1998b), *Asylum Migration in the European Union: Patterns of Origin and Destination*, office for the official Publications of the European Union, Luxembourg.

Bodemann, Y. and Spohn, W. (1990), 'The East German Revolution, German Unification, and the Left', *Critical Sociology*, Vol. 17(3), pp. 3-8.

Bonnett, A. (1996), 'Anti-Racism and the Critique of "Whiteness"', *New Community*, Vol. 22(1), pp. 97-110.

Bonnett, A. (1998), 'Who was White? The Disappearance of Non-European White Identities and the Formation of European Racial Whiteness', *Ethnic and Racial Studies*, Vol. 21(6), pp. 1029-1052.

Borrow, G. (1843), *The Zincali, or an Account of the Gypsies of Spain*, John Murray, London.

Bovenkirk, F., Miles, R. and Verbunt, G. (1990), 'Racism, Migration and the State in Western Europe: A Case for Comparative Analysis', *International Sociology*, Vol. 5(4), pp. 475-490.

Box, S. (1996), 'Crime, Power and Ideological Mystification', in J. Muncie (ed.) *Criminological Perspectives*, Sage, London, pp. 245-256.

Bozoki, A. and Sukosd, M. (1993), 'Civil Society and Populism in the Eastern European Democratic Transition Periods', *Praxis International*, Vol. 13(3), pp. 224-241.

Brand, C. (1986), 'How Are Gipsies Faring Now?', *New Law Journal*, Vol. 136, pp. 995-997.

Brearley, M. (1996), *The Roma/Gypsies of Europe: A Persecuted People*, Institute for Jewish Policy Research, London.

Brochmann, G. (1993), 'Control in Immigration Policies: A Closed Europe in the Making', in R. King (ed.), *The New Geography of European Migrations*, Belhaven, London, pp. 100-115.

Brochmann, G. (1997), 'Bosnian Refugees in the Scandinavian Countries: A Comparative Perspective on Immigration Control in the 1990s', *New Community*, Vol. 23(4), pp. 395-510.

Brubaker, R. (1991), *The Limits of Rationality*, Routledge, London.

Bunce, C. (1996), 'A Hard Road to Travel', *Nursing Times*, Vol. 92(49), pp. 34-36.

Burkitt, I. (1996), 'Civilization and Ambivalence', *British Journal of Sociology*, Vol. 47 (1), pp. 135-150.

Caffrey, S. and Mundy, G. (1997), 'Informal Systems of Justice: The Formation of Law Within Gypsy Communities', *American Journal of Comparative Law*, Vol. XLV(2), pp. 251-268.

Cain, M. (1974), 'The Main Themes of Marx' And Engels' Sociology of Law', *British Journal of Law and Society*, Vol. 1(2), pp. 136-148.

Calhoun, C. and Pfaff, S. (1998), 'The Disintegration of Yugoslavia: Nationalism, Economic Differentiation and Political Process', Conference of the American Sociological Association.

Caloz-Tschopp, M. C. (1997), 'On The Detention of Aliens: The Impact on Democratic Rights', *Journal of Refugee Studies*, Vol. 10(2), pp. 165-180.

Campbell, S. (1995), 'Gypsies: The Criminalization of a Way of Life', *Criminal Law Review*, pp. 28-37.

Carlson, H. M. and Casavant, C. M. (1995), 'Education of Irish Traveller Children: Some Social Issues', *Irish Journal of Psychology*, Vol. 16(2), pp. 100-116.

Carter, D. (1994), 'The Art of the State: Difference and Other Abstractions', *Journal of Historical Sociology*, Vol. 7(1), pp. 73-102.

Castells, M. (1996), *The Rise of The Network Society*, Blackwell, Cambridge.

Center for Reproductive Rights and Center for Human and Civil Rights (2003), *Body and Soul: Forced Sterilization and Other Assaults on Roma Reproductive Freedom in Slovakia*, Center for Reproductive Rights, New York.

Chambliss, W. (1994), 'Policing the Ghetto Underclass: The Politics of Law and Law Enforcement', *Social Problems*, Vol. 41(2), pp. 177-194.

Chartered Institute of Environmental Health (1995), *Travellers and Gypsies: An Alternative Strategy*, Chartered Institute of Environmental Health, London.

Chimni, B. (1995), 'Globalization and Refugee Blues', *Journal of Refugee Studies*, Vol. 8(3), pp. 298-299.

Chimni, B. (1998), 'The Geopolitics of Refugee Studies: A View from the South', *Journal of Refugee Studies*, Vol. 11(4), pp. 351-374.

Clark, C. (1998), 'Counting Backwards: The Roma "Numbers Game" in Central and Eastern Europe', *Radical Statistics*, Vol. (69), pp. 35-46.

Clark, C. (1997), 'New Age Travellers: Identity, Sedentarism and Social Security' in T. Acton, (ed.), *Gypsy Politics and Traveller Identity*, University Press of Hertfordshire, Hatfield, pp. 125-141.

Clark, C. and Campbell, E. (2000), 'Gypsy Invasion: A Critical Analysis of Newspaper Reaction to Czech and Slovak Romani Asylum-seekers in Britain, 1997', *Romani Studies*, Vol. 10, pp. 23-76.

Cohen, R. (1987), *The New Helots: Migrants in the International Division of Labour*, Avebury, Aldershot.

Cohen, R. (1989), 'The Detention of Asylum-Seekers In The UK', in D. Joly (ed.) *Reluctant Hosts: Europe and its Refugees*, Avebury, Aldershot, pp. 145-161.

Cohen, R. (1991), 'East-West and European Migration in a Global Context', *New Community*, Vol. 18(1), pp. 9-26.

Cohen, R. (1994), *Frontiers of Identity: The British and the Others*, Longman, London.

Collins, H. (1982), *Marxism And Law*, Clarendon, Oxford.

Collins, M. (1994), 'The Sub-Culture of Poverty: A Response to McCarthy', in M. McCann, S. O'Siochain, and J. Ruane (eds). *Irish Travellers: Culture and Ethnicity*, Queen's University Press, Belfast, pp. 130-133.

Collinson, S. (1993), *Europe and International Migration*, Royal Institute of International Affairs, London.

Colquhoun, P. (1806), *A Treatise on Indigence*, Mawman, London.

Commission for Racial Equality, (2004), *Gypsy and Traveller Sites Written Evidence: House of Commons Papers 2003-04 633-II*, Stationary Office, London.

Commission on Itinerancy (1963), *Report of the Commission on Itinerancy*, Stationary Office, Dublin.

Cooper, D. (1997), 'Fiduciary Government: Decentering Property And Taxpayers' Interests', *Social and Legal Studies*, Vol. 6(2), pp. 235-257.

Cottaar, A. (1998), 'The Making of a Minority: The Case of Dutch Travellers', in A. Cottaar (ed.), *Gypsies and Other Itinerant Groups: A Socio-Historical Approach*, Palgrave, Basingstoke, pp. 114-131.

Crang, M. (1996), 'Watching the City: Video, Surveillance, and Resistance', Environment and Planning A 28 (12): 2099-2104.

Cripps, J. (1976), *Accommodation for Gypsies*, HMSO, London.

Crowe, D. (1995), *A History of the Gypsies of Eastern Europe and Russia*, St. Martin's, New York.

Cunliffe, S. A. and Pugh, M. (1998), 'The Politicization of UNHCR In Former Yugoslavia', *Journal of Refugee Studies*, Vol. 10(2), pp. 134-153.

Cunningham, G. and Husk, W. (1980), 'White Flight: A Closer Look at the Assumptions', *Urban Review*, Vol. 12(1), pp. 23-30.

Curtis, L. P. (1997), *Apes and Angels: The Irishman in Victorian Caricature*, Smithsonian Institution, Washington.

Davis, G. (1997), 'The Historiography of The Irish Famine', in P. O'Sullivan (ed.), *The Meaning of the Famine*, Leicester University Press, London, pp. 15-39.

Davis, M. (1992), *City of Quartz: Excavating the Future in Los Angeles*, Vintage, London.

Denich, B. (1994), 'Dismembering Yugoslavia: Nationalist Ideologies and the Symbolic Revival of Genocide', *American Ethnologist*, Vol. 21(2), pp. 367-390.

Department of the Environment (1992), *Consultation Paper on the Reform of the Caravan Sites Act 1968*, HMSO, London.

Dessewffy, T. (1996), 'Strangerhood Without Boundaries: An Essay in the Sociology of Knowledge', *Poetics Today*, Vol. 17(4), pp. 599-615.

Dietler, M. (1994), 'Our Ancestors the Gauls: Archaeology, Ethnic Nationalism and the Manipulation of Celtic Identity in Modern Europe', *American Anthropologist*, Vol. 96, pp. 584-605.

Diken, B. (1998), *Strangers, Ambivalence and Social Theory*, Ashgate, Aldershot.

Dikotter, F. (1990), 'Group Definition and the Idea of Race in Modern China (1793-1949)', *Ethnic and Racial Studies*, Vol. 13(3), pp. 420-432.

Dikotter, F. (1994), 'Racial Identities in China: Context and Meaning', *China Quarterly*, Vol. 138, pp. 404-412.

Dodd, L. (1996), 'Famine Echoes', *South Atlantic Quarterly*, Vol. 95(1), pp. 97-101.

Douglas, M. (1966), *Purity and Danger: An Analysis of Concepts of Pollution and Taboo*, Routledge & Kegan Paul, London.

Douglas, M. (1992), *Risk and Blame: Essays in Cultural Theory*, Routledge, London.

Dowling, M. (1997), 'The Ireland That I Would Have: De Valera and the Creation of an Irish National Image', *History Ireland*, Vol. 5(2), pp. 37-41.

Downes, D. and R. Morgan (1997), 'Dumping the "Hostages To Fortune"?: The Politics of Law and Order in Post-War Britain', in M. Maguire, R. Morgan, and R. Reiner (eds)., *The Oxford Handbook of Criminology*, Oxford University Press, Oxford, pp. 87-134.

Duijzings, G. (1997), 'The Making of Egyptians in Kosovo and Macedonia', in C. Govers (ed.), *The Politics of Ethnic Consciousness*, Macmillan, London, pp. 194-222.

Dundes, A. (1989), 'The Ritual Murder or Blood Libel Legend: A Study of Anti-Semitic Victimization Through Projective Inversion', *Temenos*, Vol. 25, pp. 7-32.

Dunning, E. and Mennell, S. (1998), 'Elias on Germany, Nazism and the Holocaust: On the Balance Between "Civilizing" and "Decivilizing" Trends in the Social Development of Western Europe', *British Journal of Sociology*, Vol. 49(3), pp. 340-357.

Durkheim, E. (1957), *Professional Ethics and Civic Morals*, Routledge & Kegan Paul, London.

Durkheim, E. (1933), *The Division of Labour in Society*, Free Press, New York.

Eagleton, T. (1995), *Heathcliff and the Great Hunger: Studies in Irish Culture*, Verso, London.

Eagleton, T. (1997), 'Spaced Out', *London Review of Books*, Vol. 19(8), pp. 22-24.

Egmond, F. (1993), *Underworlds: Organized Crime in the Netherlands 1650-1800*, Polity, Cambridge.

Eiber, L. (1998), 'The Persecution of the Sinti and Roma in Munich, 1933-1945', in S. Tebbutt (ed.), *Sinti and Roma: Gypsies in German-Speaking Society and Literature*, Bergham Books, New York, pp. 17-33.

Elias, N. (1978), *The Civilizing Process: The Development of Manners*, Urizen Books, New York.

Elias, N. (1995), 'Technization and Civilization', *Theory, Culture & Society*, Vol. 12(3), pp. 7-42.

Ellerly, S. (1996), 'On the Road to Nowhere', *Inside Housing*, Vol. 13(45), pp. 14-15.

Emsley, C. (1997), 'The History of Crime and Crime Control Institutions', in M. Maguire, R. Morgan, and R. Reiner (eds.), *The Oxford Handbook of Criminology*, Oxford University Press, Oxford, pp. 57-86.

Engler, W. (1997), 'Contemporary Capitalism and Civilization: Questions on Norbert Elias' Civilization Theory', *Berliner Journal fur Soziologie*, Vol. 7(2), pp. 217-225.

Erikson, K. (1966), *Wayward Puritans: A Study in the Sociology of Deviance*. Wiley, London.

European Centre for Research and Action on Racism and Anti-Semitism (1994), *Political Extremism and the Threat to Democracy in Europe: A Survey and Assessment of Parties, Movements and Groups*, Institute of Jewish Affairs, London.

European Commission (1994), *Communication From the Commission to the Council and European Parliament on Immigration and Asylum Policies (COM (94) 23 final, 23 February 1994)*, European Commission, Brussels.

European Commission of Human Rights (1995), *Report On Application No. 20348/92 June Buckley Against The United Kingdom*, Council of Europe, Strasbourg.

European Roma Rights Center (1995), *Police Violence Against Roma in Romania*, European Roma Rights Center, Budapest.

European Roma Rights Center (1996), *Sudden Rage at Dawn: Violence Against Roma In Romania*, European Roma Rights Center, Budapest.

European Roma Rights Center (1997), *Time of the Skinheads: Denial and Exclusion of Roma in Slovakia*, European Roma Rights Center, Budapest.

European Roma Rights Center (1998), *A Pleasant Fiction: The Human Rights Situation of Roma in Macedonia*, European Roma Rights Center, Budapest.

European Roma Rights Center (2004a), *Five Years of Ethnic Cleansing of 'Gypsies' from Kosovo*, European Roma Rights Center, Budapest.

European Roma Rights Center (2004b), *The Non-Constituents: Rights Deprivation of Roma in Post-Genocide Bosnia and Herzegovina*, European Roma Rights Center, Budapest.

Fabijancic, T. (1995), 'The Dialectics of Modernity: Reification, Space And Vision', *Rethinking Marxism*, Vol. 8(3), pp. 90-108.

Farley, R. (1982), 'The White Flight Controversy: Policy Implications', *Research in the Sociology of Education and Socialization*, Vol. 3, pp. 207-232.

Fassman, H. and Mumz, R. (1995), 'European East-West Migration, 1945-1992', in R. Cohen (ed.), *The Cambridge Survey of World Migration*, Cambridge University Press, Cambridge, pp. 470-480.

Ferris, E. (1993), *Beyond Borders: Refugees, Migrations and Human Rights in the Post-Cold War Era*, Geneva, WCC Publications.

Fiske, J. (1998), 'Surveilling the City: Whiteness, the Black Man and Democratic Totalitarianism', *Theory, Culture & Society*, Vol. 15(2), pp. 67-88.

Flusty, S. (1997), 'Building Paranoia', in N. Ellin (ed.), *Architecture of Fear*, Princeton Architectural Press, New York, pp. 47-60.

Forrester, B. (1985), *The Travellers' Handbook: A Guide to the Law Affecting Gypsies*, Interchange Books, London.

Foucault, M. (1967), *Madness and Civilization: A History of Insanity in the Age of Reason*, Tavistock, London.

Foucault, M. (1992), *Discipline and Punish: The Birth of the Prison*, Penguin, Harmondsworth.

Franklin, A. (1993), 'Travellers on the Road to Nowhere', *Poverty*, Vol. 84, pp. 11-13.

Fraser, A. (1992), *The Gypsies*, Blackwell, Oxford.

Fraser, A. (2000), 'The Present and Future of the Gypsy Past', *Cambridge Review of International Affairs* Vol. 13, pp. 17-31.

Frederico, J. (1991), 'A Well Founded Fear of Being Persecuted', *Journal of Refugee Studies*, Vol. 4(1), pp. 83-92.

Freeman, G. P. (1994), 'Can Liberal States Control Unwanted Migration?', *Annals of the American Academy of Political and Social Science*, Vol. 534, pp. 17-30.

Freeman, M. (1995), 'Genocide, Civilization and Modernity', *British Journal of Sociology*, Vol. 46(2), pp. 207-223.

Freud, S. (1955), 'The "Uncanny" [Das Unheimliche]', in J. Strachey (ed.), *The Standard Edition of the Complete Psychological Works of Sigmund Freud*, The Hogarth Press, London, pp. 217-256.

Frey, W. (1980), 'Black In-migration, White Flight and the Changing Economic Base of the Central City', *American Journal of Sociology*, Vol. 85(6), pp. 1396-1417.

Fukuyama, F. (1992), *The End of History and the Last Man*, Hamish Hamilton, London.

Gainer, B. (1972), *The Alien Invasion: The Origins of the Aliens Act of 1908*, Heinemann, London.

Gallagher, T. (1992), 'Vatra Romaneasca and Resurgent Nationalism in Romania', *Ethnic and Racial Studies*, Vol. 15(4), pp. 570-598.

Gamble, A. (1988), *The Free Economy and the Strong State*, Macmillan, Basingstoke.

Garland, D. (1985), *Punishment and Welfare: A History of Penal Strategies*, Gower, Aldershot.

Garland, D. (1991), 'Punishment and Culture: The Symbolic Dimension of Criminal Justice', *Studies in Law, Politics and Society*, Vol. 11, pp. 191-222.

Garland, D. (1994), *Punishment and Modern Society: A Study in Social Theory*, Oxford University Press, Oxford.

Garland, D. (1996), 'The Limits of the Sovereign State: Strategies of Crime Control in Contemporary Society', *British Journal of Criminology*, Vol. 36(4), pp. 445-471.

Garland, D. (1997), 'Governmentality and the Problem of Crime', *Theoretical Criminology*, Vol. 1(2), pp. 173-214.

Garton-Ash, T. (1999), 'Cry, the Dismembered Country', *New York Review of Books*, Vol. XLVI, pp. 15-21.

Gellner, E. (1987), *Culture, Identity, and Politics*, Cambridge University Press, Cambridge.

Gerking, T. (1973), 'Vagrancy Law Alternatives', *Law and the Social Order*, Vol. 5, pp. 881-902.

Giddens, A. (1985), *A Contemporary Critique of Historical Materialism: The Nation-State And Violence*, Polity, Cambridge.

Giddens, A. (1990), *The Consequences of Modernity*, Polity, Cambridge.

Gilliom, J. (1997), 'Everyday Surveillance, Everyday Resistance: Computer Monitoring in the Lives of the Appalachian Poor', *Studies in Law, Politics and Society*, Vol. 16, pp. 275-297.

Gilroy, P. (1998), 'Race Ends Here', *Ethnic and Racial Studies*, Vol. 21(5), pp. 838-847.

Glenny, M. (1993), *The Rebirth of History: Eastern Europe in the Age of Democracy*, Penguin, Harmondsworth.

Gmelch, G. (1986), 'Irish Travellers Revisited', *Eire*, Vol. 21(4), pp. 22-28.

Gmelch, G. and Gmelch, S. (1988), 'Nomads in the Cities: Frequent Evictions Keep Britain's Gypsies on the Move', *Natural History*, Vol. 97(2), pp. 50-61.

Gmelch, S. (1982), 'Gypsies in British Cites: Problems and Government Responses', *Urban Anthropology*, Vol. 11(3-4), pp. 347-376.

Goldberg, D. (1993), *Racist Culture: Philosophy and the Politics of Meaning*, Blackwell, Oxford.

Gorz, A. (1993), 'Political Ecology: Expertocracy Versus Self-Limitation', *New Left Review*, Vol. 202, pp. 55-67.

Gottdiener, M. (1991), 'Space, Social Theory and the Urban Metaphor', *Current Perspectives in Social Theory*, Vol. 11, pp. 295-311.

Government of the Czech Republic (1997), *Resolution of the Government of the Czech Republic on the Report on the Situation of The Roma Community*, OSCE Implementation Meeting, Warsaw.

Government of the Republic of Hungary (1997), *The Situation of the National and Ethnic Minorities Living in the Republic of Hungary*, National Assembly of Hungary, Budapest.

Government of the Slovak Republic (1997), *Statement of The Government of the Slovak Republic*, OSCE Implementation Meeting, Warsaw.

Gronfors, M. (1979), *Ethnic Minorities and Deviance: The Relationship Between Finnish Gypsies and the Police*, University Press of Helsinki, Helsinki.

Gronfors, M. (1981), 'Police Perception of Social-Problems and Clients: The Case of the Gypsies in Finland', *International Journal of the Sociology of Law*, Vol. 9(4), pp. 345-359.

Gupta, D. (1983), 'Racism Without Color: The Catholic Ethic and Ethnicity in Quebec', *Race and Class*, Vol. 25(1), pp. 23-44.

Guy, W. (1998), 'Ways of Looking at Roma: The Case of Czechoslovakia (1975)', in D. Tong (ed.), *Gypsies: An Interdisciplinary Reader*, Garland, New York, pp. 14-68.

Guzzoni, U. (1997), 'Reason - A Different Reason - Something Different Than Reason? Wondering About the Concept of a Different Reason in Adorno, Lyotard and Sloterdijk', in M. Pensky (ed.), *The Actuality of Adorno*, State University Press of New York, New York, pp. 17-42.

Habermas, J. (1987a), *The Theory of Communicative Action, Vol. 2: Lifeworld and System*, Polity, Cambridge.

Habermas, J. (1987b), *The Philosophical Discourse of Modernity*, Polity, Cambridge.

Habermas, J. (1992), 'Citizenship and National Identity: Some Reflections on the Future of Europe', *Praxis International*, Vol. 12(1), pp. 1-19.

Halfacree, K. (1996), 'Out of Place in the Country: Travellers and the Rural Idyll', *Antipode*, Vol. 28(1), pp. 42-73.

Halfmann, J. (1998), 'Citizenship Universalism, Migration and the Risks of Exclusion', *British Journal of Sociology*, Vol. 49(4), pp. 513-533.

Hall, S. (1992), 'The Question of Cultural Identity', in S. Hall, D. Held, and T. McGrew (eds)., *Modernity and its Futures*, Polity, Cambridge, pp. 273-314.

Halvorsen, R. (1997), 'Collective Action by Norwegian Travellers', European Sociological Association Annual Conference, Essex University.

Hamilton, K. (1997), 'Europe, Africa, and International Migration: An Uncomfortable Triangle of Interests', *New Community*, Vol. 23(4), pp. 549-570.

Hammar, T. (1990), *Democracy and the Nation-State*, Gower, Aldershot.

Hancock, I. (1987a), *The Pariah Syndrome: An Account of Gypsy Slavery and Persecution*, Karoma, Ann Arbor.

Hancock, I. (1987b), 'Gypsies, Jews And The Holocaust', *Shmate: A Journal of Progressive Jewish Thought*, Vol. 17, pp. 6-15.

Hancock, I. (1988), 'The Uniqueness of the Victims: Gypsies, Jews and the Holocaust', *Without Prejudice: The EAFORD International Review of Racial Discrimination*, Vol. 1-2, pp. 45-67.

Hancock, I. (1997a), 'A Glossary of Romani Terms'. *American Journal of Comparative Law*, Vol. 45, pp. 329-344.

Hancock, I. (1997b), 'The Struggle For The Control of Identity', *Transitions*, http://www.ijt.cz/transitions/thestrug1.html.

Hancock, I. (2004), *Gypsy Mafia, Romani Saints: The Racial Profiling of Romani Americans*, The Romani Archives and Documentation Center, Austin.

Hannaford, I. (1996), *Race: The History of an Idea in the West*, John Hopkins University Press, Washington.

Harris, G. (1994), *The Dark Side of Europe: The Extreme Right Today*. Edinburgh: Edinburgh University Press.

Harvey, D. (1989), *The Condition of Postmodernity*, Blackwell, Oxford.

Hassner, P. (1991), 'Culture and Society,' *International Spectator*, Vol 26 (1), pp 136-153.

Hathaway, J. (1995), 'New Directions to Avoid Hard Problems: The Distortion of the Palliative Role of Refugee Protection', *Journal of Refugee Studies*, Vol. 8(3), pp. 288-294.

Hawes, D. (1986), 'Time for Gypsies to Get a Better Deal', *Municipal Journal*, Vol. 94(20), pp. 776-777.

Hawes, D. (1987), 'Gypsy Site Policy: A Failure of Both Carrot and Stick', *Policy and Politics*, Vol. 15(1), pp. 49-54.

Hay, D. (1975), 'Property, Authority and the Criminal Law', in D. Hay (ed.), *Albion's Fatal Tree: Crime and Society in Eighteenth Century England*, Allen Lane, London, pp. 17-64.

Hayden, R. M. (1996), 'Imagined Communities and Real Victims: Self-Determination and Ethnic Cleansing in Yugoslavia', *American Ethnologist*, Vol. 23(4), pp. 783-801.

Heidegger, M. (1962), *Being and Time*, Blackwell, Oxford.

Helleiner, J. (1995), 'Gypsies, Celts and Tinkers: Colonial Antecedents of Anti-Traveller Racism in Ireland', *Ethnic and Racial Studies*, Vol. 18(3), pp. 532-554.

Helleiner, J. (1998), 'For the Protection of the Children: The Politics of Minority Childhood in Ireland', *Anthropological Quarterly*, Vol. 71, pp. 51-62.

Henderson, A. (1993), *Planning as a Method of Social Control: The Discriminatory Nature of the Town Planning System in Regard to the Provision of Gypsy Sites in England*, M.Phil. Thesis, University of London.

Hetherington, K. (1993), *The Geography of the Other: Lifestyle, Performance and Identity*, Ph.D. Thesis, Lancaster University.

Hetherington, K. (1996), 'Identity Formation, Space and Social Centrality', *Theory, Culture & Society*, Vol. 13(4), pp. 33-52.

Hill, C. (1996), *Liberty Against the Law: Some Seventeenth Century Controversies*, Allen Lane, London.

Hill, H. and Pinch, T. (1993), *The Golem: What Everyone Should Know About Science*, Cambridge University Press, Cambridge.

Holgate, G. (1991), 'Adequate Accommodation: The Problem of Gypsy Site Provision', *Local Government Review*, Vol. 155(46), pp. 902-905.

Home, R. (1982), 'Planning Problems of Self-Help Gypsy Sites', *Journal of Planning and Environment Law*, pp. 212-224.

Home, R. (1993), 'Planning Aspects of the Government Consultation Paper On Gypsies', *Journal of Planning and Environment Law*, Vol. 1993, pp. 13-18.

Home, R. (1995), 'Gypsies and Development Plans After Circular 1/94', *Journal of Planning and Environment Law*, Vol. 1995, pp. 1002-1005.

Hopkinson, N. (1992), *Migration Into Western Europe*, HMSO, London.

Horkheimer, M. and Adorno, T. (1973), *Dialectic of Enlightenment*, Allen Lane, London.

Hov, B. (1993), 'Asylum in Europe: Patterns, Determinants and the Role of East-West Movements', in R. King (ed.), *The New Geography of European Migrations*, Belhaven, London, pp. 207-227.

Hudis, P. (1996), 'Bosnia in the Historic Mirror: A Commentary', *Journal of Political & Military Sociology*, Vol. 24(2), pp. 335-347.

Hughes, M. A. (1990), 'Formation of the Impacted Ghetto: Evidence from Large Metropolitan Areas, 1970-1980', *Urban Geography*, Vol. 11(3), pp. 265-284.

Hunt, A. and Wickham, G. (1994), *Foucault and Law: Towards a Sociology of Law As Governance*, Pluto, London.

Husbands, C. (1995), 'Militant Neo-Nazism in the Federal Republic of Germany in the 1990s', in L. Cheles (ed.), The Far Right in Western and Eastern Europe, Longman, London, pp. 327-353.

Huttenbach, H. (1991), 'The Romany Porjamos: The Nazi Genocide of Gypsies in Germany and Eastern Europe', in D. Crowe. (ed.), *The Gypsies of Eastern Europe*, M E Sharpe, Armonk, pp. 31-49.

Irigaray, L. (1985a), *Speculum of the Other Woman*, Cornell University Press, Ithaca.

Irigaray, L. (1985b), *This Sex Which is not One*, Cornell University Press, Ithaca.

Jackson, P. (1998), 'Construction of "Whiteness" in the Geographical Imagination', *Area*, Vol. 30(2), pp. 99-106.

Jenkins, R. (1994), 'Rethinking Ethnicity: Identity, Categorization and Power', *Ethnic and Racial Studies*, Vol. 17(2), pp. 197-223.

Jenkins, R. (1996), 'Ethnicity Etcetera: Social Anthropological Points of View', *Ethnic and Racial Studies*, Vol. 19(4), pp. 807-822.

Jessop, B. (1990), *State Theory: Putting Capitalist States in their Place*, Polity, Cambridge.

Johnston, L. (1993), 'Privatization and Protection: Spatial and Sectoral Ideologies in Modern Policing', *Modern Law Review*, Vol. 56, pp. 771-792.

Joly, D. (1996), *Haven or Hell? Asylum Policies and Refugees in Europe*, Macmillan, London.

Jurová, A. (1993), 'The Establishment of State Policy of Opinion Against Gypsies After World-War II (Czechoslovakia)', *Historicky Casopis*, Vol. 41, pp. 419-429.

Kanev, K. (1996), 'Dynamics of Inter-Ethnic Tensions in Bulgaria and the Balkans', *Balkan Forum*, Vol. 2(15), pp. 242-243.

Kayatekin, S. and Ruccio, D. (1998), 'Global Fragments: Subjectivity and Class Politics in Discourse', *Economy and Society*, Vol. 27(1), pp. 74-96.

Kaye, R. (1992), 'British Refugee Policy and 1992: The Breakdown of a Policy Community', *Journal of Refugee Studies*, Vol. 5(1), pp. 47-67.

Keith, M. and Pile, S. (1993), 'Introduction Part 2: The Place of Politics', in M. Keith (ed.), *Place and the Politics of Identity*, Routledge, London, pp. 22-40.

Kenrick, D. (1998), 'Reparations', *Index On Censorship*, Vol. 27 (4), pp. 62-63.

Klug, F., Stamer, K., and Wier, S. (1996), 'Civil Liberties And The Parliamentary Watchdog: The Passage of the Criminal Justice and Public Order Act 1994', *Parliamentary Affairs*, Vol. 49(4), pp. 536-549.

Kohn, M. (1995), *The Race Gallery: The Return of Racial Science*, Jonathan Cape, London.

Kornblum, W. and Lichter, P. (1972), 'Urban Gypsies and the Culture of Poverty', *Urban Life and Culture*, Vol. 1(3), pp. 239-253.

Kostelancik, D. J. (1989), 'The Gypsies of Czechoslovakia: Political and Ideological Considerations in the Development of Policy', *Studies in Comparative Communism*, Vol. 22, pp. 307-321.

Kumar, R. (1997), 'The Troubled History of Partition', *Foreign Affairs*, Vol. 76(1), pp. 22-40.

Kurthen, H. (1995), 'Germany at the Crossroads: National Identity and the Challenges of Immigration', *International Migration Review*, Vol. 29(4), pp. 914-938.

Kushnick, L. (1999), 'Over Policed and Under Protected: Stephen Lawrence, Institutional and Police Practices', *Sociological Research Online*, Vol. 4(1), http://www.socresonline.org.uk/socresonline/4-1/kushnick.html.

Ladanyi, J. (1993), 'Patterns of Residential Segregation and the Gypsy Minority in Budapest', *International Journal of Urban and Regional Research*, Vol. 17(1), pp. 30-41.

Lahav, G. (1998), 'Immigration and the State: The Devolution and Privatization of Immigration Control In The EU', *Journal of Ethnic and Migration Studies*, Vol. 24(4), pp. 675-694.

Laitin, D. (1995), 'Marginality: A Microperspective', *Rationality and Society*, Vol. 7(1), pp. 31-57.

Landgren, K. (1998), 'The Future of Refugee Protection: Four Challenges', *Journal of Refugee Studies*, Vol. 11(4), pp. 416-432.

Lash, S. and Urry, J. (1994), *Economies of Signs and Space*, Sage, London.

Lee, K. (2000), 'Orientalism and Gypsylorism,' *Social Analysis*, Vol. 44(2), pp. 129-156.

Lee, Raymond. (1994), 'Global Sociology Or "Ghettoized" Knowledges? The Paradox of Sociological Universalization in the Third World', *American Sociologist*, Vol. 25(2), pp. 59-72.

Lee, Ronald. (1997), 'The Rom-Vlach Gypsies and the Kris-Romani', *American Journal of Comparative Law*, Vol. 45, pp. 345-392.

Lefebvre, H. (1991), *The Production of Space*, Blackwell, Oxford.

Lemon, A. (1991), 'Roma (Gypsies) in the Soviet Union and the Moscow Teatr "Romen"', *Nationalities Papers*, Vol. 19, pp. 359-372.

Liégeois, J. P. (1987), *School Provision for Gypsy and Traveller Children*, Office for Official Publications of the European Communities, Luxembourg.

Liégeois, J. P. (1998), 'Food For Thought', *Interface*, Vol. 30, p. 2.

Liégeois, J. P. and Gheorghe, N. (1995), *Roma/Gypsies: A European Minority*, Minority Rights Group International, London.

Liska, A., Logan, J., and Bellair, P. (1998), 'Race and Violent Crime in the Suburbs', *American Sociological Review*, Vol. 63(1), pp. 27-38.

Livezeanu, I. (1995), *Cultural Politics in Greater Romania: Regionalism, Nation Building and Ethnic Struggle, 1918-1930*, Cornell University Press, Ithaca.

Lloyd, M. and Morran, R. (1998), *Failing the Test: Racial Discrimination on Caravan Parks*, Save the Children, Edinburgh.

Local Government Association (2004), *Gypsy and Traveller Sites Written Evidence: House of Commons Papers 2003-04 633-II*, Stationery Office, London.

Lorimer, D. (1988), 'Theoretical Racism in Late-Victorian Anthropology, 1870-1900', *Victorian Studies*, Vol. 31(3), pp. 405-430.

Lowe, R. and Shaw, W. (1993), *Travellers: Voices of the New Age Nomads*, Fourth Estate, London.

Lucassen, L. (1999), 'Gypsies in Germany, 1870-1945: A Critical Historiographical Overview', *Zeitschrift fur Sozialgeschichte des 20 und 20 Jahrhunderts*, Vol. 10(1), pp. 82-100.

Lutsky, K. (1995), 'When is "Obedience" Obedience? Conceptual and Historical Commentary', *Journal of Social Issues*, Vol. 51(3), pp. 55-65.

Lutz, B. D. (1995), 'Gypsies as Victims of the Holocaust', *Holocaust and Genocide Studies*, Vol. 9(3), pp. 346-359.

MacAlister, S. (1937), *The Secret Languages of Ireland*, Cambridge University Press, Cambridge.

Maciejewski, F. (1994), 'On the Psychoanalysis of the Historically Uncanny: Xenophobia and the Gypsy People', *Psyche-Zeitschrift fur Psychoanalyse und ihre Anwendungen*, Vol. 48(1), pp. 30-49.

MacLaughlin, J. (1996), 'The Evolution of Anti-Traveller Racism in Ireland', *Race and Class*, Vol. 37(3), pp. 47-63.

MacLaughlin, J. (1998), 'The Political Geography of Anti-Traveller Racism in Ireland: The Politics of Exclusion and the Geography of Closure', *Political Geography*, Vol. 17(4), pp. 417-435.

MacLaughlin, J. (1999a), 'European Gypsies and the Historical Geography of Loathing', *Fernand Braudel Center Review*, Vol. 22(1), pp. 31-60.

MacLaughlin, J. (1999b), 'Nation-Building, Social Closure and Anti-Traveller Racism In Ireland', *Sociology*, Vol. 33(1), pp. 129-151.

MacRitchie, D. (1894), *Scottish Gypsies Under the Stewarts*, D. Douglas, Edinburgh.

Malik, K. (1996), *The Meaning of Race: Race, History and Culture in Western Society*, Macmillan, London.

Mann, M. (1993), *The Sources of Social Power, Vol. 2*, Cambridge University Press, Cambridge.

Margalit, G. (2002), *Germany and its Gypsies: A Post-Auschwitz Ordeal*, University Press of Wisconsin, Madison.

Marks, J. and Fraenkel, E. (1997), 'Working to Prevent Conflict in the New Nation of Macedonia', *Negotiation Journal*, Vol. 13(3), pp. 243-252.

Marx, K. (1964), *Economic and Philosophic Manuscripts of 1844*, International Publishers, New York.

Marx, K. (1990) *Capital*, Penguin, London.

Massey, D. (1993) 'Power Geometry and a Progressive Sense of Place', in J. Bird. (ed.), *Mapping the Futures*, London, Routledge, pp. 69-69.

Mayall, D. (1988), *Gypsy-Travellers in Nineteenth-Century Society*, Cambridge University Press, Cambridge.

Mayall, D. (1992a), 'The Making of British Gypsy Identities, 1500-1980', *Immigrants and* Minorities, Vol. 11, pp. 21-41.

Mayall, D. (1992b), 'British Gypsies and the State', *History Today*, Vol. 42, pp. 6-8.

Mayall, D. (1995), *English Gypsies and State Policies*, University Press of Hertfordshire, Hatfield.

Mayall, D. (1997), 'Egyptians and Vagabonds: Representations of the Gypsy in Early Modern Official and Rogue Literature', *Immigrants and Minorities*, Vol. 16(3), pp. 55-82.

Mayall, D. (2004), *Gypsy Identities 1500-2000: From Egipcyans and Moon-men to the Ethnic Romany*, Routledge, London.

Mayhew, H. (1861), *London Labour and the London Poor, Vol. IV*, Frank Cass, London.

Mazlish, B. (1990), 'Reflections on the Eastern European Revolutions: The God That Failed', *Praxis International*, Vol. 10(3-4), pp. 236-240.

Mazower, M. (1998), *Dark Continent: Europe's Twentieth Century*, Allen Lane, London.

McCabe, S. and Wallington, P. (1988), *The Police, Public Order and Civil Liberties: Legacies of the Miner's Strike*, Routledge, London.

McCagg, W. (1991), 'Gypsy Policy in Socialist Hungary and Czechoslovakia, 1945-1989', *Nationalities Papers*, Vol. 19, pp. 313-336.

McCarthy, P. (1994), 'The Sub-Culture of Poverty Reconsidered', in M. McCann, S. O'Siochain, and J. Ruane (eds)., *Irish Travellers: Culture and Ethnicity*, Queen's University Press, Belfast, pp. 121-129.

McDonagh, M. and McVeigh, R. (1996), *Minceir Neeja in the Thome Munkra: Irish Travellers in the USA*, Belfast Travellers' Education and Development Group, Belfast.

McKinlay, A. and Taylor, P. (1998), 'Through the Looking Glass: Foucault and the Politics of Production', in A. McKinlay (ed.), *Foucault, Management and Organization Theory*, Sage, London, pp. 175-188.

McMullan, J. (1998), 'The Arresting Eye: Discourse, Surveillance and Disciplinary Administration in Early English Police Thinking', *Social and Legal Studies*, Vol. 7(1), pp. 92-128.

McMullan, J. (1987), 'Crime, Law and Order in Early-Modern England', *British Journal of Criminology*, Vol. 27(3), pp. 252-274.

Meester, M. (1992), *De Stilte Voor Het Vuur*, Meulenhoff, Amsterdam.

Melcic, D. (1994), 'The Balkans and Europe: A Philosophical Problem', *Praxis International*, Vol. 13(4), pp. 332-338.

Melucci, A. (1989), *Nomads of the Present*, Hutchinson Radius, London.

Mendras, H. (1994), 'An Image of Western Europe', *Tocqueville Review*, Vol. 15(2), pp. 131-158.

Meyer, K. (1891), 'On the Irish Origin and the Age of Shelta', *Journal of the Gypsy Lore Society*, Vol. 2, pp. 257-265.

Meyer, M. (1969), *The Origins of the Modern Jew: Jewish Identity and European Culture in Germany, 1749-1824*, National Association of Professors of Hebrew, New York.

Michie, E. (1992), 'From Simianized Irish to Oriental Despot: Heathcliff, Rochester and Racial Difference', *Novel: A Forum on Fiction*, Vol. 25(2), pp. 125-140.

Miles, R. (1994), 'Explaining Racism in Contemporary Europe', in A. Rattansi (ed.), *Racism, Modernity and Identity: On The Western Front*, Polity, Cambridge, pp. 189-221.

Milgram, S. (1974), *Obedience to Authority: An Experimental View*, Tavistock, London.

Miller, A., Collins, B., and Brief, D. (1995), 'Perspectives on Obedience to Authority: The Legacy of the Milgram Experiments', *Journal of Social Issues*, Vol. 51(3), pp. 1-19.

Millward, S. (1986), 'Travellers and the Law', *Cambrian Law Review*, Vol. 17, pp. 76-92.

Milne, S. (1994), *The Enemy Within: MI5, Maxwell and the Scargill Affair*, Verso, London.

Milton, S. (1998), 'Persecuting the Survivors: The Continuity of "Anti-Gypsyism" in Postwar Germany and Austria', in S. Tebbutt (ed.), *Sinti and Roma: Gypsies in German-Speaking Society and Literature*, Bergham Books, New York, pp. 35-47.

Ministry of Home Affairs (1948), *Report of the Committee on 'Gypsies And Like Itinerants'*, Government of Northern Ireland, Belfast.

Ministry of Home Affairs (1955), *Report on 'Itinerant Gypsies'*, Government of Northern Ireland, Belfast.

Ministry of Housing and Local Government (1967), *Gypsies and Other Travellers*, HMSO, London.

Mirga, A. (1993), 'The Effects of State Assimilation Policy on Polish Gypsies', *Journal of the Gypsy Lore Society*, Vol. 3(2), pp. 69-76.

Mirga, A. and Gheorghe, N. (1997), *The Roma in the Twenty-First Century: A Policy Paper*, Project on Ethnic Relations, Princeton.

Morris, L. (1997a), 'Globalization, Migration and the Nation-State: Towards a Post-National Europe?', *British Journal of Sociology*, Vol. 48(2), pp. 192-209.

Morris, L. (1997b), 'A Cluster of Contradictions: The Politics of Migration in the European Union', *Sociology*, Vol. 31(2), pp. 241-259.

Mouzelis, N. (1993), 'Evolution and Democracy: Talcott Parsons and the Collapse of Eastern European Regimes', *Theory, Culture & Society*, Vol. 10(1), pp. 145-151.

Mouzelis, N. (1999), 'Modernity', *British Journal of Sociology*, Vol. 50, pp. 145-151.

National Gypsy Council (1997), 'Practical Proposals for Gypsy/Traveller Law Reform', Traveller Law Reform Conference, Cardiff University.

Newburn, T. and Jones, T. (1997), *Private Security and Public Policing*, Oxford University Press, Oxford.

ni Shuinear, S. (1994), 'Irish Travellers, Ethnicity and the Origins Question', in

M. McCann, S. O'Siochain, and J Ruane (eds). *Irish Travellers: Culture and Ethnicity*, Queen's University Press, Belfast.

Nietzsche, F. (1969), *Thus Spoke Zarathustra: A Book for Everyone and no One*, Penguin, Harmondsworth.

Niner, P. (2004), 'Accommodating Nomadism? An Examination of Accommodation Options for Gypsies and Travellers in England', *Housing Studies*, Vol. 19, pp.141-159.

Nir, A. (1993), 'Gypsies in the Slovakian State', *Yalkut Moreshet*, Vol. 55, pp. 211-222.

Noonan, P. (1997), 'Travellers in Northern Ireland and Law Reform', Traveller Law Reform Conference, Cardiff University.

Novitch, M. (1984), 'Half a Million Gypsies Victims of the Nazi Terror', *Unesco Courier*, Vol. 10, pp. 24-25.

Nowicka, E. (1997), 'Exclusion or Inclusion: Education for Roma Children in Poland', European Sociological Association Conference, Essex University.

O'Nions, H. (1995), 'The Marginalization of Gypsies', *Web Journal of Current Legal Issues*, Vol. 3,
http://www.leicster.ac.uk/~nlawwww/articles3/onions3.html.

O'Kane, R. (1997), 'Modernity, the Holocaust, and Politics', *Economy and Society*, Vol. 26(1), pp. 43-61.

Okely, J. (1983), *The Traveller-Gypsies*, Cambridge University Press, Cambridge.

Okely, J. (1994), 'Constructing Difference: Gypsies as Other', *Anthropological Journal On European Cultures*, Vol. 3(2), pp. 55-73.

Okely, J. (1996), *Own or Other Culture*, Routledge, London.

Okely, J. (1997), 'Non-Territorial Culture as the Rationale for the Assimilation of Gypsy Children', *Childhood: A Global Journal of Child Research*, Vol. 4(1), pp. 63-80.

Oliner, S. and Hallum, K. (1978), 'Minority Contempt for Opors', *California Sociologist*, Vol. 1(1), pp. 41-57.

Olsen, J. (1998), *Hastened to the Grave: The Gypsy Murder Investigation*, St. Martins, New York.

Open Society Accession Monitoring Program (2001), *Monitoring the Accession Process: Minority Protection*, European Union, Brussels.

Opp, K. (1993), 'When do Authoritarian Regimes Resign? East Germany 1989', American Sociological Association.

Orkin, M. (1987), 'Othello and the Plain Face of Racism', *Shakespeare Quarterly*, Vol. 38(2), pp. 166-188.

Pahl, J. and Vaile, M. (1987), 'Health and Health Care Among Travellers', *Journal of Social Policy*, Vol. 17(2), pp. 195-213.

Parson, D. (1993), 'The Search for a Centre: The Recomposition of Race, Class and Space in Los Angeles', *International Journal of Urban and Regional Research*, Vol. 17(2), pp. 232-240.

Parsons, T. (1980), *Talcott Parsons on Institutions and Social Evolution*, University Press of Chicago, Chicago.

Pelagidis, T. (1997), 'Divergent Real Economies in Europe', *Economy and Society*, Vol. 26(4), pp. 546-559.

Petrova, D. (1997), 'Get Out, You Stinking Gypsy', *Transitions*, http://www.ijt.cz/transitions/getout1.html.

Petrova, D. (2004), 'The Roma: Between a Myth and the Future', *Roma Rights*, http://www.errc.org/cikk.php?cikk=1844.

Planning Exchange (1997), *Neighbours' Views of Official Sites for Travelling People*, The Planning Exchange, Glasgow.

Pollard, J. (1996), 'Banking at the Margins: A Geography of Financial Exclusion in Los Angeles', *Environment and Planning A*, Vol. 28(7), pp. 1209-1232.

Popov, V. (1992), 'La Conscience Ethnique Preferentielle des Tsiganes', *Etudes Tsiganes*, Vol. 38(2), pp. 38-43.

Pound, J. (1971), *Poverty and Vagrancy in Tudor England*, Longman, London.

Powell, F. (1989), 'Vagrancy and Deterrence', *Social Policy and Administration*, Vol. 23, pp. 72-83.

Powell, M. and Hewitt, M. (1998), 'The End of the Welfare State?', *Social Policy and Administration*, Vol. 32, pp. 1-13.

Pratt, J. (1998), 'Towards the "Decivilising" of Punishment?', *Social and Legal Studies*, Vol. 7(4), pp. 487-515.

Project on Ethnic Relations (1997a), *Prevention of Violence and Discrimination Against the Roma in Central and Eastern Europe*, Project on Ethnic Relations, Princeton.

Project on Ethnic Relations (1997b), *Image and Issues: Coverage of the Roma in the Mass Media in Romania*, Project on Ethnic Relations, Princeton.

Project on Ethnic Relations (1997c), *The Media and the Roma in Contemporary Europe: Facts and Fictions*, Project On Ethnic Relations, Princeton.

Puxon, G. (1973), *Rom: Europe's Gypsies*, Minority Rights Group, London.

Puxon, G. (1977), 'The Forgotten Victims', *Patterns of Prejudice*, Vol. 11(2), pp. 23-28.

Quinney, R. (1978), 'The Production of a Marxist Criminology', *Contemporary Crises*, Vol. 2(3), pp. 277-292.

Quintana, B. and Floyd, L. (1986), *Que Gitano: Gypsies of Southern Spain*, Waveland, Prospect Heights.

Rabrenovic, G. (1997), 'The Dissolution of Yugoslavia: Ethnicity, Nationalism and Exclusionary Communities', *Dialectical Anthropology*, Vol. 22(1), pp. 95-101.

Reich, W. (1972), *The Mass Psychology of Fascism*, Souvenir, London.

Reiner, R. (1997), 'Policing and the Police', in M. Maguire, R. Morgan, and R. Reiner (eds)., *The Oxford Handbook of Criminology*, Oxford University Press, Oxford, pp. 997-1049.

Rex, J. (1981), 'Urban Segregation and Inner City Policy in Great Britain', in C. Peach (eds)., *Ethnic Segregation in Cities*, Croom Helm, London, pp. 25-42.

Rex, J. (1988), *The Ghetto and the Underclass*, Avebury, Aldershot.

Rex, J. and Moore, R. (1967), *Race, Community and Conflict: A Study of Sparkbrook*, Oxford University Press, Oxford.

Rex, J. and Tomlinson, S. (1979), *Colonial Migrants in a British City: A Class Analysis*, Routledge Kegan Paul, London.

Richmond, A. (1994), *Global Apartheid: Refugees, Racism, and the New World Order*, Oxford University Press, Oxford.

Rittberger, V. (1993), 'Europe at Twentieth Century's End: Many Puzzles, Few Answers', *Praxis International*, Vol. 13(3), pp. 283-303.

Roberts, A. (1998), 'More Refugees, Less Asylum: A Regime in Transition', *Journal of Refugee Studies*, Vol. 11(4), pp. 375-395.

Robertson, R. (1995), 'Glocalization: Time-Space and Homogeneity-Heterogeneity', in M. Featherstone (ed.), *Global Modernities*, Sage, London, pp. 25-44.

Robinson, R. (1987), 'The Civilizing Process: Some Remarks on Elias' Social History', *Sociology*, Vol. 21, pp. 1-17.

Robinson, V. (1995) 'The Changing Nature and European Perceptions of Europe's Refugee Problem', *Geoforum*, Vol. 26(4), pp. 411-427.

Rodriguez, C. E. and Corderoguzman, H. (1992), 'Placing Race in Context', *Ethnic and Racial Studies*, Vol. 15(4), pp. 523-542.

Rogers, R. (1992), 'The Future of Refugee Flows and Policies', *International Migration Review*, Vol. 26(4), pp. 1112-1143.

Rose, N. and Valverde, M. (1998), 'Governed By Law?', *Social and Legal Studies*, Vol. 7(4), pp. 541-551.

Roth, A. (1995), 'Ethno-Nationalism: The Romanian Version', *Anthropological Journal on European Cultures*, Vol. 4(2), pp. 7-36.

Rudge, P. (1989), 'European Initiatives on Asylum', in D. Joly (ed.), *Reluctant Hosts: Europe and its Refugees*, Avebury, Aldershot, pp. 212-215.

Russell, B. and Lewis, H. (1900), *The Jew in London: A Study of Racial Character and Present Day Conditions*, T. Fisher Unwin, London.

Said, E. (1978), *Orientalism*, Routledge and Kegan Paul, London.

Salecl, R. (1993), 'The Fantasy Structure of Nationalist Discourse', *Praxis International*, Vol. 13(3), pp. 213-223.

Salo, M. (1979), 'Gypsy Ethnicity: Implications of Native Categories and Interaction', *Ethnicity*, Vol. 6(1), pp. 73-96.

Samuels, A. (1985), 'A Confounded Nuisance ... To Everyone?', *Local Government Review*, Vol. 149(16), pp. 303-314.

Sandford, J. (1973), *Gypsies*, Abacus, London.

Sandland, R. (1996), 'The Real, the Simalcrum and the Construction of "Gypsy" in Law', *Journal of Law And Society*, Vol. 23(3), pp. 383-405.

Scammell, G. V. (1991), 'Essay and Reflection: On the Discovery of the Americas and the Spread of Intolerance, Absolutism, and Racism in Early-Modern Europe', *International History Review*, Vol. 13(3), pp. 502-521.

Schmeidl, S. (1997), 'Exploring the Causes of Forced Migration: A Pooled Time-Series Analysis, 1971-1990', *Social Science Quarterly*, Vol. 78(2), pp. 284-308.

Schoen, D. (1977), *Enoch Powell and the Powellites*, Macmillan, London.

Seidman, S. (1985), 'Max Weber: A Classic Analyzed', *Contemporary Sociology*, Vol. 14(6), pp. 673-677.

Shamir, R. (1993), 'Formal and Substantive Rationality in American Law: A Weberian Perspective', *Social and Legal Studies*, Vol. 2(1), pp. 45-72.

Shamir, R. (1996), 'Suspended In-Space: Bedouins Under the Law of Israel', *Law & Society Review*, Vol. 30(2), pp. 231-257.

Sheleff, L. (1975), 'From Restitutive Law to Reive Law: Durkheim's "The Division of Labour In Society" Revisited', *European Journal of Sociology*, Vol. 16(1), pp. 16-45.

Shukra, K. (1998), *The Changing Pattern of Black Politics in Britain*, Pluto, London.

Shurmer-Smith, P. and Hannam, K. (1994), *Worlds of Desire, Realms of Power: A Cultural Geography*, Arnold, London.

Sibley, D. (1981), *Outsiders in Urban Societies*, Basil Blackwell, Oxford.

Sibley, D. (1988), 'Survey 13: Purification of Space', *Environment and Planning D: Society and Space*, Vol. 6(4), pp. 409-421.

Sibley, D. (1990), 'Urban Change and the Exclusion of Minority-Groups in British Cities', *Geoforum*, Vol. 21(4), pp. 483-488.

Sibley, D. (1994), 'The Sin of Transgression', *Area*, Vol. 26(3), pp. 300-303.

Sibley, D. (1998), 'Sensations and Spatial Science: Gratification and Anxiety in the Production of Ordered Landscapes', *Environment And Planning A*, Vol. 30(2), pp. 235-246.

Simmel, G. (1950), 'The Stranger', in K. Wolff (ed.) *The Sociology of Georg Simmel*, Free Press, New York, pp. 402-408.

Simmel, G. (1971), 'The Metropolis and Mental Life', in D. Levine (eds). *On Individuality and Social Forms: Selected Writings of Georg Simmel*, Chicago University Press, London, pp. 324-339.

Simmel, G. (1994a), 'Bridge and Door', *Theory, Culture & Society*, Vol. 11(1), pp. 5-10.

Simmel, G. (1994b), 'The Picture Frame: An Aesthetic Study', *Theory, Culture & Society*, Vol. 11(1), pp. 11-17.

Simon, J. (1998), 'Refugees in a Carceral Age: The Rebirth of Immigration Prisons in The United States', *Public Culture*, Vol. 10(3), pp. 577-607.

Sims, B. (1997), 'Crime, Punishment, and the American Dream: Toward a Marxist Integration', *Journal of Research in Crime and Delinquency*, Vol. 34(1), pp. 5-24.

Solomos, J. and Back, L. (1996), *Racism and Society*, Macmillan, London.

Soravia, G. (1984), 'A Wandering Voice', *UNESCO Courier*, Vol. 10, pp. 21-23.

Sorkin, M. (1992), *Variations on a Theme Park: The New American City and the end of Public Space*, Noonday, New York.

Soulis, G. (1961), 'The Gypsies in the Byzantine Empire and the Balkans in the Late Middle Ages', *Dumbarton Oaks Papers*, Vol. 15, pp. 141-165.

Soysal, Y. (1997), 'Changing Parameters of Citizenship and Claims-Making: Organized Islam in European Public Spheres', *Theory and Society*, Vol. 26(4), pp. 509-527.

Stasiulis, D. (1997), 'International Migration, Rights, and the Decline of "Actually Existing Liberal Democracy"', *New Community*, Vol. 23(2), pp. 197-214.

Stewart, M. (1990), 'Gypsies, Work and Civil Society', *Journal of Communist Studies*, Vol. 6(2), pp. 140-162.

Stewart, M. (1997), *The Time of The Gypsies*, Macmillan, London.

Stock, M. (1994), 'Youth Culture in East-Germany: From Symbolic Dropout to Politicization', *Communist and Post-Communist Studies*, Vol. 27(2), pp. 135-143.

Sutherland, A. (1997), 'Complexities of U.S. Law and Gypsy Identity', *American Journal of Comparative Law*, Vol. 45(2), pp. 393-405.

Sutherland, A. (1975), *Gypsies: The Hidden Americans*, Free Press, New York.

Sway, M. (1975), 'Gypsies as a Perpetual Minority: A Case Study', *Humbolt Journal of Social Relations*, Vol. 3(1), pp. 48-55.

Sway, M. (1981), 'Simmel's Concept of the Stranger and the Gypsies', *Social Science Journal*, Vol. 18(1), pp. 41-50.

Sway, M. (1984), 'Economic Adaptability: The Case of the Gypsies', *Urban Life*, Vol. 13, pp. 83-98.

Swyngedouw, M. (1995), 'The "Threatening Immigrant" in Flanders 1930-1980: Redrawing the Social Space', *New Community*, Vol. 21(3), pp. 325-340.

Tabboni, S. (1995), 'The Stranger and Modernity: From Equality of Rights to Recognition of Difference', *Thesis Eleven*, Vol. 43, pp. 17-27.

Taras, R. (1993) 'Making Sense of Matrioshka Nationalism', in I. Bremner (ed.) *Nation and Politics in the Soviet Successor States*, Cambridge University Press, Cambridge, pp. 525-536.

Taylor, A. J. (1972), *Laissez-Faire and State Intervention in Nineteenth-Century Britain*, Macmillan, London.

Taylor, P. (1996), 'Embedded Statism and the Social Sciences: Opening up to New Spaces', *Environment and Planning A*, Vol. 28(11), pp. 1917-1928.

Tebbutt, S. (1998) 'Piecing Together the Jigsaw: The History of the Sinti and Roma in Germany', in S. Tebbutt (ed.), *Sinti and Roma: Gypsies in German-Speaking Society and Literature*, Bergham Books, New York, pp. 1-16

Thomas, P. and Campbell, S. (1992), *Housing Gypsies*, Cardiff University Law School, Cardiff.

Thompson, E. P. (1993), *Customs in Common*, Penguin, London.

Thranhardt, D. (1995), 'Germany: An Undeclared Immigration Country', *New Community*, Vol. 21(1), pp. 19-36.

Tiilikainen, T. (1995), 'The Problem of Democracy in the European Union', in A. Rosas (ed.), *A Citizens' Europe: In Search of a New Order*, Sage, London, pp. 19-38.

Todd, R. (1984), *Gypsies, the Community and the State: Conflict And Negotiation in the Development of Social Policy Towards Gypsies in England And Wales 1970-80*, Ph.D. Thesis, University of Bradford.

Todosijevic, B. (1998) 'Authoritarianism as a Predictor of Anti-Semitism and Anti-Gypsy Attitudes: The Case of Hungary', *International Sociological Association Conference*.

Toffler, A. (1980), *The Third Wave*, Collins, London.

Toibin, C. (1998), 'On the History of the History of the Irish Famine', *London Review of Books*, Vol. 20(15), pp. 17-23.

Tomova, I. (1995), *The Gypsies in the Transition Period*, International Center for Minority Studies and Intercultural Relations, Sofia.

Trumpener, K. (1992), 'The Time of the Gypsies: A "People without History" in the Narratives of the West', *Critical Inquiry*, Vol. 18, pp. 843-884.

Tuitt, P. (1996), *False Images: Law's Construction of the Refugee*, Pluto, London.

Ulc, O. (1991), 'Integration of the Gypsies in Czechoslovakia', *Ethnic Groups*, Vol. 9, pp. 107-118.

Urry, J. (1995), *Consuming Places*, Routledge, London.

Urry, J. (1996), 'Is The Global a New Space of Analysis?' *Environment and Planning A*, Vol. 28(11), pp. 1977-1982.

Usher, P. (1976), 'The Class System, Metropolitan Dominance and Northern Development in Canada', *Antipode*, Vol. 8(3), pp. 28-32.

van de Port, M. (1998), *Gypsies, Wars & Other Instances of the Wild: Civilization and its Discontents in a Serbian Town*, Amsterdam University Press, Amsterdam.

van de Port, M. (1999), 'It Takes a Serb to Know a Serb: Uncovering the Roots of Obstinate Otherness in Serbia', *Critique of Anthropology*, Vol. 19(1), pp. 7-30.

van den Berghe, P. (1997), 'Rehabilitating Stereotypes', *Ethnic and Racial Studies*, Vol. 20(1), pp. 1-16.

Verdery, K. (1993), 'Nationalism in Romania', *Slavic Review*, Vol. 52(2), pp. 179-203.

Vertovec, S. (1999), 'Conceiving and Researching Transnationalism', *Ethnic and Racial Studies*, Vol. 22(2), pp. 447-462.

Vesey-Fitzgerald, B. (1944), *Gypsies of Britain: An Introduction to Their History*, Chapman & Hall, London.

Wacquant, L. (1991), 'From "Black Metropolis" to "Hyper-Ghetto": Race, State and Economy in the Transformation of the Black Ghetto in the Post-Fordist Era', Poverty, Immigration and Urban Marginality in the Advanced Societies Working Conference, Paris.

Wallace, C., Chmouliar, O., and Sidorenko, E. (1996), 'The Eastern Frontier of Western Europe: Mobility in the Buffer Zone', *New Community*, Vol. 22, pp. 259-286.

Wallace, R. (1996), *Refugees and Asylum: A Community Perspective*, Butterworths, London.

Waters, M. (1995), *Globalization*, Routledge, London.

Watts, M. (1994), 'Youth and Xenophobia: Traditions and Transitions', International Sociological Association Conference.

Webber, F. (1991), 'From Ethnocentrism to Euro-Racism', *Race and Class*, Vol. 32(3), pp. 11-17.

Webberly, G. (1986), *A Report on the Analysis of Responses to Consultation on the Operation of the Caravan Sites Act 1968*, HMSO, London.

Weber, M. (1927), *General Economic History*, Greenberg, New York.

Weber, M. (1968a), *Economy and Society, Vol. 2.*, Bedminster, New York.

Weber, M. (1968b), *Economy and Society, Vol. 1.*, Bedminster, New York.

Weinerman, E. (1994), 'Racism, Racial Prejudice and Jews in Late Imperial Russia', *Ethnic and Racial Studies*, Vol. 17(3), pp. 442-495.

Welsh, J. (1994), 'The Role of the Inner Enemy in European Self-Definition: Identity, Culture and International Relations Theory', *History of European Ideas*, Vol. 19(1-3), pp. 53-61.

Weyrauch, W. O. (1997), 'Oral Legal Traditions of Gypsies and Some American Equivalents', *American Journal of Comparative Law*, Vol. 45(2), pp. 407-442.

Willems, H. (1995), 'Right-Wing Extremism, Racism or Youth Violence? Explaining Violence Against Foreigners In Germany', *New Community*, Vol. 21(4), pp. 501-523.

Willems, W. (1997), *In Search of the True Gypsy: From Enlightenment to Final*

Solution, Frank Cass, London.

Willems, W. (1998), 'Ethnicity as a Death-Trap: The History of Gypsy Studies', in A. Cottaar (ed.), *Gypsies and Other Itinerant Groups: A Socio-Historical Approach,* Palgrave, Basingstoke.

Williams, E. M. and Harper, P. S. (1977), 'Genetic Study of Welsh Gypsies', *Journal of Medical Genetics,* Vol. 14(1), pp. 172-176.

Wilpert, C. (1991), 'Migration and Ethnicity in a Non-Immigration Country: Foreigners in a United Germany', *New Community,* Vol. 18(1), pp. 49-62.

Wilson, M. (1998), *Directory of Planning Policies for Gypsy Site Provision in England,* The Policy Press, Bristol.

Wilson, T. (1983), 'White Response to Neighborhood Racial Change', *Sociological Focus,* Vol. 16(4), pp. 305-318.

Wilson, W. (1987), *The Truly Disadvantaged: The Inner City, the Underclass and Public Policy,* University Press of Chicago, Chicago.

Wilson, W. (1997), *When Work Disappears: The World of the New Urban Poor,* Alfred A. Knopf, New York.

Wilton, R. D. (1998), 'The Constitution of Difference: Space and Psyche in Landscapes of Exclusion', *Geoforum,* Vol. 29(2), pp. 173-185.

Wirth, L. (1966), *The Ghetto,* University Press of Chicago, Chicago.

Wolff, L. (1994), *Inventing Eastern Europe: The Map of Civilization and the Mind of The Enlightenment,* Stanford University Press, Stanford.

Wood, E. M. (1997a), 'Labor, the State, and Class Struggle', *Monthly Review,* Vol. 49(3), pp. 1-17.

Wood, E. M. (1997b), 'A Note on DuBoff and Herman', *Monthly Review,* Vol. 49(6), pp. 39-43.

Woodiwiss, A. (1997), 'Against "Modernity": A Dissident Rant', *Economy and Society,* Vol. 26(3), pp. 1-21.

Wydra, H. (1998), 'Violence and its Causes in New Eastern Europe Democracies', International Sociological Association Conference.

Yelling, A. (1977), *Common Field and Enclosure in England, 1450-1850,* Macmillan, London.

Zelizer, V. (1996), 'Payments and Social Ties', *Sociological Forum,* Vol. 11(3), pp. 481-495.

Zetter, R. (1991), 'Labelling Refugees: Forming and Transforming a Bureaucratic Identity', *Journal of Refugee Studies,* Vol. 4(1), pp. 39-62.

Zukier, H. (1996), 'The Essential "Other" and the Jew: From Anti-Semitism to Genocide', *Social Research,* Vol. 63(4), pp. 1110-1154.

Index